Much has been written upon behavioral and cognitive approaches to the understanding of choice, the general process of making decisions. Furthermore, consumer decision-making is central to understanding consumer behavior and consumer product and service adoption, purchase, use and to post-purchase behaviors. In his new book, *Addiction as Consumer Choice: Exploring the Cognitive Dimension*, Gordon Foxall makes a highly significant addition to the body of literature on consumer choice by offering a specifically formulated blend of cognitive and behavioral forms of understanding, which comes out of his ongoing multidisciplinary research project.

Foreword by Paul M.W. Hackett, *Professor, Emerson College, Boston, USA*

Based upon a coherent epistemology, the book presents an integrated interpretation of addiction that draws on concepts and findings from operant behavioral-economics, consumer behavior analysis, neuroscience and cognitive psychology. Using clear and friendly language, this scholarly, groundbreaking endeavor will be a milestone in the field.

Jorge M. Oliveira-Castro, *Professor, University of Brasilia, Brazil*

Despite harmful consequences, addiction remains prevalent in society. But can it be conceived as 'consumer choice'? Gordon Foxall discusses this question in his insightful, multidisciplinary portrayal of addiction – a must for researchers in the areas of Addiction and Consumer Behavior.

Mirella Yani-de-Soriano, *Senior Lecturer, Cardiff University, UK*

Addiction as Consumer Choice

A striking characteristic of addictive behavior is the pursuit of immediate reward at the risk of longer term detrimental outcomes. It is typically accompanied by the expression of a strong desire to cease from or at least control consumption that has such consequences, followed by lapse, further resolution, relapse, and so on. Understood in this way, addiction includes substance abuse as well as behavioral compulsions like excessive gambling or even uncontrollable shopping. Behavioral economics and neurophysiology provide well-worn paths to understanding this behavior and this book regards them as central components of this quest. However, the specific question it seeks to answer is: What part does *cognition* – the desires we pursue and the beliefs we have about how to accomplish them – play in explaining addictive behavior?

The answer is sought in a methodology that indicates why and where cognitive explanation is necessary, the form it should take, and the outcomes of employing it to understand addiction. It applies the Behavioral Perspective Model (BPM) of consumer choice, a tried and tested theory of more routine consumption, ranging from everyday product and brand choice, through credit purchasing and environmental despoliation, to the more extreme aspects of consumption represented by compulsion and addiction.

The book will advance debate among scholars of consumer behaviour, behavioural scientists and cognitive psychologists about the nature of consumption and compulsion.

Gordon R. Foxall is Distinguished Research Professor at Cardiff University, and Visiting Professor in Economic Psychology at the University of Durham, UK.

Routledge Studies in Marketing

This series welcomes proposals for original research projects that are either single- or multi-authored or an edited collection from both established and emerging scholars working on any aspect of marketing theory and practice, and provides an outlet for studies dealing with elements of marketing theory, thought, pedagogy and practice.

It aims to reflect the evolving role of marketing and bring together the most innovative work across all aspects of the marketing 'mix' – from product development, consumer behaviour, marketing analysis, branding and customer relationships, to sustainability, ethics and the new opportunities and challenges presented by digital and online marketing.

Addiction as Consumer Choice

Exploring the cognitive dimension

Gordon R. Foxall

Routledge
Taylor & Francis Group

LONDON AND NEW YORK

First published 2016 by Routledge

2 Park Square, Milton Park, Abingdon, Oxon OX14 4RN
605 Third Avenue, New York, NY 10017

Routledge is an imprint of the Taylor & Francis Group, an informa business

First issued in paperback 2021

Publisher's Note

The publisher has gone to great lengths to ensure the quality of this reprint
but points out that some imperfections in the original copies may be apparent.

British Library Cataloguing in Publication Data
A catalogue record for this book is available from the British Library

Library of Congress Cataloging in Publication Data
Names: Foxall, G. R., author.
Title: Addiction as consumer choice : exploring the cognitive
dimension / Gordon R. Foxall.
Description: Abingdon, Oxon ; New York, NY : Routledge, 2016. |
Series: Routledge studies in marketing | Includes bibliographical
references and index.
Identifiers: LCCN 2015036212 | ISBN 9780415703208 (hardback) |
ISBN 9780203794876 (ebook)
Subjects: LCSH: Consumer behavior. | Compulsive behavior. |
Consumption (Economics)–Psychological aspects.
Classification: LCC HF5415.32 .F6778 2016 | DDC 362.29–dc23
LC record available at http://lccn.loc.gov/2015036212

ISBN: 978-0-415-70320-8 (hbk)
ISBN: 978-0-367-33902-9 (pbk)

Typeset in Bembo
by Wearset Ltd, Boldon, Tyne and Wear

Agnolo Bronzino, *An Allegory with Venus and Cupid* (*c*.1545). The National Gallery, London. Venus and Cupid, mother and son, are shown in illicit passion, surrounded by symbols of the consequences of licentiousness. The hybrid beauty on the right proffers honeycomb with one distorted gesture while concealing a stinging scorpion in her other hand. A grinning youth rushes to fling sweet blossoms, heedless of the thorn piercing his foot, while opposite him is shown the haggard head of one in utter despair. At the top, winged Time pulls away the veil of concealment held by Oblivion. The masks on the ground serve two purposes, not only enabling the intemperate to deny their folly, to themselves and to others, but also hiding the cruel consequences of excess until escape is impossible. (Jean Foxall)

Contents

Illustrations

Figures

Table

Boxes

Foreword

Much has been written about behavioral and cognitive approaches to the understanding of choice, the general process of making decisions. Furthermore, consumer decision-making is central to understanding consumer behavior and consumer product and service adoption, purchase, use, and to post-purchase behaviors. In his new book, *Addiction as Consumer Choice: Exploring the Cognitive Dimension*, Gordon Foxall makes a highly significant addition to the body of literature on consumer choice by offering a specifically formulated blend of cognitive and behavioral forms of understanding, which comes out of his ongoing multidisciplinary research project.

It may seem unusual to find addiction and consumer decision-making together in a single research monograph. However, the book amply justifies the juxtaposition of the two areas of study in its conception of addiction as an extreme modality of consumer choice, which differs in degree though not in kind from more routine modes of consumption. It is important to note right at the start of my comments that Foxall introduces the many layers of his argument in a skillful manner that gently introduces the reader to each of the multiple disciplines upon which he draws, culminating in dexterous elaborations upon these as is necessary. Through the lens of intentional behaviorism he considers the possible role of cognition in understanding addiction which he views as a consumption modality characterized by steep temporal discounting, reversed preferences, and the committing of behavior, even though these behaviors may obstruct daily life and be economically irrational.

By establishing addiction as an extreme form of consumer choice, Foxall provides insight into addiction-related decision-making mechanisms and processes in which consumer choice is governed by the pursuit of immediate rewards at the expense of long-term outcomes. He commences by offering an operant explanation of behavior where the rate of repetition of a given behavior is seen as being a function of the consequences that this form of behavior has produced in the past in similar circumstances. For many years, Gordon Foxall has investigated and developed behavioral explanations of consumer decision-making and other forms of consumer activity. In many ways this book represents the pinnacle of these enquiries. Over the preceding decade, his work has increasingly sought to broaden the explanatory power of the behavioral predictions implicit in his writing through the amalgamation of cognition within his magnum opus: the Behavioral Perspective Model to understanding behavior. He critiques the utility of cognitive interpretations in his wider research program, and here in this book he questions whether cognitive explanations are required to produce explanations that incorporate intentionality, where the consumer is understood as someone who attempts to maximize utility and allows a reasoned explanation for the individual's current condition. Following this, he asks whether a facilitative cognitive explanation is necessary to produce understanding.

In this book, Gordon Foxall extends his arguments that have been put forward in his extensive writing on consumer decision-making, all of which is couched within the methodological approach of intentional behaviorism. The author claims that this methodology is of particular worth, since it provides explanations of human behavior that fulfill Ockham's call to not multiply causal accounts without good reason as the methodology does not impose additional explanatory mechanisms in its accounts. In adopting such frugality, he is able to sustain cognitive insights that are extant and in a symbiotic relationship with the predictive power of behavioral accounts and which together provide a wider and deeper understanding of the behaviors associated with instances in which we have to choose from among a number of options.

Throughout the text, Foxall includes boxes that contain further elaborations upon areas that are of central importance to his arguments, such as *Operant Behavior, Compulsion and Addiction, the Nervous System, Drugs of Abuse,* and *Incentive Salience*. Readers are thus able to find information that delves into the finer points of these concepts.

It has often been my experience that explanations of human behavior, including consumer behavior, when derived solely from behavioral understandings, have the possibility of yielding hackneyed, derivative, and dead-end explanations. However, in his ongoing research program, the results of which are reported in this book, I believe Foxall makes an important and seminal contribution to the understanding of both consumer decision-making and behavioral addiction, through his proposition of an account of consumer behavior that distinctively blends behavioral mechanisms with insights from cognitive approaches. He employs research studies, and his reflections upon these studies, to open further consideration of addictive behavior, and illustratively incorporates a rule-governed situation to depict the intentional behaviorist approach. Throughout his research Gordon Foxall has attempted to develop a frugal behavioral system in his establishment of explanations of consumer behavior. The result of his endeavors is an unequalled body of understanding in regard to consumer choice that should stand at the fore of teaching and research in this area for many years to come.

Paul M.W. Hackett
Professor of Consumer Ethnography, Emerson College, Boston, MA
Visiting Academic, Department of Philosophy, University of Oxford

Acknowledgments

The frontispiece, Bronzino's *An Allegory with Venus and Cupid*, is reproduced by kind permission of The National Gallery, London.

Figure 2.2 is reproduced from E.K. Miller and J.D. Wallis (2009) Executive function and higher-order cognition: Definition and neural substrates. In L.R. Squire (Ed.) *Encyclopedia of Neuroscience*, Vol. 4 (pp. 99–104), by kind permission of Academic Press.

Figure 5.5 is reproduced from K.E. Stanovich (2011) *Rationality and the Reflective Mind*, by kind permission of Oxford University Press, USA.

Figure 5.7 is reproduced from P.J. Corr (2008) Reinforcement sensitivity theory (RST): Introduction. In P.J. Corr (Ed.) *The Reinforcement Sensitivity Theory of Personality* (pp. 1–42), by kind permission of Cambridge University Press.

In Chapters 2 and 3, I have drawn on and revised extensively portions of my "Accounting for consumer choice: Inter-temporal decision-making in behavioral perspective," *Marketing Theory*, 10, 315–345.

In Chapter 4, in drawing on material from G.R. Foxall and V. Sigurdsson (2012), "When loss rewards: The near-miss effect in slot machine gambling," *Analysis of Gambling Behavior*, 6, 5–22, I have added to and substantially rewritten it, and propose an alternative interpretation to that of the original. I am grateful to my co-author.

Chapter 6 draws on revised versions of material published in my "Cognitive requirements of competing neuro-behavioral decision systems: Some implications of temporal horizon for managerial behavior in organizations," *Frontiers in Human Neuroscience*, Vol. 8, Article 184, 1–17.

The material on reward prediction errors in Box 4.2 is based on material in my "The marketing firm and consumer choice: Implications of bilateral contingency for levels of analysis in organizational neuroscience," *Frontiers in Human Neuroscience*, Vol. 8, Article 472, 1–14.

I should like to thank Sally Osborne, my secretary at Cardiff University, and Sinead Waldron and Jacqueline Curthoys at Routledge, for their help and encouragement as I have worked on this book. I am also profoundly grateful to Dr. Mirella Yani-de-Soriano, and Professors Paul Hackett and Jorge Oliveira-Castro for their invaluable comments on earlier drafts.

It is, as ever, an especial delight to thank my wife Jean for her invaluable comments on earlier drafts, and the opportunities we have had to discuss the subject matter.

Having thanked so many people, I must claim one supreme accolade for myself: the remaining errors are mine alone.

Introduction

Bronzino's painting that forms the frontispiece to this book, and which is sometimes known as *Venus and Cupid, Folly and Time*, is not in my view defeatist. For, although the immediate is tempting, it is not inevitable. While it reflects stimulus–response reactions to the imperatives of environmental opportunities and threats, inculcated in the course of a long phylogenetic history, the lure of the immediate *can* be overridden, not only by the learning that occurs during the ontogenetic development of the individual, but also through the contemplation of alternative futures. The painting captures the moment of choice, the unconsummated instant whose outcome is uncertain, at least to the naïve observer. It is this moment with which we are here concerned: the point of decision in which either passion or restraint will prevail, when one course of action, together with its aftermath, will be determined. In inquiring further of this moment, we shall not solve the problem of free will versus determinism, but, by understanding better the cognitive dimension of addiction, we may at least clarify the nature of choice.

Intentional Behaviorism

This book adopts the perspective of *Intentional Behaviorism* (Foxall, 2004, 2007a, 2007b) toward addiction conceived of as a mode of consumer choice. The function of Intentional Behaviorism is to supply the explanation of behavior with cognitive insights where this becomes necessary through the inability of extensional behavioral science to supply an account that is intelligible on its own terms, namely showing behavior to be a function of appropriate environmental variables. The method does not, therefore, juxtapose behaviorism and cognitivism as alternatives between which one must choose, but regards the former as both a useful paradigm in itself for understanding consumer choice and a means of delineating the context in which the contribution of the latter becomes both necessary and enlightening. In applying this procedure to addiction, the book describes and elucidates three stages of the methodology: *Theoretical minimalism* which seeks to establish at what point an explanation of behavior in terms of the three-term contingency (Box I.1) of radical behaviorism breaks down; *Intentional interpretation* which provides an account of the consumer's behavior by treating him or her as an idealized system, a maximizer of utilitarian and informational reinforcement, and ascribing the intentionality the system ought to have given its observed behavior pattern and its accompanying learning history and current consumer behavior setting; and *Cognitive interpretation* which provides the cognitive structure that would account for the system's behaving in this way. These latter two stages comprise *psychological explanation*.

The aspects of consumer behavior to which this methodology is applied are the explanation of temporal discounting and preference reversal which are characteristics of akrasia and addiction. The three examples explored represent a spectrum, from the most basic aspect of intertemporal valuation which lies at the heart of all temporal discounting, through consideration of the basic strategies involved in trying to allay temptation and pursue consistently one's original preference for a greater good, to the cognitive distortions inherent in a highly addictive activity, namely slot-machine gambling. In each case, I argue that, while they play a part in the process of learning and the maintenance of behavior, the contingencies of reinforcement cannot be related sufficiently closely to the observed pattern of behavior to provide a convincing operant explanation (Box I.1).

Box I.1 Operant behavior

Operant behavior is behavior that *operates* on the environment, producing consequences (reinforcers and punishers) that influence the future rate at which the behavior is repeated. The fundamental explanatory device of operant psychology is the *three-term contingency*, $S^D \rightarrow R \rightarrow S^{r/a}$, in which the rate of emission of a response, R, occurring in the presence of a setting or discriminative stimulus, S^D, is determined by the reinforcing and aversive stimuli, $S^{r/a}$, that have previously followed it (Skinner, 1953, 1971, 1974). Stimuli which control the entire three-term contingency have also been identified (e.g., Sidman, 1994), leading to the idea of the *n*-term contingency. Some pre-behavioral stimuli, known as motivating operations (MO) have the effect of enhancing the relationship between the response and its reinforcing consequences. An operant is actually not a single response but a class of responses that are maintained by similar consequences.

Operant and respondent conditioning

Operant behavior should be distinguished from *respondent* behavior: that which is shaped and maintained by classical or Pavlovian conditioning. The starting point for this is a stimulus–response event that is biologically determined (i.e., inborn or innate, and therefore unlearned). A puff of air into the eye is a stimulus of this kind, since it automatically brings about (in a physically unimpaired individual) the response of blinking. Since no conditioning has occurred, we refer to the air puff as an *unconditioned stimulus* (UCS) and the blink as an *unconditioned response* (UR). If a neutral stimulus such as a click is paired for a time with the onset of the air puff, the individual comes to blink upon hearing the click, even after the air puff has been discontinued. The click, in other words, produces a *similar* response to that of the air puff; it is usually not identical to it, being a somewhat weaker blink, perhaps. The blink in this case, since it has been learned or conditioned, is known as a *conditioned response* (CR), the click as a *conditioned stimulus* (CS). Skinner (e.g., 1974) named this form of conditioning *respondent conditioning* to distinguish it from *operant conditioning*.

Reinforcement and reward

The terms *reward* and *reinforcer* are variously defined in the literatures of neuroscience and psychology. Each usage has its merits but perhaps the least confusing is Skinner's in which *reinforcer* refers to any environmental stimulus that follows the emission of a response and which has the effect of increasing the rate at which that response is performed (e.g., Skinner, 1974). This is in line with the usual meaning of a reinforcer as something that strengthens, in this case something that strengthens a response by increasing the probability of its recurrence. This usage is also consonant with the understanding of a reinforcer as something for which an organism will work to achieve. A *punisher* is a consequent stimulus, contingent upon the performance of a response, which has the effect of decreasing that response's rate of occurrence. Positive reinforcement involves the reception of a reinforcer; negative reinforcement, escape from or avoidance of an aversive consequence. In both cases, the behavior is "strengthened"; hence, it is reinforced in each case. An aversive consequence may also be understood, therefore, as something an organism will work to avoid or escape from.

Avoidance and escape are behaviors that are negatively reinforced. If a behavior leads to the reception of an aversive consequence (e.g., incurring a fine for not returning a library book), the behavior is punished (it is likely to occur less often in future), and the aversive consequence is therefore a punisher. Some usages employ the term "reinforcer" to refer to rewards and punishers. This seems particularly confusing in view of what has been said of reinforcement's meaning strengthen: punishers hardly do this. Skinner is precise in defining reinforcement and punishment in terms of their contingent effects upon behavior; he argues also that a reward is a beneficial effect received by the individual that may or may not be contingent upon behavior and that is not systematically related to the rate at which behavior is subsequently enacted.

However, this book generally employs the term *reward* to refer to emotional reactions that may affect the rate of behavioral performance and which are elicited by reinforcing stimuli provided by the external environment (Rolls, 1999). In a sense, therefore, emotions are the ultimate biological reinforcers and punishers. They are of a particular kind, however, and this has implications for the explanation of behavior. Emotions are private (though their effects may be public) and not amenable to the third-person observation that is generally held necessary for scientific analysis. If they are to be used in the explanation or interpretation of behavior, it is necessary therefore be set the criteria for their ascription.

The intentional interpretations provided involve treating the individual as a rational utility maximizer and discovering the intentionality that would be consistent with the resultant complex of behavioral motivations. From this it is possible to raise questions about the mental apparatus that would be necessary for this kind of intentionality to be forthcoming and to provide an acceptable interpretation of behavior. The tripartite model of cognitive structure and functioning developed in the book is intended to provide a means of justifying the intentionality applied to the three target behaviors. As it has been developed here, it has the advantages, first, that it is closely related to the behaviors under consideration (the range of normal and addictive behaviors that are the subject of neurobehavioral decision theory), and second, that its association with this theory provides links with the neuroscience and behavioral science that are required to maintain the relevance and focus of cognitive explanation.

While the examination of slot-machine gambling provides a template for the place of cognitive explanation in addiction (since many other kinds of addiction entail cognitive distortions of the kind encountered in the near-miss phenomenon), the examination of the decision strategies emanating from picoeconomic interests applies to a wider range of addictive and nonaddictive patterns of behavior, and the necessity of accounting for intertemporal valuation in cognitive terms is near-universal in consumer research. The analysis undertaken in this book is, therefore, relevant to the analysis of the spectrum of consumer behaviors summarized in the Continuum of Consumer Choice, from routine everyday brand choices, through credit purchasing and environmental spoliation, to compulsive purchasing and addiction, each of which has elements of temporal discounting and preference reversal which impinge upon consumer decision-making in different ways.

These considerations may come as no surprise to many who are involved in theoretical and practical work on addiction, and for whom the use of cognitive terminology is an everyday necessity. But there are at least two reasons for not taking for granted the role of cognition in the explanation of addiction (as well as in other modes of consumption). First, cognition is often conflated with other variables, neurophysiological and behavioral, which have their own influence on behavior and yet belong conceptually to a quite different realm of discourse from that of cognition. Second, and partly as a result of this, the role of cognitive psychology is probably less well developed in the explanation of addictive behavior than those of behavioral science and neuroscience. It is these matters that the book seeks to address and redress.

Outline of the book

The first three chapters are concerned to clarify the nature of the investigation, to understand the implications for explanation of the temporal discounting and preference reversal that are characteristic of addiction, and its methodological basis, Intentional Behaviorism, which presents the explanatory procedure outlined above in which theoretical minimalism provides a framework for the development of intentional and cognitive interpretations of behavior.

Chapter 1, "Speaking of addiction," is concerned with the characterization of addiction and aspects of theory development and explanation that are involved in its understanding. Human behavior generally and addiction in particular are often discussed in terms of *choice*, a term that has numerous connotations, from the description of a sequence of behaviors to behavior occasioned by mental information processing and decision-making, to actions stemming from the exercise of free will. Chapter 1 sets the scene for the pursuit in later chapters of the argument that the questions raised by viewing addiction as choice may be elucidated by placing addiction within the context of consumer behavior, as an extreme mode of consumption which contrasts with the routine purchasing typified by everyday brand selection. Indeed, consumer behaviors may be arrayed on a continuum that spans these polar limits. Similar influences affect the rate at which consumption occurs whatever place it occupies on this continuum. Useful insight is available to us in our quest to understand addiction by viewing its commonalities with other forms of consumer choice.

This raises far-reaching methodological questions. The required cognitive dimension of a comprehensive model of addiction entails a different approach to explanation from that assumed by the other components of such a model, the behavioral and the neurophysiological. What form should cognitive interpretation take and how is its inclusion in a model of addiction justified? The analysis of consumer behavior, especially with respect to the incorporation of a cognitive dimension of explanation, is invaluable as a guide to the kind of cognitive interpretation required by a theory of addiction and its implications.

Although the question of whether (and if so how) consumers might exercise autonomous choice is beyond the scope of this book, that of how far a cognitive analysis of consumer behavior can contribute to understanding the responsibility consumers may have for their behavior, especially their extreme consumption, is central to it.

Chapter 2, "Temporal preference," discusses differences in delay discounting and preference reversal as the bases of broad modes of consumer choice. Despite the plethora of definitions of addiction, there is a common factor: a tendency to discount the future which is at the heart of impulsive, compulsive, and addictive behaviors. The chapter takes a broad perspective on the role of temporal discounting in human societies and suggests that the urgency with which we seek reward has not always been as great as it often is now. With temporal discounting goes preference reversal and the apparent irrationality of choice, manifesting in persistence in behavior that has deleterious consequences, that is characteristic of addiction. Understanding addiction requires our accounting for this apparent irrationality. Again, a cognitive account seems the inevitable avenue to accomplishing this. Once again, however, the inclusion of cognition into general theories of addiction can easily be piecemeal, underdeveloped, and confusing, especially where neurophysiological elements of addiction are both emphasized and conflated with the intentional explanation upon which cognitive accounts necessarily rest. This chapter argues that temporal discounting is influenced by contextual factors, by neurophysiology, and by evolutionary changes that have facilitated the development of prefrontal cortex (PFC) and thus spurred the capacity to exercise executive functions as a means of countering the demands of steep discounting.

Chapter 3, "Consumption and addiction," describes the structure of an extensional model of consumer choice, the behavioral economic research that has been concerned with its testing, and its relationship to emotional responses to consumer settings and to the course of addiction. The purpose of the Behavioral Perspective Model (BPM) of consumer choice is to elucidate the problem of identifying when cognitive explanation is required, and the form it should assume may be addressed by considering the way in which similar problems have been approached in consumer research. The problem identified by the behaviorists, namely that it is too easy to multiply intentional idioms and, in particular, cognitive re-descriptions of behavior, does not need to propel us into a fixed radical behaviorist mode of explanation but it deserves to be taken seriously. This approach to psychological explanation, *theoretical minimalism*, involves building an extensional model of consumer choice and testing it rigorously in order to identify the points at which intentional interpretation becomes necessary and the form it must take. Chapter 3 summarizes that extensional model, the BPM, and reviews its positive contributions to understanding consumer behavior generally and addictive behavior in particular.

The remaining chapters are concerned with the use of psychological explanation to elucidate addictive behavior. Chapter 4, "Psychological explanation: intentional interpretation," opens with a discussion of psychological explanation, comparing and contrasting the approach taken in this book with that of Bermúdez (2003). Chapter 4 discusses three aspects of addiction which require cognitive explanation. The first is *intertemporal valuation:* only an intentional interpretation captures what is happening when one compares two outcomes, both of which are in the future. The stimulus field that would be essential for a radical behaviorist explanation is unavailable, and the interpretation of the behavior requires an understanding of the personal level of exposition if its implications for the continuity/discontinuity of behavior are to be appreciated and if a speculative behavioral interpretation is to be guarded against. Intertemporal valuation therefore requires a cognitive explanation despite its portrayal in behaviorist accounts as an extensional phenomenon. The import of intertemporal valuation derives from its position as a fundamental component of both the understanding of addictive behavior and the cognitive explanation of how individuals overcome the temptation to continue to choose behaviors that provide short-range rewards but which beget longer range deleterious outcomes.

The second, *picoeconomic strategization*, describes the mental operations involved in overcoming addictive behavior (Ainslie, 1992). These entail pre-commitment to courses of deliberation, emotion, and action that will pre-clude the temptation to select short-term gain which either excludes a greater gain or incurs harmful consequences in the longer term future. Again, the stimulus field is unavailable and the behavior, which entails discontinuity with the individual's previous pattern of behavior, requires understanding in terms of the intentionality at the personal level of exposition and the inadequacies of a behaviorist interpretation. The import of picoeconomic strategizing derives from the positive ways in which it entails the intertemporal re-evaluation of future behaviors. This has far-reaching implications for the cog-nitive interpretation of addiction-related behavior.

The third involves the "*near-miss*" effect in slot-machine gambling, i.e., the tendency for a score that resembles a winning score (say, the visual presenta-tion of two identical symbols plus one maverick symbol when three identicals are required to win) to motivate further play. Despite its being, objectively, an outright failure, this score is often interpreted by the player as indicating that he or she has "almost won." This well-documented phenomenon is dis-cussed in terms of its neurophysiological basis and the possibility that it may be regarded as operant behavior. Despite the contributions of neurophysiol-ogy and operancy to its understanding, however, the conclusion is reached that only an explanation that includes cognitive distortion can account for the near-miss effect. The kinds of interpretation of this behavior in terms of con-tingencies of reinforcement rely more on the fanciful imagination of the rein-forcers, which may account for the player's continuing to gamble. An intentional interpretation seems a more intellectually honest means of accounting for the behavior, since the behavior can be made intelligible only by attributing its control to the cognitive distortions of the player.

Chapter 5, "Psychological explanation: cognitive interpretation," is con-cerned to show how the second stage of cognitive explanation, the construction of a cognitive framework that supports the intentional interpretations presented in Chapter 4, may proceed. It examines the role of the competing neurobehav-ioral decision systems model, which provides the main vehicle for probing this kind of theory in view of its incorporation of neurophysiology, cognition, and behavior. An understanding of addiction that is anywhere near adequate in terms of the necessary disciplinary structure must rest heavily on neuroscience, behavioral science, *and* cognition (Gould, 2010). My vehicle for deriving and expanding upon the implications of this is the *competing neurobehavioral decision systems* (CNDS) model of Warren Bickel and his colleagues, which understands addiction in terms of the hyperactivity of an impulsive system based on the limbic and paralimbic systems and the hypoactivity of an executive system based on PFC (e.g., Bickel and Yi, 2008). The interactions of these neurophysiologi-cal systems are held in this model to determine the rate at which the individual discounts the future. However, this does not explain all aspects of addictive behavior, which calls for a more explicit cognitive component of the model.

Chapter 5 explores the relevance of Stanovich's (2011) tripartite cognitive theory to the kind of mental architecture required to account for the intentional interpretations proposed in Chapter 4. The model encompasses conceptually both the impulsive and executive systems that comprise the CNDS model and a further echelon of cognitive processes, Reflective Mind, which exerts metacognitive control over the dual processes that are fundamental to both picoeconomics and the CNDS approach. This tripartite theory is adapted in light of the CNDS model and applied to the three areas of interest to akrasia and addiction in terms of individual differences in the capacity for hypothetical thinking that is necessary for the cognitive rehearsal of novel scenarios for future behavior that lies at the heart of both intertemporal valuation and picoeconomic strategizing.

The investigation undertaken here is necessarily multidisciplinary, drawing on neuroscience, psychology, philosophy, and economics as well as consumer research. I have therefore sought to build the argument, layering themes rather than presenting them en bloc the first time they become relevant. This involves reiteration of some points but I have tried to differentiate the discussions of overlapping themes.

The multidisciplinary approach I have adopted means that not all readers may be equally familiar with the economic psychology, behavioral science, cognitive psychology, behavioral economics, philosophy, neurophysiology, and study of addiction, all of which enter into the argument. I have sought to overcome this in two ways: through the layering of material so that themes are introduced earlier and built upon later, and a small amount of repetition where this is necessary to pursue detailed arguments without necessitating frequent referral to earlier sections.

1   Speaking of addiction

Nay, but this dotage of our general's
O'erflows the measure.

William Shakespeare, Antony and Cleopatra

Addictive behavior

A striking characteristic of addictive behavior is the pursuit of immediate reward at the expense of longer term deleterious outcomes. Moreover, addiction is typically accompanied by the expression of a strong desire to cease from or at least control consumption that has such consequences, followed by lapse, further resolution, relapse, and so on (Ainslie, 1992). Understood in this way, addiction is said to include not only substance abuse but also behavioral compulsions like excessive gambling or even uncontrollable shopping, which bring immediate short-lived rewards followed by the possibility of longer term aversive consequences (Müller and Mitchell, 2011; Ross *et al.*, 2008, 2010). While profound preference reversal may not amount to a definition of addiction, its prevalence among addicts has led to the understanding that their behavior is explicable in terms of competing brain regions which in turn engender heightened saliency of immediate rewards and awareness of the longer term consequences of indulgence.

From another perspective, addiction has been described as a "disorder of choice," as "voluntary behavior" (Heyman, 2009), albeit in Skinner's (1953) sense of such behavior as that determined by its consequences in the process of operant learning rather than elicited by preceding stimuli as in classical or Pavlovian conditioning. Given Skinner's argument that operant behavior is no less environmentally determined than that produced in classical or Pavlovian conditioning, Heymann's use of the word "choice" is interesting. From the point of view of radical behaviorism, there is no suggestion that the behavior of the addict is chosen in the sense that it reflects free moral agency. Rather, the implication is that such behavior is the result not of a medical condition or underlying physiological susceptibility to the effects of ingested substances but of the contingencies of reinforcement and punishment within which it is embedded. Hence, if the response costs of obtaining and ingesting such substances increases sufficiently, the behavior will occur less frequently or even cease. Its consequences are its causes. More accurately, its rate of repetition is a function of the consequences which similar behavior has generated in similar circumstances in the past. This is the essence of operant explanation.

Intriguing as the debate about free will and determinism in the context of addiction may be, it raises but leaves unresolved the proper role of mental language in the description and understanding of addiction. Cognitive psychology is generally conceived of as a deterministic science but its practitioners have trafficked nonetheless in such intensional concepts as desires and beliefs, information processing and decision-making, which to the layperson imply at least a phenomenological level of understanding and often a sense of personal agency.

This book speaks of addiction as an extreme mode of consumer choice, different in degree though not in kind from more routine modes of consumption; that is, consisting in the use of products and services that serve as reinforcers, engendering similar neurophysiological responses and emotional rewards, but in the case of drug and process addictions generating also craving and compulsion that go well beyond the usual desire for more economic goods until the addict's life is seriously disrupted (Box 1.1).

Box 1.1 Compulsion and addiction

Compulsion implies an inability to control one's behavior despite awareness of its deleterious consequences. Compulsive drug use has several causes: *biological*, both genetic predisposition and current physiological pressures; *contextual*, social pressures and substance availability (including classical and operant conditioning which determine the efficacy of environmental stimuli); and *cognitive*, beliefs that rationalize behavior (Altman *et al.*, 1996). The view that all are implicated in drug addiction is insufficient for understanding and treating addiction which require a precise model of causal interaction (Carlson, 2010). Moreover, any attempt to differentiate among these sources of causation raises questions of free will and determinism which involve the nature of choice and invite consideration of the role of the alternative causes. In examining the role of neurobiology as the basis of compulsion, therefore, it becomes necessary to set this particular perspective within the context of the other influences on choice.

The first consideration of a biological perspective on addiction is why this phenomenon could have evolved through natural selection. Evolutionary logic suggests that the results of ingesting certain substances would have been adaptive and that the hedonic associations of such ingestion would have provided immediate reinforcement for the whole chain of behaviors that produced them (Panksepp, 1998). But the genetic structures preserved in this process play a limited role in influencing current behavior: while genes may specify the general adaptive goals of behaving by determining primary reinforcers, they do not determine specific behaviors or the secondary reinforcers that control their incidence

(Rolls, 2005). Heritability measures apply to whole populations and have limited if any explanatory value for individual behavior (Joseph, 2003). It cannot be denied that genetic factors influence the etiology of addiction (Heyman, 2009, p. 93), since studies of fraternal and identical twins indicate that shared genes increase the probability that twins share drug dependency (Kendler *et al.*, 2000; Tsuang *et al.*, 1998, 2001), but their influence is far from straightforward.

Evolutionary considerations are, however, implicated in the ways in which brain systems register the current reinforcing/punishing consequences of drug ingestion and thus the likelihood of future drug use. Two examples are presented to illustrate the extensive role that biogenic factors play in addiction: the tendency of a drug such as cocaine to induce craving for its continued self-administration, and the role of the insula in evoking urges to use drugs based on representations of interoceptive phases of ingestion. Dopamine (DA) is associated with wanting or craving a drug rather than with the hedonic pleasure of taking it (Berridge and Robinson, 1995). This is especially apparent in the case of cocaine which interferes with the re-uptake of DA, permitting it to influence its receptors over time. The cocaine rush or high that is the result of this is thus prolonged and strengthened. The outcome is that the behavior of cocaine use which precedes such reinforcement is continually evoked, with the result that the individual experiences a craving for the drug (Hyman and Malenka, 2001).

The resulting focus of research has been on the mesolimbic dopaminergic system (Box 3.2) and other brain regions such as the amygdala and ventral striatum involved in emotional responses. But there is recent evidence that the insula is important because of its relation to the conscious craving for drugs (Naqvi and Bechara, 2008). This role has been revealed by correlation-based fMRI studies which show the increased activity of the insula during self-reported urges to ingest drugs. Such activity is related to the emergence of the secondary reinforcers which tie drug use to specific behavioral and contextual factors and to the cognitive drivers of drug use. "Over time, as addiction increases, stimuli within the environment that are associated with drug use become powerful incentives, initiating both automatic (i.e., implicit) motivational processes that drive ongoing drug use and relapse in addiction to conscious (i.e., explicit) feelings of urge to take drugs" (Naqvi and Bechara, 2008, p. 61). The ritualistic practices involved in the preparation of drugs, associated with specific places, apparatus, packages, lighters, and so on, thus become sources of the pleasure that reinforces not only those activities but the consummatory acts of drug ingestion. These processes, which elicit specific memories of encounters with the contexts and the drugs, are also responsible for differences in the subjective experience of urges for various drugs be they cigarettes, cocaine, or gambling. By ensuring that the individual keeps particular goals in mind, the insula is also involved in (thwarting) the executive functions that might overcome drug urges (cf. Tiffany, 1999). The learning process includes the development of neural plasticity through DA priming with respect to the impending chain of appetitive events; Naqvi and Bechara (2008) propose that this DA dependency invokes activity in the insula and associated regions such as the ventromedial prefrontal cortex (VMPFC) and amygdala. The plasticity involves the establishment of representations of the interoceptive outcomes of using drugs and thus engender relapse even after long periods of non-use.

These neurobiological processes appear sufficient to account for compulsion, the indulgence in immediate pleasures in the knowledge that they will eventuate in severely unpleasant consequences. Behavior enacted in the face of impending contingent punishment which we have previously experienced and of which we are cognitively aware seems so irrational as to be explicable only in terms of chemical forces over which we have no immediate control. But reinforcement and punishment suggest an alternative explanation. Brain-based emotions, urgings and cravings, which are the ultimate rewards and motivators of behavior, are the endpoint of a sequence of behavior–environment relationships that make addiction controllable. Heyman (1998, 2009) points out that, whereas the biogenic influences which lead to the definition of addiction as a disease beyond the control of individuals, an alternative model is based on the existence of choice. The environmental contingencies that are the immediate regulators of operant responses control "voluntary" behavior that is selected by its consequences, rather than elicited by antecedent stimuli. This in turn gives rise to the idea of choice as behavior that is determined by its costs and benefits, and even by cognitive consideration of its costs and benefits. The import of Heyman's proposal is that since operant behavior can be modified by the manipulation of its consequences, particularly by increasing the immediate costs of acquiring and taking drugs, it is under the control of the individual. This shift in the locus of control from internal chemistry to the person acting in a context of rewards and sanctions indicates, according to Heyman (2009), that addiction is not a disease but a choice.

Heyman is correct in raising the possibility of treating addiction by changing its consequences but it must be noted that he uses terms such as "voluntary" and "choice" in ways that are likely to mislead non-behaviorists. Skinner (1953, pp. 110–112) distinguished reflexive or "involuntary" behavior from that which is operant or "voluntary." It is in this sense that behaviorists distinguish voluntary behavior, and Skinner was at pains to point out that "voluntary" behavior is as much under the control of environmental contingencies as "involuntary." Heyman's proposal seems disingenuous if he does not make explicit his understanding of the terminology of choice. His emphasis on the need to research environmental determinants of behavior and their interactions with biological functioning is nevertheless overdue.

This book applies a methodological approach to the explanation of consumption based on *Intentional Behaviorism* (Foxall, 2004, 2007a, 2007b, 2008, 2015c, 2015d) with the overall objective of understanding better both addiction and its explanation. Intentional Behaviorism is a methodology which incorporates the parsimonious model of behavior advanced by radical behaviorism in order to ascertain the point at which intentional interpretation, including cognitive narratives, becomes necessary to account for observed behavior. Hence, the method is not confined to the investigation of consumption via the extensional sciences. Rather, the objective is to learn from this process not only where intentional language and explanation are appropriate, and hence avoid their unnecessary proliferation but also to understand better the unique contribution to understanding that the parsimonious model, which avoids intentional idioms, can make.

This theme of addiction permits, above all, an opportunity to test and evaluate the theory of consumer choice. Most of the empirical research which has founded the model has been concerned with routine aspects of consumer choice such as product, brand, and store selection, and with the interpretation of relatively routine aspects of consumer behavior like spending and saving, the adoption and diffusion of innovations, environmental conservation, and the role of marketing management in shaping and maintaining patterns of consumer choice. My overriding aim is, therefore, to evaluate the model itself as a theory in terms of its applicability to the phenomenon of addiction. This investigation of addiction as consumer choice is not simply a case study for the testing of conclusions drawn elsewhere: it is part of an extension of the thinking inherent in the research program itself and its applicability to understanding human consumption.

The Consumer Behavior Analysis research program

When I began to study, teach, and undertake research in consumer behavior, there was a strong tendency to explain choice in cognitive terms and to do so somewhat uncritically on the understanding that any behavior was necessarily preceded by a mental attitude or intention. This assumption derived naturally from everyday folk psychology and was reinforced by the ascendancy of cognitive psychology at the very time when modern consumer behavior studies were coming to the fore. (Realization that a suitable framework of conceptualization and analysis for this purpose was Skinner's radical behaviorism (1945, 1953) led to a critical examination of the epistemological basis of radical behaviorism in terms of its distinctive ontology and methodology and to an assessment of its role in the interpretation of consumer choice (Foxall, 2010b)).

The cognitive explanation of consumer choice has since then become more sophisticated but I believe there is still a need for the research program I inaugurated in order to reach more stable and reasoned conclusions about the nature of cognition and its role in social scientific explanation. The procedure of this program was to employ a behaviorist model of consumer choice, one which entirely eschewed cognitive and other intentional variables, and to ascertain how far one could go by using it to understand consumer choice. In this way, by testing the behaviorist model to destruction, it would be possible to ascertain the point at which behaviorist assumptions broke down, and the nature and role of the required cognitive variables would be revealed. At the same time, any positive contribution of the more parsimonious model would also become apparent. These expectations are being met and the results of the research program provide a foundation for continuing investigation.

Mindful of the behaviorist dictum that allusion to mental entities is unnecessary to explain observed behavior (Skinner, 1950, 1963, 1974), it becomes necessary to employ intentionality with care and consideration in order to generate a plausible and responsible psychological explanation of choice. It is here that the conceptualization of addiction as consumer behavior comes into its own, since the approach to consumer research with which I have been associated for some decades has been intimately concerned with the probity of a cognitive approach to the explanation of consumer choice.

The Behavioral Perspective Model (BPM; Foxall, 1990/2004, 2010a) is a means of exploring and explaining consumer choice in relationship to its environmental determinants. As the research program was designed to demonstrate, the application of this model to consumer choice has revealed both the advantages of a parsimonious approach to the explanation of certain aspects of consumer behavior and the bounds of behaviorism: the points at which an intentional or cognitive intentional interpretation of consumer behavior becomes necessary and the form it should take (Foxall, 2004, 2007a, 2008b). The opportunity has accordingly been taken to develop further models and methodologies which incorporate intentional interpretations (Foxall, 2007b, 2007c, 2013).

The methodology of Intentional Behaviorism

The methodological procedure entailed in Intentional Behaviorism, which is described at greater length in Foxall (2016a), has three stages (Figure 1.1). Stage One, *Theoretical Minimalism/Contextual Explanation*, is marked by the use of extensional behavioral science in a spirit of theoretical minimalism to establish the bounds of behaviorism. At this stage, choice is conceived of as behavior in the context of alternative behaviors: the ratio of a person's performance of behavior *A* as a proportion of his or her performances of all

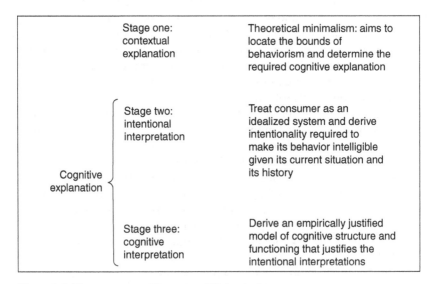

Figure 1.1 The sequence of Intentional Behaviorism.

other behaviors: $A:A'$, for example, the number of times a consumer pur-chases a standard pack of a particular brand of breakfast cereal compared with the number of his or her similar purchases of other brands. The purposes of this stage are, first, to determine the extent to which a parsimonious, behav-iorist model can account for aspects of consumer choice that are not revealed by other models; and second, to identify where an intentional account of behavior becomes necessary as a result of the inability of the extensional model to explain observed activities, and the form that that intentional account must take in order to interpret the behavior. Usually, this entails that the stimulus conditions necessary to predict and control the behavior are not empirically available. Three such bounds of behaviorism have been identified: in accounting for the continuity/discontinuity of behavior, in providing a personal level of exposition to interpret behavior, and to delimit the scope of behavioral interpretation (Foxall, 2004, 2007a, 2007b, 2007c).

The problem of accounting for behavioral continuity/discontinuity arises when the antecedent and consequent stimuli needed to explain observed behavior by means of the n-term contingency cannot be reliably identified with interpersonal agreement. The problem of developing a personal level of exposition arises in response to the behaviorist's notion of private events (thoughts and feelings) in an attempt to account for behavior in terms of a subjective phenomenology. Private events are inherently intentional con-structs and require a treatment in terms of intentional interpretation. Delimi-tation of behavioral interpretation is necessary because such an account of behavior lacks a means of establishing limits for the environmental events that can count as reinforcers and antecedent stimuli in interpreting behavior that is not amenable to an experimental analysis. How distant in time and/or space can a stimulus be and still credibly provide a plausible account of behavior? The limit can only be determined by considering what the individual can reasonably have known at the time he or she acted.

Extensional explanation, which is amenable to a high degree of empirical evaluation by means of experimental and correlation-based statistical methods, is the starting point for the investigation of behavior (Fagerstrøm and Sigurds-son, 2015). It is typified by the three-term contingency of radical behaviorism (an explanatory device in which the rate at which observed behavior is per-formed is accounted for by the nature of its previous consequences and the current stimulus field in which it occurs; see Box 1.1). The goals of such ana-lysis are limited to the prediction and possibly the control of the behavior. The first stage of Intentional Behaviorism consists in the formulation and testing to destruction of a parsimonious behaviorist model of choice.

In Stage Two, *Intentional Interpretation*, the consumer is treated as an inten-tional system, i.e., idealized as a utility maximizer to which is attributed the intentionality it "ought" to have, given its learning history and current behavior setting. This construction of an idealized account of the behavior of the indi-vidual is to a degree consonant in its objectives and procedure with Dennett's (1978) *intentional system theory (IST)*: it consists in ascribing the desires and beliefs, the perceptions and emotions that the consumer, viewed as a rational system, "ought" to have given its history and current circumstances. It is exactly these variables that the model produced in the context of theoretical minimalism has identified as consistently related to the consumer's observed behavior patterns. Hence, the procedure of intentional interpretation has the advantage of being able to call upon a tranche of empirical research results which enable the idealized account of the consumer behavior to be constrained in its use of intentional idioms rather than being permitted to run free in the woods of psychological speculation. Dennett argues that his IST should be tested according to how accurately it can predict the system's behavior. Intentional interpretation within the Intentional Behaviorism methodology is concerned to present an interpretation of observed consumer behavior, for which the stimulus conditions necessary for a behaviorist explanation are not available, in a way that may be evaluated according to the empirical findings of the extensional model of consumer choice (the BPM). In other words, the interpretation produced in the absence of the stimulus field necessary to generate an extensional *explanation* of the behavior in question (to the extent that it could be predicted and controlled) is assessed in terms of its plausibility as an explicator of the class of behavior for which such an explanation is possible. Hence, the intentional behaviorist approach differs from Dennett's in several ways, to which I will return after describing the final stage.

Stage Three, *Cognitive Interpretation*, proposes an empirically justified model of cognitive structure and functioning which would be necessary to effect the behavior of a system that merited the intentionality interpretation constructed in Stage Two. The rationale for this is that the intentional interpretation be shown to be consistent with the underlying cognitive psychology that accounts for consumer decision-making and, on a cognitive view therefore, for consumer behavior. This component of Intentional Behaviorism takes two forms: the construction of a micro-cognitive psychology which reflects the consistency of the intentional interpretation with sub-personal considerations, predominantly those identified and studied by neuroscience, and a macrocognitive psychology which reflects the consistency of the intentional interpretation with super-personal considerations, predominantly those identified and studied by behavioral science. Taken together, Stages Two and Three constitute Psychological Explanation.

Dennett (1978, 1987) identifies IST as a competence theory, one which lays out what mechanisms would be required to account for behavior, notably the intentionality in terms of which it would be accounted for, but which does not inquire into the nature and operations of those mechanisms. In other words, it specifies the desires and beliefs the system would have to have had to bring it to its current position. Dennett also proposes that the system would be predictable on the basis of this ascribed intentionality, which takes the form of *abstracta* that are logically derived constructs. The underlying structures and functions that would account for this intentionality belong to what Dennett styles sub-personal cognitive psychology, in which cognition is justified on the basis of neurophysiological links which proceed in terms of the more specific *illata*, causally interacting entities that enter into empirically testable theories and interpretations. Sub-personal cognitive psychology is a performance theory, one which specifies the precise mechanisms that justify the intentional interpretation that is IST; it represents the sophisticated application of the intentional stance at the level of the sub-personal, notably that of neurophysiology. Sub-personal units are treated as predictable from the attribution to them of contentful terms. Employing as its constructs the illata which Dennett defines as the specific and refined variables that can enter into scientific theories, sub-personal cognitive psychology is a performance theory, one which explores the structure and functioning of the cognitive mechanisms that account for behavior.

This study employs existing theories that are relevant to addictive behavior and cognitive processing as the sources of intentional interpretation and cognitive interpretation. This avoids my constructing theories in support of my own methodology, and in addition it promotes integration among theories of cognitive processing. It means, furthermore, that the theories may not fit exactly the strictures I have set for these components of psychological explanation; this is not an impediment to my task, since it will provide one source of critical evaluation of this approach to cognitive explanation. It is desirable that the intentional interpretation consist in a theory that is closely related to akrasia and addiction, while the cognitive interpretation provides a broader understanding of cognitive functioning. Chapter 4, therefore, establishes the case for an intentional interpretation by demonstrating the limitations of a behavioral explanation of intertemporal valuation, picoeconomic strategizing, and the near-miss, while Chapter 5 develops cognitive treatments of these phenomena.

It is essential that the cognitive interpretation be consistent with findings and theories in neuroscience and behavioral science, since these are a prime source of constraint on speculative cognitive explanation. For this reason, I have used as my template for the development of a cognitive interpretation *the competing neurobehavioral decision theory* (CNDS; Bickel *et al.*, 2013) which has firm connections with these extensional sciences. This choice is entirely for positive reasons, notably because of the three elements which the model contains, pointing to the integration of neuroscience, behavioral science, and cognitive psychology. It is a central tenet of Intentional Behaviorism that, although intentionality must not be ascribed at the sub- or super-personal levels of exposition, any intentional interpretation offered at the personal level must be consistent with and indeed constrained by the findings and theories of the extensional sciences. The CNDS model is eminently suitable for this intellectual quest.

An example: schedule insensitivity

An example of the problem is provided by experimental performances on so-called matching tasks. Matching will be explicated in greater depth in Chapter 2 but its essence is captured by the following example. The behavior of adult human beings on matching tasks may be explained by the kinds of schedule of reinforcement in operation. Known as "concurrent" schedules, they consist of two keys, A and B, each of which produces a reinforcer after a different interval of time has elapsed provided that at least one response has been made on that key during the period. If, in phase 1 of an experiment, pressing key A is reinforced every 10 seconds as long as at least one press has been made and pressing key B once every 20 seconds as long as at least one press has been made, then the matching law predicts that the participant will allocate 66.6 percent of responses to key A and 33.3 percent to B. In addition, he or she will obtain similar proportions of reward, respectively, from each key. Similar results are obtained for human and nonhuman animals. Hence, the term *matching* (Herrnstein, 1997). But if, in phase 2 of the experiment, the schedules are modified so that different periods must elapse before responding receives reinforcement, nonhumans adapt quickly to the new schedule while human participants tend to retain the former response pattern. We cannot explain human beings' insensitivity to the altered schedules by reference to the discriminative and reinforcing stimuli now in operation, since their behavior is clearly not influenced by them. The sole explanatory factor within the scope of radical behaviorism is the private events (thoughts and feelings) that are a central, even defining, element in this philosophy of psychology. The rules that participants devise for themselves in order to comply with the schedules in force during phase 1 of the experiment and that are enshrined in their thoughts, are held to be carried over to the new situation defined by phase 2 and to lead the individual to continue the behavior pattern that was reinforced in phase 1 but not in phase 2. An alternative strategy of explanation might be to maintain that it is the individual's learning history that carries over from phase 1 to phase 2, that he or she is constrained by previous reinforcement patterns to repeat the behavior under the new stimulus conditions (Foxall and Oliveira-Castro, 2009).

However, neither of these explanations is acceptable within a science of behavior because each deals in unobservables that cannot enter into either an experimental or correlational analysis. Any statements about the verbal rule formulations that entered into the decision-making of an experimental participant are mere fabrications, untestable conjectures, explanatory fictions. Similarly, any appeal to a learning history that is not empirically available is not an entity that can enter into a scientific explanation. They are speculations, the purpose of which is to save the theory upon which the accompanying explanation of behavior rests. These are precisely the sorts of explanatory fiction that behaviorists such as Skinner sought to eliminate from scientific inquiry. The fact that they proceed in the terminology of behavior analysis may seduce the reader into thinking that they do not "appeal to events taking place somewhere else, at some other level of observation, described in different terms, and measured, if at all, in different dimensions" (Skinner, 1950, p. 193). In fact, they contravene Skinner's strictures on every count. Resort to private verbal behavior or to an unobserved learning history is necessarily an appeal to otherwise located events, observed by who knows whom, and discriminable only in different dimensions. It would be intellectually dishonest to provide accounts of this kind simply in order to prop up the radical behaviorist ideology of explanation or to appeal to some form of "action-at-a-distance" to fill in the gaps that scientific observation is unable to fill. The fact of the matter is that the behavior cannot be explained in terms of the extensional language that is the hallmark of behaviorist psychology and perhaps its very *raison d'être* (Foxall, 2004). More satisfactory is to acknowledge the explanatory gap that arises when the stimuli responsible for a behavior pattern cannot be identified and to employ intentional language to account for the behavior. That is the problem with which Intentional Behaviorism is concerned. But how is such an interpretation to be constructed and justified?

In terms of the model of psychological explanation just explicated, we would arrive at an *intentional interpretation* by treating the experimental participant as someone who seeks to maximize the returns from his or her behavior. The reinforcers used in experiments of this kind are typically points or small sums of money. We assume that the player is an optimizer, a person who maximizes utility by attempting to gain as many points or coins as possible. We then ascribe to him or her the intentionality with which such behavior would be consistent: the *desire* to maximize returns, and the *beliefs* that by playing in this way, pressing these keys in these time frames, the goal will be achieved. This ascription of intentionality provides a plausible intentional account of the behavior. The next stage is to ground this account in what is known of the cognitive architecture that would be consistent with such behavior and the ascribed intentionality; the necessary *cognitive interpretation* would consist, therefore, in an account of decision-making based on cognitive theories for which empirical evidence had accrued.

The necessity of psychological explanation

Only when the stimulus conditions that account for the behavior cannot be identified should we seek elucidation of the behavior in psychological terms (those that refer to intentionality, including cognition). The rationale for this rests on the more reliable knowledge that may be obtained from the extensional sciences of behavior and neurophysiology. My reasons for taking this stance are primarily epistemological: I do not wish to support imperious views of science, but it is important when making interpretations of behavior to have some idea of the kind of knowledge that is being generated and its status. The overriding question, therefore, is what kinds of knowledge can we have of consumer choice and addictive behavior? As a rough-and-ready guide I distinguish three broad kinds of knowledge.

First, *scientific knowledge* is that which gives rise to justified explanation based on replicated experimental analysis which establishes functional relationships between dependent and independent variables. I will refer to this simply as explanation. This is not to overlook the imperfections of scientific experimentation; it is simply to recognize that such extensional explanation, partly by virtue of its being corrigible, has a very high degree of reliability. The essential characteristic of scientific knowledge is its amenability to disconfirmation through empirical investigation: it is falsifiable (Popper, 1959). This kind of knowledge is at the heart of the radical behaviorist philosophy of psychology, the empirical research component of which was long known as the "experimental analysis of behavior." Although this is quintessentially the scientific method, and yields, as I have said, high reliability, it has the downside that it is confined to telling us about how people behave in experimental settings and therefore can lack the verisimilitude required to understand how people act amid the complexities of natural settings.

Second, *statistical analysis of data*, typically by means of regression-based methods, also evinces a high degree of reliability and may have enhanced validity insofar as it reflects independent variables present in natural settings that cannot be reproduced in experimental settings. While the radical behaviorism paradigm enjoins single-subject research design upon its adherents, there are instances where data must be aggregated over subjects simply because they have learning histories of such diversity that studying one at a time would make their behavior very difficult to relate to the environmental contingencies under investigation (Foxall, 1998, 2010a; Curry *et al.*, 2010). This is also an extensional explanation and may be especially valuable when its basic premises can be demonstrated experimentally. This has not found a ready place in radical behaviorism, since it usually requires aggregated data for many subjects rather than the single-subject research paradigm that has dominated that approach. Nevertheless, it is sometimes essential to aggregate data for multiple subjects in order to observe behavioral regularities that can be consistently related to patterns of reinforcement. Moreover, this methodology provides insights into real world behavior that cannot be gleaned from experimental analyses. The outcomes of this form of enquiry as quasi-explanation may be thought of as quasi-experimentation.

Third, there is interpretation. This may take the form either of a *behavioral interpretation* or an *intentional interpretation*. The former is couched in the extensional language of radical behaviorism, an extrapolation of the behavioral principles gained in the laboratory or through correlation-based statistical analysis. The difficulty with behavioral interpretation is that when it is impossible to subject environmental variables of which behavior may possibly be a function to experimental or quasi-experimental tests, it is tempting to assume too great an influence on the part of events that are interpreted as consequences of the behavior (Foxall, 2004). One of the most important functions of intentional interpretation arises under such conditions: that of delimiting the urge toward behavioral interpretation in circumstances beyond the scope of a laboratory or tightly controlled statistical study. It also becomes necessary whenever a behavioral interpretation cannot be undertaken with the rigor required to ensure intellectual integrity. This would be the case whenever the elements of the three-term contingency cannot be reliably applied in the process of interpretation to the extent of achieving intersubjective agreement within the scientific community.

The *intentional interpretation* of observations, undertaken when extensional explanation within the rigorous requirements of radical behaviorism is not feasible, is also a route to knowledge in its own right. It is not possible for this mode of research to demonstrate functional relationships between the intentional concepts used to make the behavior intelligible. Interpretation was a key preoccupation of some radical behaviorists like Skinner (1953, 1969) who, nevertheless, failed to provide much of a framework for its systematic accomplishment. Although his interpretation of verbal behavior (Skinner, 1957) attempts a systematic analysis, his other interpretations tended to take the form of rather undisciplined extrapolations (e.g., Skinner, 1953). In this book I am going to be concerned primarily with intentional interpretation and I seek above all a reasoned methodology by which it may be achieved. The focus is on what the development of an interpretive method reveals of consumer choice so that we can gauge how this elucidates addiction in particular. It is precisely because I see the importance and necessity of intentional interpretation that I contrast the kind of knowledge of which it is capable with those produced by alternative methodologies. It is necessary to be aware of the status of that in which one believes.

Psychological accounts take the form of *interpretation* of the behavior rather than its *explanation*, since the rigor that would be imposed by experimental and quasi-experimental methods is not accessible to the interpreter. Any tests of hypotheses derived from the psychological interpretation are couched in the terminology of either behavioral science or neurophysiology; the testing itself belongs to the realm of behavioral science or neuroscience rather than to that of psychological interpretation.

While understanding addiction requires contributions from neurophysiology, behavioral science, and cognitive psychology, however, some current models often tend to downplay or confuse the role of cognition in addiction. The following analysis seeks, therefore, to redress this balance in view of the centrality of cognition to understanding consumer choice in general and addiction in particular.

Having said this, the treatment of cognition, even simply the use of cognitive terms, has the problems that (1) they tend to proliferate all too easily as a result of their readiness to fill gaps of psychological explanation, and (2) they are often confused with neurophysiological terms and occasionally behavioral terms, even though intentional – including cognitive – terms belong to another realm of discourse and explanation. My analysis is also intended, therefore, to contribute to the clarification of the use of intentional terms in general and cognitive terms specifically.

Conceptual clarification

The nature of cognition

Definitions of cognition differ considerably in their ontological and methodological breadth and my aim at this stage is to suggest a spectrum within which the various cognitive operations may be understood. Heyes (2000, p. 4) writes, in the context of the evolution of cognition:

> cognitive states and processes are (1) theoretical entities, which (2) provide a functional characterization of operations of the central nervous system, (3) may or may not be objects of conscious awareness, (4) receive inputs from other cognitive states and processes and from perception, and (5) have outputs to other cognitive states and processes and to behavior.

Emphasizing the distinctiveness of a cognitive explanation from the sort produced by behaviorism, Tomasello (2014, p. 8) argues:

> [C]ognition evolves not from a complexifying of stimulus–response linkages, but, rather, from the individual organism gaining (1) powers of flexible decision-making and behavioral control in its various adaptive specializations, and (2) capacities for cognitively representing and making inferences from the causal and intentional relations structuring relevant events.

Writing also in an evolutionary context, Shettleworth (2000, p. 43) proposes a broader conception that comprehends perception within cognition:

> [A] full account of the evolution of cognition should embrace all mechanisms that invertebrates and vertebrates have for taking in information through the senses, retaining it, and using it to adjust behavior to local conditions.

Cognition, she notes, citing Terrace (1984) and McFarland (1991), respectively, is said to involve "explicit representations of absent stimuli" or "declarative as opposed to procedural knowledge." Hence, cognition is "information processing in the broadest sense, from gathering information through the senses to making decisions and performing functionally appropriate actions, regardless of the complexity of any internal representational processes that behavior might imply" (Shettleworth, 2000, p. 43). Even these portrayals of cognition do not represent the whole continuum, however; for, as Tooby and Cosmides (1992) argue, emotion may under some circumstances be regarded as an aspect of cognition. The import of this further broadening of the scope of cognition stems not only from arguments that affect has a cognitive component but also from the evolutionary logic which permits the treatment of emotionality in modular terms (Faucher and Tappolet, 2008).

For present purposes, the more restricted standpoint of Heyes and the more embracing standpoint that includes perception and emotion as integral parts of cognition provide a spectrum of definitions which may prove applicable in different explanatory contexts. I will make use of them singularly and finally attempt a synthesis.

Any attempt to integrate cognitive psychology, behavioral science, and neurophysiology into a single framework of analysis, however, comes up against the difficulty that the discourse which is ordinarily the stock in trade of experimental science and the intentional language of beliefs and desires belongs to quite distinct modes of explanation (Bennett and Hacker, 2003). This identification may be argued philosophically but, if the researchers in question are acting in response to the necessary arguments, they seldom make this fact explicit. The impression given is that the two are equivalent, even though no attempt has been made to justify this assumption. If cognition is kept separate from neurophysiology, the difference in the kinds of explanation each offers is usually overlooked, even though the ascription of cognition to an individual follows canons of judgment that are quite distinct from those that lead to the acceptance or rejection of a hypothesis in the neurological sciences.

The definitions I have quoted above are valuable for more than their ontological range, however. For instance, Heyes's statement that cognitive states and processes are *theoretical* entities is based on the understanding that cognitive terms refer to unobservables which, though not directly amenable to experimental analysis, are used by investigators to increase the intelligibility of their subject matter. Although cognitive activity appears to be real on the basis of our personal experience therefore, it is not part of a causal explanation of behavior. Cognition is not a directly demonstrable property of individuals but is ascribed on the basis that their beliefs will be consistent with their behavior patterns and current situation, including their neurophysiological functioning. Thus Dennett (1987) argues that we can predict the behavior of an intentional system by adopting the intentional stance, ascribing to it the beliefs and desires it may be expected to have, given its current situation and learning history. Although the present aim is to explain behavior rather than necessarily to predict it, a similar logic of ascription applies. Hence, the purpose of a cognitive analysis is to reconstruct the beliefs and desires by which an individual most probably acted. This is neither a causal nor an experimental analysis: it is an *interpretation* rather than an explanation. Especially pertinent here is the proposition that cognitive states and processes are theoretical entities, which implies that they refer to "unobservables," terms employed to make behavior more intelligible in the absence of directly observable variables of which it may be shown experimentally to be a function.

Moreover, cognitive explanation requires a conception of thinking in terms of the desire-belief notion of rationality, as Tomasello (2014, p. 9) puts it: "a goal or desire coupled with an epistemic connection to the world (e.g., a belief based on an understanding of the causal or intentional structure of the situation) creates an intention to act in a particular way." *Individual intentionality*, as he terms this model, proposes that

> thinking occurs when an organism attempts, on some particular occasion, to solve a problem, and so to meet its goal, not by behaving overtly but, rather, by imagining what would happen if it tried different actions in a situation – or if different external forces entered the situation – before actually acting. This imagining is nothing more than or less than the "off-line" simulation of potential perceptual experiences.

This prebehavioral contemplation makes three cognitive demands: namely, the capacities to (1) represent experiences to oneself "off-line," (2) simulate representations of this kind in terms of causality, intentionality, and logic, and (3) monitor one's putative behavior and appraise the outcomes of these simulated behaviors so that a reasoned decision could be made (Tomasello, 2014, p. 9). These are considerations to which we will return when considering dual-process and tripartite models of cognition in Chapter 5.

Another observation is that, although cognitive activity is real in the first-personal phenomenological sense that it certainly seems to be real to each of us at a subjective level, it does not *cause* behavior in the strong sense which could be demonstrated by, say, an experimental analysis. I assume a materialist purview in which mental events are functional specifications of brain processes or, more accurately, as Heyes points out, processes of the central nervous system (Box 1.2). What, then, is the role of cognition in a theory of behavior? Rational beings (and there are evolutionarily consistent arguments for humans to be expected to act rationally: Dennett, 1995) may be predicted to behave *in accordance with* the beliefs and desires which can be logically ascribed to them on the basis of their phylogenetic and ontogenetic histories. The purpose of a cognitive analysis is thus to reconstruct the beliefs and desires that are consistent with the manner in which individuals have been observed to act, given their evolution by natural selection and their experience. Such an account supposes no more than a weak form of cognitive-behavioral causality and may better merit the term *interpretation* than explanation.

Box 1.2 The nervous system

The nervous system is conceptually divisible into two intimately connected parts which interact to ensure that inputs via the senses are centrally processed and thereby converted into behavioral outputs. The central nervous system (CNS) comprises the brain and the spinal cord, while the peripheral nervous system (PNS) is the entire nervous system beyond the CNS such as the neurons that influence skeletal muscles to produce movement. The CNS comprises some 10^{11} to 10^{12} neurons ("nerve cells"), each of which communicates with many others (Cabanac, 2010). The two systems are vitally interconnected, however: for instance, motor neurons are located in the spine but interact with elements of the PNS that effect muscular movement. The term *afferent* is used to describe activity directed toward the CNS, such as inputs from sensory organs; *efferent* denotes activity from the CNS, such as innervation of more remote nerves.

The brains of vertebrates contain three major divisions: the *hindbrain*, *midbrain* (the mesencephalon), and *forebrain* (Figure 1.2). Comparison of the human brain with the brains of fish, amphibians, reptiles, and most mammals including primates indicates that the former is marked by a disproportionately expanded forebrain. We will consider each of these in turn and then their interconnectedness, especially in the production of behavior. As a generalization, the hindbrain and midbrain subdivisions, which are known together as the *brainstem*, perform non-cognitive functions such as regulating breathing and blood flow, and locomotion. The brainstem is a receptor for sensory information and acts to integrate the motor output of super-neck areas via the *cranial* nerves (not the spinal nerves). The midbrain is also involved in the initial processing of some sensory information. The forebrain is the seat of rational or executive functioning which, on the basis of the sensory inputs it receives from the midbrain, and stored information regarding past behavior and its outcomes, underpins the cognitive activities we designate coordination, evaluation, and decision-making. It is worth noting even at this stage, since my later argument will make much of it, that we have shifted here from an account of the brain in purely neurophysiological terms to one that describes its functions using cognitive expressions. Of course, the forebrain is as much a physical structure as any part of the brain, one that contains cells that convey chemical signals to other cells. Yet most accounts of forebrain function at all levels of biological sophistication resort to the language of the mind in order to express the effects of this neurological functioning on behavior. This shift has important theoretical and philosophical implications.

Even though the hindbrain, midbrain, and forebrain evolved in quite different time frames and play different roles in organizing the behavior of fish,

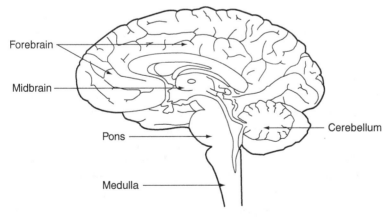

Figure 1.2 Hindbrain, midbrain, and forebrain.

amphibians, reptiles, and mammals (and, among the mammals, human beings), all three regions contribute to the cognitive functioning of modern consumers. Information concerning vibration and orientation is transmitted from the ear and organs of balance to the *hindbrain* which is composed of the *cerebellum*, the *pons*, and the *medulla*. The *cerebellum* coordinates movement and the learning and enactment of motor capabilities. The *pons*, which connects the hindbrain and midbrain, is instrumental in communication of information from the cerebellum to the forebrain. The *medulla*, which is important to the control of automatic operations like digestion, swallowing, breathing, and heart rate, integrates the brain with the other major component of the nervous system, the spinal cord.

The *midbrain* is especially concerned with the integration of sensory and motor functions. It controls response to visual and auditory information, receiving information from the eyes and translating it into appropriate motor responses. Hindbrain and midbrain are connected in the form of the *reticular formation*, which also forms part of the medulla. Other components of the midbrain are the *substantia nigra*, the *inferior colliculus*, and the *superior colliculus*. The colliculi are concerned, respectively, with auditory and visual sensation. That is, the superior colliculi receive mainly visual stimuli and the inferior colliculi receive mainly auditory stimuli. In addition, the superior colliculi receive nociceptive (related to tissue damaging) and tactile input, and are involved in eye movement and orientation to external stimuli. Together, the colliculi form the topmost part or "roof" of the midbrain. Because they are collectively concerned primarily with vision, the cell layers that compose them are known as the *optic tecta*. The "floor" is composed of the *tegmentum* which is implicated inter alia in motor function. The *substantia nigra* is also concerned with motor function, notably with voluntary movement.

The *forebrain* comprises the *telencephalon* (the foremost part of the brain, containing the *cerebral hemispheres*; the *cerebral cortex* is the outmost part of the hemispheres, the large enfolded layer); and the *diencephalon* mediates the flow of information from the spinal cord to the telencephalon. The cerebral cortex (or "neocortex") is involved in the control of both sensory and motor functions.

A problem that arises in the ascription of cognition in accounting for behavior is that the entities that are proposed to do the work of explanation are theoretical; they are by their very nature unobservables, inferred on the basis of observations of behavior, its environmental determinants, and the neurophysiology that undergirds it. Whereas the entities proposed by behavioral science and neuroscience may for the most part be directly observed and are amenable to direct experimental analysis – and where they are not, the scientists involved strive to make them so – cognitive concepts are not tangible in this way and cannot be made so. They may be translated into behavioral or neurophysiological variables but these remain proxies, and the experimental and other methods of examining them empirically belong to behavioral science and neuroscience, respectively. Verbal responses generated by attitude surveys are behaviors under the control of the stimulus conditions that influence all behavior; the increased firing of dopaminergic neurons when a reward is signaled are neurophysiological events rather than expectations. For these reasons, the ascription of cognition in accounting for behavior requires caution and tentativeness. It is something to be undertaken only when the extensional sciences of behavior and neurology have been shown to be unable to explain the behavior in question. Even then, intentional ascription must be consonant with, and hence both inspired and constrained by, the findings of these extensional sciences.

Intentional and extensional languages and explanations

The adoption of intentional interpretation requires more than the haphazard use of terms such as "desire" and "belief," "perception" and "emotion." Nor can intentionality be swept aside, as it often is by behaviorists, as having no import in the context of behavioral explanation, if only because behaviorists frequently resort to it themselves in their expositions of behaviorism (Foxall, 2007b, 2008b, 2009). Psychological, as opposed to behaviorological, explanation has a logic and a purpose peculiar to itself which entails criteria that must be carefully observed in its execution (cf. Bermúdez, 2003 with LeDoux, 2015).

"Intentionality," in the philosophical context in which I am using the word, refers to the "aboutness" of some entities like thoughts and feelings; they represent something other than themselves. As a rule we think about *something*, feel *something*, believe or desire or perceive *something*. This is not always the case: in the case of feelings such as general anxiety or depression it can be difficult to identify the object of intentionality. Hence, Brentano's (1874) idea that intentionality was the inescapable mark of the mental and that therefore it distinguishes the physical from the non-physical founders (Crane, 1998). But that does not affect my purpose here. Most emotions however display intentionality – being angry *about* the price of food, or loving a significant other – and anxiety and depression are probably best regarded as meta-emotions or moods.

Intentionality is a linguistic phenomenon, something which inheres in grammatical sentences rather than substances (Chisholm, 1957; Dennett, 1969). (Sometimes, the term "intensional" is reserved for this linguistic usage; Crane, 2009). Theories of behavior are a matter of how language is deployed to make a subject matter intelligible: they are methodological devices rather than ontological descriptions. The essence of intentional interpretation is the explanation of an individual's behavior in terms of what he or she *desires* and what he or she *believes* about the availability of the desired object and the means to attain it. That is, we explain my retrieving a particular book by my desire to read it and my belief that it is on a particular shelf in my library. Such intentional explanation is also at the heart of social and behavioral science: if A *desires* x and *believes* that doing y will lead to x, he or she will do y (Rosenberg, 1988). As I have said, the "attitudes" represented by the italicized words enter into sentences that are *about* something other than themselves: we do not simply "expect" or "desire" or "like" per se; we "expect that p," "desire that p," or "believe that p." The "p" represents a proposition such as "That my book is in the library," while the mentalistic verb preceding it is known philosophically as an "attitude." Hence, the predicate of the statement "The author believes that the book is in the library" is known as a propositional attitude.

Intentional and extensional sentences differ in several regards, all of which are central to the kind of explanation they present. First, extensional language allows the *substitution of coextensive terms* without altering the truth value of a sentence. Confining myself to extensional language, if I say, "Ed McBain wrote the 87th Precinct novels," I can also say "Salvatore Albert Lombino wrote the 87th Precinct novels," since Ed McBain was a pseudonym used by Salvatore Albert Lombino for these famous police procedurals. Substituting "Salvatore Albert Lombino" for "Ed McBain" does not affect the truth value of the sentence; the names are synonyms or *coextensives*: in each case the extension of the author named is the particular man who wrote police procedurals. However, intentional language does not permit the substitution of coextensives without a change in the truth value of the sentence. So, it does not follow from my saying "John *believes* that Ed McBain wrote the 87th Precinct novels" that I can say, "John *believes* that Salvatore Albert Lombino wrote the 87th Precinct novels" without altering the truth value of the sentence. In these statements about John, the two names for this author are different *intensions*, linguistic referents of a particular person, and it does not follow that they are in this guise coextensives. One way of saying this is that John may simply not know that Ed McBain is Salvatore Albert Lombino, so one is not substitutable for the other. Sentences that do not permit the substitution of coextensives, intentional sentences, are said for this reason to exhibit *referential opaqueness*; extensional sentences display *referential transparency*.

Therefore, extensional language consists in sentences, the truth value of which inheres in the substitutability of coextensive terms. Rephrasing "This consumer has purchased Brand X" as "This consumer has purchased Product Y" when X is the sole member of the Y product category is an example of the substitution, *salve veritate*, of synonymous terms which is the hallmark of extensionality. This is the language which is generally taken to be that of hypothetico-deductive science: it leads directly to statements that can be tested by their correspondence with empirical evidence (Quine, 1960). By extensional language is meant, therefore, sentences that are "referentially transparent," that conform to the normal usages of science, contain no intentional terms, sentences that allow substitution of identicals.

Second, intentional objects possess *intensional inexistence* (Brentano, 1874). This does not mean that they do not exist (though that is a point we shall return to). It means that they refer to, represent or are about something other than themselves which is said to exist *in* them. The intentional terms possess intentional in-existence therefore in the sense that the intentional item exists *in* the proposition. "Peter is thinking about the shoes he is going to buy" implies that the shoes he is imagining exist within his thoughts. If Santa Claus rather than Peter's shoes is the intentional object of a sentence, the truth value of the sentence is not affected by the nonexistence of Santa. "Peter believes that Santa is going to bring him a pair of shoes" is true, regardless of the existential status of Santa Claus.

This brings us to the third difference between the extensional and the intentional. If Peter is thinking about the golden mountain rather than his shoes, the intentional object in question does not of course exist in reality. In intentional language and behavioral interpretation there is no implication that the intentional object, in this case the golden mountain, actually exists, has existed, or will ever exist anywhere. As noted above, what we have said about the characteristics of intentional sentences does not imply real existence. Santa Claus has intentional "in-existence"; he "exists" within the intentional idiom contained in the sentence that refers to him. But extensional sentences entail an existential reality that can be checked by the senses: the extensional statement "Peter is going to buy those shoes" is true only if there is a pair of shoes for Peter to purchase.

Another reason why intentional and extensional languages involve distinct modes of explanation is that an intentional sentence cannot be translated into an extensional sentence without altering its meaning, usually by adding information. The sentence, "John said that it was a weekday" might be rendered extensionally as "John said, 'It is Wednesday,'" "John said, 'It isn't Sunday,'" "John said, 'Today is a school day,'" and so on. Each of these extensional sentences adds information not present in the original intentional rendering.

The question of how language is to be used in the explanation of behavior is raised also in the context of the mind–body problem which arises from the differences in kind between knowledge by acquaintance and knowledge by description. The resolution of this problem would require bridging concepts that belong to both categories but we lack such conceptual sophistication. Any proposed bridging concept would in practice belong to one or other category and could not therefore perform the necessary boundary-spanning work. The result is not substance dualism, since the problem is ultimately verbal rather than ontological, but it does mean that conceptual dualism is inevitable. This means that our languages of exposition and explanation will belong to one category or the other and that the temptation to smuggle in the language of one to seemingly elucidate the other must be rigorously resisted.

Levels of exposition

Dennett (1969) distinguishes the *sub-personal level of explanation*, that of "brains and neuronal functioning," from the *personal level of explanation*, that of "people and minds." The sub-personal level, which refers to the neurophysiological processes that underlie reinforcement, thus entails a separate kind of scientific purview and approach to explanation: by encompassing neuronal activity it is the domain of the neuroscientist and entails an extensional account (Box 1.3). The personal level of exposition, as I use this term, refers to the domain of mental phenomena and is the explanatory concern of the psychologist; it requires an intentional account. I have also proposed a third level of exposition in order to cover the whole range of phenomena and sciences that deal with them in a comprehensive approach to the explanation of behavior (Foxall, 2004, 2007a, 2007b, 2007c). This is the *super-personal level of exposition* which encompasses operancy, the respect in which the rate of behavior is contingent upon its reinforcing and punishing consequences; this is the field of extensional behavioral science. ("Operancy" refers to the effect on behavior of environmental contingencies of reinforcement and punishment. As a term which refers specifically to the *process* of reinforcement and punishment of behavior it avoids the theoretical notion of "conditioning" and is therefore more consistent with an extensional portrayal.)

Box 1.3 Neurons and neurotransmission

Neurons are central to how information is translated from inputs received through the senses into information that leads to bodily movement, emotions, and other forms of activity. The human brain contains about 100 billion neurons. Two types of projection emanate from opposing ends of the cell body. *Dendrites* input information from other neurons; they divide repeatedly into smaller fibers that link to the *axons* of other nerve cells. Each neuron has a single axon which carries electrical and chemical messages to the dendrites of receiving neurons.

The cell body contains the nucleus, the myelin sheath that covers the axon in order to increase the speed with which it conveys electrical currents, and the dendrites that are innervated by the axons of other neurons (Figure 1.3).

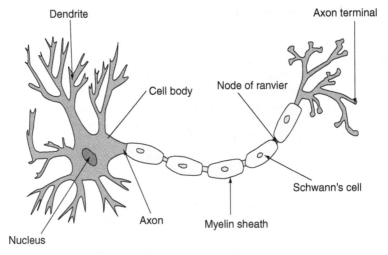

Figure 1.3 The structure of a typical neuron.

Myelin is a thick, white, fatty substance formed as a result of the cytoplasm in the oligodendrocyte membranes in the central nervous system (CNS) and the Scwhann cells of the peripheral nervous system (PNS). It provides a sheath around some vertebrate axons which insulates them electrically. Its function is to permit the rapid propagation of *action potentials* over long distances. An action potential is a sudden increase ("spike") in the electrical activity of a neuron, usually engendered by a sensory input such as acute heat. The neuron is said to be "firing" when its action potentials increase in this way. Neurons communicate via chemicals (neurotransmitters) with large numbers of other neurons, influencing their tendency to fire or produce action potentials.

The point at which the dendrite of one neuron interacts with the axon of another is known as a *synapse*, and each neuron in the human brain is linked to others via some 1000 synapses (Figure 1.4). The small gap between the terminal buttons of the presynaptic cell and the receptors of the postsynaptic cell is the *synaptic cleft*. At this point, the action potential of the presynaptic cell releases a neurotransmitter which enters the synaptic cleft and comes into contact with appropriate *receptors* positioned on the postsynaptic cell. As a result of a neurotransmitter entering the second cell, information is transferred within the nervous system. (Neurons are categorized by the neurotransmitters they release: hence, dopaminergic, glutamatergic, and cholinergic neurons respectively release dopamine, glutamate, and acetylcholine.) Terminal buttons, located toward the end of the axon, contain *synaptic vesicles*. These contain the neurotransmitters, which communicate with other neurons. An action potential in the presynaptic cell engenders the ejection of the neurotransmitter into the synaptic cleft. Communication between neurons is thus both an electrical and chemical process. A neurotransmitter may have either an excitatory or inhibitory effect on the postsynaptic neuron; i.e., it may facilitate or impede the normal functioning of the cell by increasing or decreasing the action potentials it produces.

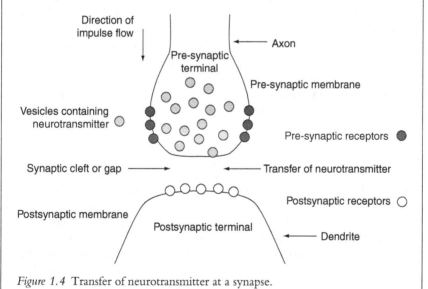

Figure 1.4 Transfer of neurotransmitter at a synapse.

The essence of super-personal explanation is the operant paradigm and the description of the BPM which is an extensional model of consumer choice. In empirical work and in the explanation of behavior, it is commonplace now to employ a molar conception of operant behavior (i.e., to consider sequences of responses in relation to sequences of reinforcers), rather than to look at behavior in a molecular fashion (i.e., in terms of a single response under the control of a single discriminative stimulus and a single reinforcer), as the three-term contingency presents the contingencies of reinforcement (Baum, 1973, 2015).

Great care is necessary to maintain the separation of these three levels, since the mode of explanation which each entails is unique and cannot be combined with the others in a simple fashion (Hornsby, 2000). The fundamental difference in mode of explanation which must be constantly recognized is as follows. The sub- and super-personal levels, which are based on the neuro- and behavioral sciences respectively, require the use of extensional language and explanation, both of which are in principle amenable to experimental ("causal") analysis, or failing this to the quasi-causal analysis made possible by statistical inference. They differ from one another in terms of the kinds of stimuli and responses (independent and dependent variables) that must be taken into consideration in empirical testing of the hypotheses to which they give rise. They differ more fundamentally from the personal level of explanation, which attracts a wholly different mode of analysis, namely that of intentional psychology; the approach to explanation in this case relies on the ascription of beliefs, desires, and feelings on the basis of non-causal criteria. The intentional explanation which underlies cognitive accounts, and which interprets behavior in terms of ascribed beliefs and desires, belongs at the personal level of analysis: that of persons and their inferred mental operations.

Although it may be permissible in everyday discourse to mix these explanatory modes, as when we employ *une façon de parler* to describe the car in front as having decided to brake suddenly, in scientific discourse the distinct levels of analysis and explanation which they connote must be kept separate. This does not mean that intentional language should occupy no place whatever in scientific accounts but it does implies that if a theory incorporates both modes of explanation it must make clear the relationship(s) between them and show how their joint use explicates the subject matter to which the theory is directed. Murphy and Brown (2007, p. 23) employ the term "semantic hygiene" for the practice of using "mentalist language only to describe what the whole person is doing or experiencing, not to refer to the activity of some part of the person (such as the brain)." "In our terms," they continue, "applying mentalist language to the brain is a category mistake – another version of Cartesian materialism" (ibid.). To deviate from this dichotomy of the personal and sub-personal/super-personal by employing intentional language at the sub- and super-personal levels which are the province of the extensional neuro- and behavioral sciences, respectively, is to be guilty of what Bennett and Hacker (2003) term the *mereological fallacy*, the attribution to parts of a system of features that properly belong only to the system as a whole (Bennett, 2007; Bennett and Hacker, 2007; Foxall, 2007b, 2008a).

The basis of these differences in explanation is the intentional language that is appropriate at the personal level and the extensional language that is appropriate at the sub-personal and super-personal levels of exposition. The difference in the truth value of sentences expressed in each explanatory language marks them off as distinct, probably incommensurable sources of explanation. This strengthens the stricture on mixing language from one realm with the explanation of elements that belong to the other.

As I have noted above, it is particularly tempting to refer to sub-personal elements and their functions in cognitive terms, and there is a long-standing tendency to make ad hoc use of cognitive and other intentional terms to account for behavior. This calls for a more exacting approach to the use of intentional terminology. The appropriateness of intentional language may be established by exhausting the capacity of extensional language to explain behavior, thereby revealing the place and nature of intentional and cognitive interpretation.

Nor does Intentional Behaviorism embrace Dennett's definitions of IST and sub-personal cognitive psychology, per se. Since the distinction between the personal level of exposition denoted by the use of intentional language and the sub-personal level of exposition that speaks of brains and neurons is strictly maintained in Intentional Behaviorism, the two elements of psychological explanation which it employs (intentional interpretation and cognitive interpretation) are both competence theories and their variables are abstracta. The abstracta–illata distinction which has been heavily criticized by adherents of Dennett's system as well as detractors is thus avoided (Ross, 2000, 2002b). Intentional Behaviorism regards the extensional behavioral and neurosciences as providing the performance theories which can be empirically tested. The purpose of the cognitive interpretation is indeed to "cash out" the intentional interpretation by providing, on the basis of empirical evidence as well as theoretical reasoning, an account of the cognitive structures and functions that are theoretically feasible.

Implications for Intentional Behaviorism

Dennett (2006) points out that behavior is all we have to study; to that extent we are all "behaviorists" of one sort or another. The first sort of behaviorism is that which eschews entirely any mention of the mental in explaining behavior, adhering strictly to the attempt to describe behavior only in extensional language. This is the radical behaviorism of Skinner (1945). The second is that which finds it necessary to resort to intentional language in order to describe and explain observed behavior. This latter is the approach taken by Intentional Behaviorism.

For Dennett (1987), an entity is an intentional system if its behavior can be predicted by the ascription to it of appropriate desires and beliefs. That is all there is, he says, to being intentional, to having a mind. I agree that the key consideration in our ascribing intentionality to a system is that this is the sole means we have of rendering its behavior intelligible. Such a system is an intentional system. But I differ from Dennett in two respects. First, I do not make prediction the criterion, since I believe that predictions made at this level will be gross, uninteresting, and largely unfalsifiable. I would hold, rather, that an intentional interpretation be judged on how far it is consistent with knowledge gained from neurophysiology and behavioral science. Hence, while Dennett's emphasis on prediction may lead to the hypothesis that the system will maximize utility in general, the search for intelligibility in Intentional Behaviorism would require that the behavior of a consumer be consistent with the maximization of some combination of utilitarian and informational reinforcement.

Second, I do not hold that becoming more intelligible as a result of being ascribed intentionality is *all* there is to having mentality and being an intentional system. I am ultimately a realist rather than an instrumentalist about the existence of intentional entities; though they may be largely verbal and affective, they actually exist in others as I believe them to exist in me. (I do not believe this ontological point differs much in practice from that which Dennett would make: Dennett, 1991b, 2006). My inference about their existing in me (at least as discernible patterns of my private behavior) is based on knowledge by acquaintance and is therefore not empirically available for scientific scrutiny, any more than are the private events of radical behaviorism. I can only report that I seem to have desires and beliefs, perceptions and emotions, and that they seem to be responsible for my behavior or at least consistent with it. On this basis and on the basis of the knowledge by description I receive from others about their desires, beliefs, emotions, and perceptions, I am willing to attribute intentionality to others and to assume that it has a similar impact upon their behavior, either causing it or at least, in rational persons, being consistent with it. Moreover, it is difficult to understand where the notions of desires and beliefs would have originated if not in their seeming to be real in one's experience.

Third, for a system's intelligibility to be increased by the ascription of intentionality, it is necessary to show that it is capable of making intentional inferences and modifying its behavior accordingly. If this is not the case, then there is another stance which may be applied to rendering the system's behavior intelligible. Dennett mentions the physical stance (which applies to the operation of physical entities), and the design stance (which applies to designed entities); we might add the contextual stance which portrays entities' behavior as determined by the consumer situation (the interaction of their learning histories and the stimulus field constituted by their current behavior setting; Foxall, 1999a. This is the heart of the extensional Behavioral Perspective Model described in Chapter 3). Although there is bound to be controversy over the range of species to which an intentional stance may therefore be employed, it is probably safe to assert that in addition to human beings, the nonhuman great apes, particularly bonobos and chimpanzees, but also gorillas and orangutans qualify (Tomasello, 2014), though, on the basis of the apparent capacities to analogize and innovate, this may well not be an exclusive list (Reader and Laland, 2003). My aim is to establish a principle rather than to demarcate the applicability of an intentional stance. The point is that many behaviors, including those of species to which an intentional stance is applicable, may be rendered more intelligible by alternative stances prior to the point at which we need to ascribe intentionality to them. But that point will become apparent as we observe the capacities of the species to employ intentional reasoning themselves. This confines the entities that can be treated as intentional systems to those that can themselves apparently show the capacity to reason intentionally.

The contextual stance

The *contextual stance* (Foxall, 1999a) is the philosophical position which portrays behavior as the result of contingencies of reinforcement and punishment, more particularly in terms of the *n*-term contingency in which a discriminative stimulus sets the occasion for particular behavioral consequences contingent upon the performance of a given response. Some consequences of responding have the effect of increasing the probability of the emission of a similar response in similar circumstances in future; these consequences are known as reinforcers and the procedure described is positive reinforcement. An aversive consequence produced by a response reduces the rate of the behavior and is known as a punisher. Action that serves to avert an aversive consequence is said to be negatively reinforced: it is still reinforced because it is strengthened (repeated) but negatively because it has the effect of avoiding or escaping from the aversive consequence. The sequence seems superficially contradictory, since the variable of which behavior is a function follows the response but the point is that it is the individual's history of reinforcement that determines his or her current behavior. This stance translates into the consumer situation, as presented in Chapter 3 in terms of an extensional model of consumer choice, in which the probability of a response is decided by the intersection of that learning history and the current stimulus setting. In essence, the context stance states that a "contextual system" or "operant system" is an entity that is predictable from its learning history and the behavioral outcomes made possible by its current situation (Foxall, 1999b, 2015e). This approach has been employed widely in consumer research.

Consumer choice

Temporal discounting and preference reversal

While there are multiple definitions of addiction (Ross *et al.*, 2010; Poland and Graham, 2011; West and Brown, 2013), preference reversal entailing steep discounting (exaggerated devaluation) of the future is a constant theme.

The two behavioral tendencies are related but not identical. Preference reversal entails the abandonment of an individual's inclination to patiently await the LLR when the opportunity to consume becomes imminent; steep discounting entails a dramatic reduction in the subjective value of the LLR on account of its not being available for some time. As will be discussed in Chapter 3, all but the most routine and everyday consumer behaviors involve both: buying on credit, for instance, especially if large debts are thereby incurred; and disposing of waste products in ways that make life easier at the moment but damage the physical environment in the longer term. This is not to underestimate the differences between addictive consumption and other forms of consumer choice, to ignore the facts that addiction is widely conceived of as a disease, that its consequences may be more devastating than those of any other kind of consumption, and that addictive behavior may be immensely difficult if not impossible to reverse. Hence, Koob *et al.* (2014) present a neurophysiological and behavioral understanding of addiction, couched in terms of drug dependency but applicable also to process or behavioral addictions. For these authors, "drug addiction is a disease and, more precisely, a *chronic* relapsing disease" (Koob *et al.*, 2014, p. 4, emphasis in original). They define addiction more completely as "a chronic relapsing disorder characterized by compulsive drug seeking, a loss of control in limiting intake, and emergence of a negative emotional state when access to the drug is prevented" (Koob *et al.*, 2014, p. 26). This is not, of course, to say that environmental factors play no part: McKim and Hancock (2013) outline two approaches to the acquisition of the disease of addiction. *Predisposition theories* propose that people may be born with the disease or at least acquire it before they begin abusing the drug. Hence, the disease predisposes some people to become addicts once they start using the drug. *Exposure theories* portray addiction as caused by repeated exposure to the drug. Addicts were not born with the disease: they acquire it by exposure to the drug. Recreational drug use may then develop into harmful use and addiction with the result that this causes changes in the brain that further encourage addiction. The former approach emphasizes genetic and neurophysiological predispositions to drug addiction; the latter, the consumer situations in which drug use may begin and, in some people, develop further. There are numerous variations on these themes, most of which draw attention to a range of biological and situational imperatives in the development and treatment of addiction.

Drawing attention to addiction as an extreme mode of consumption is to recognize that the most visible aspect of addiction is its irrationality (in economic terms) in that it entails high levels of investment in behaviors intended to overcome it, followed by larger investments in its continuance. The motivation that follows from this is to understand better how cognitive factors may be used to explain such preference reversal. The analysis therefore takes as its primary focus temporal discounting and preference reversal, using them as templates for the explanation of consumption in general and addiction in particular, tracing specifically the implications for a cognitive explanation of this behavior pattern.

Addiction as consumption

Viewing addiction as a mode of consumption behavior has the advantage that it enables us to compare the factors that account for it with those that are relevant to the explanation of more routine forms of consumption. In particular, the role and nature of cognitive explanation as it has been developed in the context of consumer theory may be relevant to determining the role of cognition in the explanation of addiction. The development of the consumer theory has concentrated on the responsible use of cognitive terms and the ways in which neurophysiological and behavioral factors prescribe and circumscribe cognitive usages. In treating addiction as a form of consumption, the analysis applies to it the same logic of theory development with respect to cognitive explanation as has been employed in theoretical consumer research generally.

By treating addiction as consumer choice, I do not wish to trivialize it. "Consumer choice" is a term that sometimes brings to mind insignificant selections among myriad brands that are virtually identical to one another, belonging to product classes that no one may need and possibly would not even want in the absence of the pressures of marketing persuasion. These are not my views, even of consumer choices that entail far less serious consequences than does habitual drug taking, problem gambling, compulsive shopping, or whatever form addiction takes. My primary aim is, rather, to understand better how we can speak of choice in a complicated area of human experience, one that may have far-reaching deleterious outcomes for the individuals involved and the members of their social networks.

Addiction is centrally concerned with *reinforcement* or reward, which is also at the heart of economic behavior, including consumption (Hursh *et al.*, 2012). Both operant psychology and economics are essentially concerned to understand the allocation of scarce resources among multiple opportunities to obtain satisfaction or utility (Foxall, 2015a; Foxall and Sigurdsson, 2012). *Consumer Behavior Analysis* (Foxall, 2001, 2002, 2015b) is concerned with understanding the allocation of behavior among different opportunities for purchase and consumption, and in doing so it refines the idea of reinforcement by bifurcating it into its purely functional or utilitarian benefits and its social benefits which convey information about one's status and prestige. Addiction is not only conceivable as an extreme form of consumption; it is also open to analysis in the same terms as other kinds of consumption. It is amenable to analysis on the basis of the same disciplines and the same underlying causal factor as any other form of consumption. The idea of reinforcement links them all, and reinforcement generally exerts a more potent effect upon behavior the more immediate it is. Addiction differs from many other modes of consumption in degree rather than in kind.

Characterizing addiction

Let us recap on what addiction means, by asking at what point akrasia, or weakness of will, may be said to have become addiction, which implies a degree of compulsion to behave in a particular way. Preference reversal, based on temporal discounting, and hyperbolic discounting at that, is an obvious component of both akrasia and addiction. But more is required for addiction. There must also be economic irrationality: the heavy investment in a course of action that is then voided by the adoption of a contradictory path. More than even that, the irrationality must be pursued to the extent that it entails the breakdown of one's lifestyle: loss of livelihood, loss of close relationships, loss of self-esteem. This progression must occur before we can speak of addiction, and there must be consonant evidence in terms of the sources of reinforcement and neurophysiological functioning. But the process is not irreversible; folly and time do not necessarily capture a person's being to the extent that they preclude change. Sometimes, the hold of a drug or pattern of behavior are situationally determined, as in the case of American soldiers in Viet Nam who were apparently addicted to heroin by the time they returned home but who settled into their indigenous environment and foreswore the drug (Robins *et al.*, 1975; Heyman, 2009). Sometimes, the addiction is indeed a chronic relapsing medical disorder (Koob *et al.*, 2014), but there are those who have also moved away from this pattern. Chapters 2 and 3 explicate these themes.

2 Temporal preference

I wasted time, and now doth time waste me.

William Shakespeare, *Richard II*

Akrasia

As I scan my daily newspaper over breakfast, I note the television programs scheduled for the evening. It is easy at so early an hour to vow that I will under no circumstances allow myself to watch what is on offer. Tidying my sock drawer or deadheading the roses seem more valuable uses of my time, and serious reading or writing infinitely preferable. Comes the evening, however, the opportunity to relax and be passively entertained wins out. Am I speaking here of "myself" as one person whose preferences are reversible simply with the passage of time, or of two separate agents warring to gain the upper hand? If the latter, how are they related and how do they influence each another? Perhaps there is some superordinate level of decision-making that arbitrates between them; or perhaps they reflect no more than differing histories of operant reinforcement.

Preference reversal

The problem of preferences that change with time lies at the heart of many comparatively trivial daily decisions. What seems perfectly reasonable when we begin becomes absurd simply because other options, ultimately less valuable than the initial longer term objective, have become immediately accessible (Rachlin, 2000a). Apparently for that reason alone, these short-term choices temporarily assume an irresistible level of attractiveness: the result may be excessive consumption leading to obesity or procrastination leading to failure to achieve (Ainslie, 2010; Kennett, 2001; Radoilska, 2013). The problem, namely akrasia or weakness of will, occurs also in the more serious contexts of substance abuse and problem gambling, even when the individuals concerned know from experience the deleterious outcomes of their behavior and have the "best intentions" of changing it. It is interesting that when

Searle (2001, p. 10) quips that "akrasia in rational beings is as common as wine in France," he should allude to weakness of will as a common characteristic of *rational* beings. In what sense are we to understand this rationality that underlies such self-defeating behavior? Once again, the questions of the apparently "divided self" or "multiple selves" arise (Ainslie, 2001; Elster, 1987; Ross *et al.*, 2008). These questions, which are central to my investigation in this book, raise a number of additional considerations: for instance, in what sense can addiction be judged to be a "choice"? Who or what (the individual, the environment, neurophysiology) is responsible for addictive behavior? Can we attach moral responsibility for the excessive consumption that often characterizes addiction to another "self," one that was in control of my being and behavior at some earlier time but which is now disempowered by the self I currently am, a "self" that is, perhaps, not to blame (Hanson, 2009)?

The initially self-controlled and subsequently impulsive behaviors involved in preference reversal may be traced to neurophysiological and cognitive bases of competing decision systems. Jentsch and Taylor (1999) propose that drug seeking stems from amygdala-based reward processing that intensifies the incentive value of potentially addictive substances, accompanied by the weakened capacity of frontal cortical processes to impede such behavior. Bechara (2005) similarly argues that the extent of an individual's willpower to resist drugs depends on the relationship between an impulsive system based on the amygdala which indicates the immediate outcomes of behavior and a reflective system, based in turn on the ventromedial prefrontal cortex (vmPFC) which indicates delayed outcomes (Bickel and Yi, 2010; Mischel and Ayduk, 2013; Euston *et al.*, 2012). This relationship has been most comprehensively described, however, in the competing neurobehavioral decision systems (CNDS) model which hypothesizes that two competing neural systems respectively exert excitatory or inhibitory control over potentially addictive behavior (Bickel *et al.*, 2013).

Competing neurobehavioral decision systems

The CNDS model proposes that imbalance between an individual's "impulsive" and "executive" systems influences his or her rate of temporal discounting. Hyperactivity of the impulsive system, based on limbic and paralimbic brain regions, coupled with hypoactivity of the executive system, based in the prefrontal cortex (PFC), results in a tendency to discount the future steeply and to engage in addictive behavior (Bickel and Yi, 2008). A major premise of the CNDS model is, therefore, that the impulsive and executive systems must be in some respects antipodal and yet contribute in a complementary manner to the determination of the individual's temporal discounting behavior and valuation of currently and potentially available reinforcers. These have been concerns of the CNDS model's authors who also emphasize the role of metacognition (i.e., "cognition about cognition" or "thought about thought") in the regulation of inter-system connectivity

(Jarmolowicz *et al.*, 2013). In attempting to clarify further the factors responsible for the achievement of a relative balance between the impulsive and executive systems, this paper explores further the antipodality of the model's component decision systems and, in particular, the nature and role of metacognition in their relationships.

The CNDS model has two important implications for the resolution of the question of multiple selves. First, by incorporating *cognitive* or decision-making contributors to the extent of an individual's temporal discounting tendency, it links to the capacity to regulate behavior through goal setting and maintenance, social cognition (understanding why others behave as they do), and insight (taking one's own imperfections into account in judging behavioral outcomes). Second, the model's incorporation of operant behavioral economics and neuroeconomics (Bickel *et al.*, 2007a, 2007b, 2011a, 2011b, 2011c, 2012b) facilitates its integration with the economic reasoning which underlies another significant contribution to the explanation of multiple selves and their interaction, namely *picoeconomics* (Ainslie, 1992, 2001; Foxall, 2014a, 2014b; Ross, 2012).

Picoeconomic interests

Ainslie (1992) speaks of the problem of akrasia by reference to separate *interests* that are in conflict: one concerned with our gaining long-term benefits such as engaging in productive work, the other with short-term pleasures like undemanding amusement. One's experience as the locus of this clash of interests is often marked by a sturdy resolve to undertake the more rewarding activity, followed by a lapse into the other just as it becomes available, followed by regret, further resolution and perhaps inevitable relapse. This cycle is characteristic of addiction but it also marks many everyday switches of preference involved in less extreme behavior. What is so preferable when we make our plans is edged out by an alternative that is initially unthinkable but of immense value as it heaves into sight. Even though we know full well that the activity which we were determined to undertake when we set out will bring greater benefit, the fact that it is delayed while the less beneficial activity can be obtained immediately raises the value of the latter sharply until it exceeds the current worth of the other. An intriguing facet of Ainslie's approach is the possibility that, by "bundling" together the combined benefits of a series of later-appearing rewards and comparing these *in toto* with the immediate benefit of a current, less valuable choice, it is possible to overcome the temptation to make a sub-optimal decision (i.e., to exercise "willpower" or "self-control"). Hence, picoeconomics has implications for the role of cognition and metacognition in relationships between neurobehavioral decision systems and the place of agency in understanding their interaction (see also Elster, 2015).

Some of these implications are taken up by Ross (2009), who defines the situation in economic terms by reference to two rewards available at different times such that *a* is, for example, taking a short vacation starting in a week [t_1], and *b* is, for instance, starting a two-year course of study for a higher degree [t_2]. Looking well into the future, the person's utility function indicates that *b* is preferable to *a*. At this point, the person discounts the future rather gently. However, as the time of the vacation becomes closer, the person's utility function indicates a preference for *a* over *b*. Ross (2012) models the various picoeconomic interests in two ways depending on whether these interests are conceived of as acting synchronously or diachronically. In the first case they may be seen as sub-agents that have either conflicting utility functions or divergent time preferences. Agents with conflicting utility functions may be modeled in terms of a Nash equilibrium game among these agents. Modeling the behavior of sub-agents whose time preferences diverge adverts to the sub-personal level of neurophysiology in which a hyperbolic time preference emerges from "competition between steeply exponentially discounting 'limbic' regions and more patient (less steeply exponentially discounting) 'cognitive' regions" (Ross, 2012, p. 720). Like the CNDS model, this picoeconomic portrayal depends heavily on the findings of a key experiment in neuroeconomics based on fMRI scans of human beings choosing between SSR and LLR (McClure *et al.*, 2004).

Neuroeconomics of decision systems

The study by McClure *et al.* (2004) required students to choose reinforcers varying with temporal delay and size. When making decisions relating to immediate reinforcers, the regions of the students' brains that were highly activated were located in the limbic and paralimbic areas (including the ventral striatum, the medial orbitofrontal cortex, the medial prefrontal cortex, and posterior cingulate cortex); however, when making decisions about reinforcers that were delayed, the relevant brain regions were located in lateral prefrontal brain regions (including the dorsolateral prefrontal cortex, the ventrolateral prefrontal cortex, and the lateral orbitofrontal cortex).

Rolls (2008, p. 517) shows that McClure *et al.* (2004) represent the rational and emotional elements in decision-making as:

$$r\,(t) = \beta_\gamma{}^t r(0) \tag{1}$$

where $r\,(t)$ = the time discounted reward value at time t, $r\,(0)$ = the value of the reward if received immediately at time $t = 0$. β is interpreted as reflecting the impulsive element in decision-making (representing emotionality, based in the limbic system), while γ is the standard exponential discount rate (representing the rational element, based in PFC). In the process of scrutinizing immediate rewards, participants activated brain regions that involve emotion, namely the medial orbitofrontal cortex, medial prefrontal cortex/pregenual cingulate cortex, and ventral striatum. However, while examining longer term payoffs, they activated areas of the lateral prefrontal cortex (implicated in higher cognitive functioning), and part of the parietal cortex related to quant-itative reasoning. In his modeling of picoeconomic conflict in terms of dia-chronically appearing multiple selves, Ross (2012) speculates briefly about the cognitive demands of such a portrayal: each sub-agent is portrayed as tempor-arily in control of the person's behavior, with its own utility function and incomplete knowledge of the other, though its utility is constrained by the investments made by earlier-appearing agent(s).

In seeking to clarify the issue of multiple selves, this book draws upon recent investigations of antipodality between components of the impulsive and executive systems (Bickel *et al.*, 2012a). This work is invaluable for iden-tifying the elements of a theory of behavior that would account for both normal and excessive (addictive) consumption of substances such as alcohol and other drugs and activities such as gambling. Importantly, it demonstrates which elements of the impulsive system are antipodal to elements of the executive system (and may, therefore, be properly considered components of these antithetical tendencies), as well as those which play a broader role in the execution of appropriate behaviors. Prominent among the latter are what the CNDS model identifies as metacognition and the goal-directed regulation of behavior (Jarmolowicz *et al.*, 2013).

Later chapters build on the results of this work to propose a model of cog-nitive functioning in addiction which places the impulsive and executive systems in a framework consistent with recent developments in multi-process theories of cognition (Stanovich, 2009a, 2009b, 2011; Stanovich and West, 2000). It thereby incorporates a broader domain of theory on the cognitive control of behavior which acknowledges a long-standing division of thinking into that which is rapid and intuitive as opposed to that which is slow and deliberative (Evans and Stanovich, 2013). This dichotomy is similar to that which marks the distinction between impulsive and executive systems and is consistent with the account of behavioral control which the examination of the CNDS model in terms of antipodality reveals. The advantage of such a framework is that it allows for a forum within which the competing demands of the impulsive and executive systems interact so that conflict is resolved and behavior that generates more acceptable long-term consequences is selected over short-term expediency. The central focus is, therefore, on the structure of the CNDS model and, in particular, its incorporation of the metacognitive control of behavior. In the following sections the CNDS model is described in greater detail and the implications of antipodality for the construal of deci-sion systems is discussed. The questions of how metacognition is depicted in the model and a potential tripartite model are the foci of the following sec-tions. Finally, the implications of the analysis for understanding the multiplic-ity of selves involved in the decision process are discussed by critically examining the emergent framework in terms of picoeconomic bundling behavior.

My failure to resist television programs may reveal weakness of will but it is not a case of addiction. As long as I manage to live a generally effective life, an occasional indulgence in mass entertainment is another expression of my preferences as a consumer. It involves choosing the easier of two options, of devaluing the benefits of additional intellectual involvement with my work. But as long as television does not totally prevent my working effectively, giving in to infrequent viewing is no more than an expression of the human condition. Addiction would require a pattern of behavior that went much further than this: very steep discounting of the future despite costly involvement in efforts designed to overcome this state of affairs. The first manifests *hyperbolic discounting*; the second, *economic irrationality*. While these may not be sufficient in themselves to *define* addiction, together they form an inescapable component of addictive behavior, and uncovering their implications for the cognitive explanation of addiction is a central objective of this book.

Temporal discounting

What causes the adoption or rejection of the drugs, people, and technologies that lead to addictive patterns of behavior is the subject of an immense literature. Even defining addiction is an undertaking which has generated considerable heat as well as some light. In this book I seek to unite the disciplinary interests upon which these models rest by concentrating on steep temporal discounting as an important index (though not necessarily a definition) of addiction and tracing the implications of this phenomenon for the role of cognition in the explanation of preference reversal. Since addiction is one mode, albeit an extreme one, of consumer choice, I am also working with ideas on the role of cognition in the explanation of consumer behavior more generally.

Temporal discounting (also known as delay discounting) is concerned with the *current subjective value* of a reward that will be received in the future (i.e., the value of that future reward as it is rated in the present moment). I might be offered $100 but, frankly, this seems like just $90 to me right now because I have got to wait six months for it. If my benefactor offered me the $90 now, I would be indifferent between taking that money immediately and waiting six months for the $100. If he or she offered more than $90 (but presumably less than $100) now, I would accept it straight away. If I could obtain the $100 in less than six months, I would take that deal instead of waiting. Another way of putting it is that if someone owed me $90 now but could not pay me for six months, I would require him or her to give me $100 at that time to compensate me for having to wait.

Delay discounting, then, relates to the declining subjective value of a reward as a result of the delay until its receipt. The interesting question is: *How much* will I discount or devalue the $100 in view of the time I have to wait for it? This is interesting because the (subjectively imagined) present value of a reward that will be received after a long wait is less than the same reward received more immediately, but we would like to know by how much. The lower the present value of a future reward that is to be delivered at a specific future date, the more the individual is said to be discounting or devaluing the eventual reward, and people who devalue the future a great deal are said to discount the future *steeply* or at least more steeply than those who value it more highly.

Another reason an individual's discounting behavior is of interest is that it signals or reflects his or her willingness to forgo a more immediate benefit in favor of a greater future benefit. No doubt it is oversimplifying matters to put it so starkly, but choosing the later, larger reward (LLR) is said to embody self-control, while choosing the sooner, smaller reward (SSR) embodies impulsivity, and the balance between the two may indicate proneness to weakness of will, which at its most extreme may manifest as addiction. "Self-control," "impulsivity," and "weakness of will" are all loaded terms, of course, but attempting to understand them in light of how we value the future can bring at least a modicum of rigor to the way in which we understand both consumption and addiction. Determining how far an individual is responsible for his or her behavior is fraught with difficulties but appreciating the role of cognition in explaining consumer behavior can improve understanding by charting human capacities for accountable action. For, although cognitive psychology and cognitive science are often treated by their practitioners as deterministic sciences, they are concerned with the role of rationality and foresight in decision-making and may thus indicate whether individuals could sensibly be judged to have any control over their behaviors.

An intriguing aspect of the way in which individuals approach the choice of immediate and delayed rewards is the tendency to switch their preferences from one to the other. Weakness of will, manifesting at the extreme in addiction, is characterized by an initial preference for the LLR which abruptly morphs into a preference for the SSR just as it becomes available. It is also true, however, that individuals switch preferences in the opposite direction, as when a heavy drinker chooses sobriety (or, in our terms, chooses the delayed reward of better health or finances over the immediate pleasures of alcohol).

That which we seek to explain, therefore, is the observable behavior of preference reversal which, broadly speaking, may take two forms: *first*, a pattern of behavior in which SSR is chosen in preference to LLR even though an initial preference was for LLR; and *second*, a reformulation of this pattern such that LLR is now chosen over SSR. In the first instance, we can conceptualize and measure the behavior in terms of temporal discounting, which quantifies the rate of discounting. In the second, we have to think in terms of metacognitive processes exerting control. Taking stock of one's situation, forecasting and reviewing the future consequences of one's behavior pattern, weighing the deleterious effects of continued indulgence against the pleasures of immediate consumption – all these require metacognition; that is, thoughts and feelings about future thoughts and feelings.

Exponential and hyperbolic discounting

Decision-making under conditions of risk is modeled by subjective utility theory while, in the case of intertemporal choice, by discounted utility theory which portrays the rational decision-maker as discounting delayed outcomes by a constant rate for each unit of elapsed time (Kacelnik, 1997; Read, 2003; Samuelson, 1937). The commonplace form of discounting assumed in economics and finance is exponential, in which the rate of discounting is constant at all delays:

$$V_i = A_i e^{-kDi} \tag{2}$$

where V_i is the present value of a delayed reward, A_i is the amount of a delayed reward, k is a constant proportional to the degree of temporal discounting, D_i is the delay of the reward, and e is the base of natural logarithms. The significance of the constant rate of discounting in the exponential model is that the value of a larger reward which is delivered later is at all times greater than that of a smaller reward which is received earlier: the larger-but-later reward (LLR) is always preferred by an individual to a smaller-but-sooner reward (SSR) in this choice situation. However, in the hyperbolic form of discounting displayed in many human situations, while the LLR is initially preferred (i.e., at t_0), as indicated by the initially higher line in Figure 2.1, shortly before the SSR becomes available (just prior to t_1), its value increases dramatically, the lines cross, and the individual selects the objectively inferior reward.

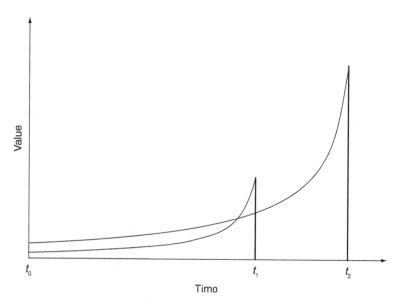

Figure 2.1 Hyperbolic discounting.

In many consumption contexts, consumers' temporal discounting is accurately described by this hyperbolic function: the later occurring of two rewards is diminished in an individual's subjective estimation even though it is the larger, with the result that the more immediate reward is selected in preference despite its being by definition the smaller of the two. This "impulsive" behavior is described by the hyperbolic discounting function

$$V_d = A / (1 + kD) \tag{3}$$

where V_d is the discounted value of a reward of a particular magnitude or amount, A, received after a delay, D (Mazur, 1987; Madden and Bickel, 2010). In this case, the rate of discounting varies with the extent of the delay faced by the consumer (e.g., Ainslie, 1992, 2001; Rick and Loewenstein, 2008). In this case, while the LLR is initially more highly valued, as the SSR becomes available its value surpasses that of the LLR and it is selected. The k parameter indicates the extent to which the value of the LLR diminishes compared to that of the SSR over time (Stein and Madden, 2013). The major behavioral characteristic of choice described hyperbolically is that the individual is likely to reverse preferences as time advances, an observation which is highly relevant to the extreme drug use and gambling already mentioned, the making of resolutions to change, and the yielding to temptation that may follow (Sayette and Griffin, 2013). Behavior that discounts the future is of central importance to the CNDS model insofar as temporal discounting is an index of the extent to which behavior is under the control of the tendency toward disinhibited impulsivity (the selection of an SSR rather than an LLR) as opposed to the inhibiting influence of the executive functions which results in the choice of LLR over SSR ("self-controlled" behavior) (Bickel and Yi, 2008; Barkley, 2012, 2013).

The basis of preference reversal

The operant paradigm treats choice simply as a matter of the relative frequencies exhibited by alternative behavior sequences which does not make recourse to any underlying mental decision-making. As de Villiers and Herrnstein (1976, p. 1131) put it, "[O]ur position is that choice is merely behavior in the context of other behavior, *not* a distinctive psychological process of its own." The result of thinking about choice in this manner is exemplified by the phenomenon of *matching* and its explanation in terms of *melioration*.

Choice as relative responding: the matching law

The underlying mechanism of temporal discounting in consumer choice appears to be the phenomenon of behavioral matching discovered by Herrnstein (1970, 1979, 1997; Davison and McCarthy, 1988). The matching law

(Equation 4) is based on the observation that the rate of responding on two choices matches the rate of reinforcement obtained from each:

$$\frac{B_a}{B_a + B_b} = \frac{R_a}{R_a + R_b},$$

(4)

where B_a and B_b are behaviors on each of two choices a and b, and R_a and R_b are the amounts of reinforcement obtained from each of these choices, respectively.

The strict matching equation (Equation 4) is a special case of the equivalence of the behavior ratio (B_a / B_b) and the reinforcement ratio (R_a / R_b). In order to encapsulate empirical findings in which strict matching of this kind was not the case, Baum (1974, 1979) proposed the generalized matching law:

$$\frac{B_a}{B_b} = c \left(\frac{R_a}{R_b} \right)^a,$$

(5)

where B_a, B_b, R_a, and R_b represent behavior and reinforcers as in the previous equations. The free parameters c and a are estimated via the logarithmic transformation of data for relative response (choice behavior) and relative reinforcement received:

$$\log \frac{B_a}{B_b} = a \log \frac{R_a}{R_b} + \log c$$

(6)

The parameter a (the exponent, representing the slope of the line) accounts for the sensitivity of preference to changes in the independent variable; the parameter c represents bias, namely any tendency for the respondent to favor one or other of the response alternatives for reasons not programmed through the schedules of reinforcement governing the relationship between responding and receipt of reinforcement. The strict matching detailed in Equation (4) is found only when both a and c equal unity (see also Baum, 1979, 2015).

Numerous independent variables may be employed to account for the degree of matching revealed empirically by the application of Equation (7). They can be any variables that research indicates to affect behavior and include the rate, amount, immediacy (delay), and quality of the reinforcers that influence behavior (Fisher and Mazur, 1997). The following concatenated generalized matching equation (Equation 7) accounts for this diversity:

$$\log \frac{B_a}{B_b} = a_r \log \left(\frac{R_a}{R_b} \right) + a_m \log \left(\frac{M_a}{M_b} \right) + a_q \log \left(\frac{Q_a}{Q_b} \right) + a_d \log \left(\frac{D_b}{D_a} \right) + \log c,$$

(7)

where R, M, Q, and D represent, respectively, reinforcer frequency, amount, quality, and delay (Curry *et al.*, 2010; Sigurdsson and Foxall, 2015).

The relationship between delay and choice (the D and B, respectively, of Equation (7) lies at the heart of hyperbolic discounting. Matching behavior involves the choice of the option offering the greater or faster reward. Matching and discounting have been found to characterize a whole swathe of consumer behavior beyond that of routine everyday purchasing and consumption. Yet the latter is also marked by matching (Foxall, 1999b; Foxall *et al.*, 2004; Foxall and Schrezenmaier, 2003; Wells and Foxall, 2013). Consideration of the underlying decision process is important for understanding matching behavior in different contexts such as those treated here. Herrnstein (1982; Herrnstein and Vaughan, 1980; Vaughan and Herrnstein, 1997) proposes that the process is melioration in which the decision-maker maximizes immediate (or, as he calls them, local) returns; that is, at each choice point he or she selects the alternative that offers the higher level of reward. Over a series of choices, melioration may not yield the kind of global maximization assumed by rational choice economics, though in many consumer buying contexts the assumptions of both approaches are similar.

Because impulsivity is often indexed by measures of the extent to which an individual discounts the future, much interest has focused on the extreme forms of consumer choice in which discounting is substantial, such as addictions (e.g., Ainslie, 2001; Rachlin, 2000). But a theory of consumer behavior should be able to demonstrate the underlying causal features of choice at the routine, everyday end of the spectrum in similar terms to those used to explain the more extreme forms of consumption. To the extent that addiction lies on the same continuum as other modes of consumer behavior, the requirements for a theory of one impacts the development of a theory of the other.

Melioration

Matching provides an interpretation of complex economic choice. Notably, it does so at the molar level of analysis, correlating not single responses but sequences of responding with sequences of reinforcement. Herrnstein argued that this level of analysis was required to be underpinned by a molecular mechanism that accounted for the patterns observed at the more abstract level. This molecular process he terms *melioration*, described by Davison and McCarthy (1988, p. 136) as "the process in which the difference between local rates of reinforcement leads to a continuous change in the distribution of behavior in the direction of an equality of local reinforcement rates." An everyday example is the way in which drivers on a major highway frequently switch lanes, selecting the clearest and fastest way forward, returning to the original lane or entering a third when that becomes the most advantageous. Overall, such a driver may not reach the final destination quicker than had another route through the lanes been chosen but immediate advantage (the local rate of reinforcement) leads to an averaging of the rates of reinforcement over all choices made. An equilibrium is reached when the average reinforcement rates of each lane are finally equalized. In a two-lane example, if T_a and

T_b are the times allocated to the two responses, R_a and R_b, respectively, the local difference in reinforcement rates, R_d, is

$$R_d = (R_1 / T_1) - R_2 / T_2).\tag{8}$$

Time allocation changes as a result of the sensitivity of behavior to local rates of reinforcement; stabilization is reached when $R_d = 0$. Melioration, in which the behavior offering the immediately higher or highest rate of reinforcement is chosen, may result, in certain circumstances, in the maximization of overall reinforcement, but it is more often likely to lead to sub-optimization at that global level. It is, however, a process of maximizing local reinforcement: at each choice point, the individual selects the more or most advantageous source of reinforcement by allocating his or her behavior accordingly. In this way, melioration provides a molecular-level mechanism to explain the behaviors to which matching refers (Herrnstein and Vaughan, 1980).

Hyperbolic discounting as a hallmark of addiction

The underlying assumption behind much which follows is that extreme consumption, exemplified by addiction, is explicable in terms of a rate of temporal discounting that is high in comparison with other modes of consumption. It is important, therefore, to examine the empirical evidence for or against this proposition.

Dependence on drugs is a function of the interaction of drugs with the limbic brain areas which control the individual's response to reinforcers. These natural circuits of reinforcement can be requisitioned by drugs of abuse (Box 2.1) that are often held to hijack the mesocorticolimbic system, with the result that the consumer craves the emotional highs induced by such chemical rewards (Bickel and Johnson, 2003; Nester and Landsman, 2001; Robbins and Everitt, 1999). Although there seems to be a natural tendency for human beings to devalue future rewards in favor of more immediately appearing rewards, this discounting of the future is inflated by persons dependent on drugs of abuse. Hence, drug dependence, like other addictions, appears to be a "disorder of discounting." Given that so many of us are subject to akrasia even in mild degree, the notion of a disorder of discounting implies a marked tendency to discount delayed rewards or to incur longer term deleterious effects of behavior for the sake of sooner appearing benefits.

Box 2.1 Drugs of abuse

Drugs of abuse are powerful reinforcers whose emotional effects invest their ability to enact behavior that leads to their acquisition and use with added potency. Both drugs of abuse (including alcohol and nicotine) and other manifestations of addiction such as pathological gambling and compulsive consumption rely on neurophysiological systems that underlie the processing of reward or reinforcement. The stages in the process of addiction are described in terms of the brain regions and their functions that appear closely associated with reinforced behaviors.

The consumption of drugs of abuse follows several patterns, ranging from infrequent and irregular use when the individual remains in control of his or her level of intake, through more sustained using in which some of the harmful effects of the drug are felt, to addiction, by which time the individual has come to depend upon the drug (Koob *et al.*, 2014). Some people remain at the initial stage, displaying considerable self-control: perhaps they smoke or drink only on particular social occasions and feel no desire to do so at other times. Some may dabble rather than persist. However, the neuro-circuitry responsible for ultimate reinforcement and which subserves full addiction functions when *any* reward is received by the individual and has powerful effects especially over the emotions which make continued consumption more likely. Although comparatively few reach the stage of dependence in which they are preoccupied with seeking out and consuming the substance, the situational and neurophysiological influences on their behavior is instructive for understanding consumer choice in general. In the course of shifting from occasional use to full addiction, the individual's relationship with the substance changes profoundly. At first, the drugs act as positive reinforcers: they are sufficiently pleasant to encourage further use in order to obtain these enjoyable outcomes. At the point of dependence, however, the effects are almost totally unpleasant. The drug is sought now only to allay the craving that motivates the search for both the substance and the situations associated with its procurement and consumption, and the deleterious feelings that result from the drug's absence. It has become a negative reinforcer, one whose use serves merely to assuage the aversive outcomes of previous consumption, including its cessation (Koob, 2013; note that the approach of Baum (2015) contains some similarities with that of Koob). Cognitively and behaviorally, the dependence manifests in typical patterns of preference reversal.

Hijacking of the dopaminergic system[*]

The effect of drugs of abuse and the behaviors that comprise process addictions are often said to operate by "hijacking" the mesocorticolimbic system (Box 3.2). What this means is that the drugs and the behaviors as a result of which their own incentive value and capacity to act as reinforcers intensifies. Increased dopamine release is associated with greater craving, since it is implicated in the salience of stimuli that have been associated with it in the past. Normally, dopamine remaining in the synaptic cleft is broken into its constituents by enzymes so that its effect on the postsynaptic neuron diminishes. Alternatively, its effect on the postsynaptic neuron is reduced by its being reuptaken into the presynaptic neuron from whence it came. Any chemical or behavioral means of reducing the analytical effect of the enzyme or otherwise prolonging the presence of dopamine (e.g., by inhibiting reuptake) increases the rewarding effect of the neurotransmitter and promotes addiction. The drug itself and any places or artifacts with which it is associated acquire incentive salience and increase the likelihood that the drug user will seek out and obtain the substance, having already sought out the situations and accoutrements associated with it by experience. The greater the effect of the drug or behavior in inhibiting the removal of dopamine, the greater the likelihood of both addiction as a direct consequence and the salience of the situational cues that promote it. Cocaine acts by preventing the reuptake of dopamine, an excitatory neurotransmitter, by the presynaptic cell. The postsynaptic cell is therefore stimulated by dopamine to a greater extent than is ordinarily the case. Nicotine by contrast has an indirect effect on dopamine retention: it binds to receptors on the dopamine neuron that normally bind the neurotransmitter acetycholine and thereby increases the release of dopamine (Subramaniyan and Dani, 2015). Nicotine also reduces the presence of an enzyme that breaks down dopamine, and hence increases it efficacy at the postsynaptic neuron. The opiate, heroin, which as the term suggests is chemically similar to the opioids naturally produced in the body, binds to opioid receptors which are located on GABA neurons. GABA is an inhibitory neurotransmitter which works by impeding dopamine release. The binding of heroin to opioid receptors on the GABA neurons has the effect of obstructing the release of GABA, with the result that the DAergic neuron is no longer restrained.

★ This section is based on Toates and Dommett (2011).

Bickel and Johnson (2003) argue that discounting delayed rewards is a fundamental behavioral process in drug dependence. They reach this conclusion by noting that a large number of empirical studies indicate, *first*, that evolutionarily old brain areas demonstrate cross-species contributions to hyperbolic delay discounting and that their effects are apparent for a wide range of drug reinforcers; *second*, that drug-dependent individuals discount to a greater degree than non-drug-dependent individuals, and that this is the case for a large number of communities and of drug types; and *third*, that the high levels of discounting found among the drug dependent are modulated by manipulations of the conditions of drug deprivation (e.g., ex-dependent individuals and those who are to some extent abstemious discount less than those who are currently dependent and those who never had any dependence); hence, discounting is flexible, fluctuating in line with changes in the circumstances surrounding drug use.

Certainly, the analysis of delay discounting is particularly apposite to the analysis of addictive behavior (Yi *et al.*, 2010). The decision whether to use a drug, for instance, resolves into a number of binary decisions – to consume or not to consume on each occasion that presents an opportunity. The benefits of any one act of consumption are small and concrete compared with those of abstaining (i.e., the promised long-term positive outcomes of increased health and well-being). However, given that the drug user continues to consume, his or her subjective valuation of doing so must be greater than that of abstinence. While the benefits of consuming the drug now are immediate or nearly so, those of abstaining are delayed, a factor that reduces their power to influence the current decision. These delayed outcomes are not even promised for delivery at a specific date in the future and they are poorly specified in terms of their exact nature. For some drugs such as nicotine and alcohol it may even appear that heavy users incur no or minor disadvantages in the course of their lives. Not only does the delay of the healthier reinforcer, the D of Equation (7), exceed that of the object of addiction: the amount of the delayed reinforcement, the A of Equation (7), is poorly specified in that it is more hazily defined and its magnitude questionable. The possibility arises that persons who are already more prone to discount the future are more likely to seek the immediacy of drug-induced highs over the possible long-term benefits of abstinence. There is increasing evidence that this is the case – so much so that Peters and Büchel (2011) argue that the evidence that a tendency toward steep discounting is implicated in the development of addictions is so strong as to make discounting a reliable marker for addiction. The argument has two components: establishing the fact of the matter and determining the causal relationship.

A wide range of addictive behaviors are associated with the tendency to discount steeply (Bickel *et al.*, 2007a, 2007b; Businelle *et al.*, 2010; Madden and Bickel, 2010; Yi *et al.*, 2010). Evidence that addicts tend to discount much more steeply than controls is available for both drug-related and nondrug addictions, including among the drug-related examples: *opioid and dependency* (Kirby *et al.*, 1999; Madden *et al.*, 1997; Monterosso *et al.*, 2007; Kirby and Petry, 2004; Odum *et al.*, 2000; Coffey *et al.*, 2003; Heil *et al.*, 2006; Hoffman *et al.*, 2006); *nicotine* (Audrain-McGovern *et al.*, 2009a, 2009b; Bickel *et al.*, 1999, 2007a; Johnson *et al.*, 2007; Mitchell, 1999; Peters and Büchel, 2011; Odum *et al.*, 2002; Baker *et al.*, 2003; Reynolds *et al.*, 2004; Ohmura *et al.*, 2005); *unhealthy consumption* (Story *et al.*, 2014), and *alcohol consumption* (Petry, 2001a; Mitchell *et al.*, 2005), and, as an example of a nondrug addiction, *gambling pathology* (Alessi and Petry, 2003; Bjork *et al.*, 2004; Dixon *et al.*, 2003; Petry, 2001b; Petry and Casarella, 1999; Mitchell *et al.*, 2005; Vuchinich and Simpson, 1998).

But does a tendency to discount steeply increase the likelihood of addiction or does becoming an addict make it more probable that one will become a heavy discounter? Consideration of the possible biological bases of both behaviors raises intriguing possibilities of explanation. Peters and Büchel (2011) note the possibility raised by Wills *et al.* (1994) that individuals may be predisposed to both steep discounting and addictive behavior by an underlying genetic propensity toward impulsivity. There seems little or no evidence however to support the view that increasing consumption of drugs is associated with an augmenting inclination to discount at higher rates.

Economic irrationality and addiction

Simply opting for an SSR that precludes achieving the LLR for which I have expressed a preference is not of itself irrational in an economic sense, eccentric as it may be. Nor does it of itself constitute addiction, even if it is a behavior pattern that is highly recursive. Gambling inevitably has a negative expected value, given that, over an extended number of gambles, the accumulation of debt is inescapable (Clark, 2010). But, as Ross *et al.* (2008) point out, economists understand irrationality in terms of inconsistent preferences: attempting to live by one rule at one time and a contradictory rule at a later point. Suppose I set out with the firm intention to save enough money by the end of the month to take a short activity break, spend time actively planning the holiday, carefully comparing destinations, costs, transport and accommodation options, and the opportunities for walking on offer. My aim is to raise my fitness level as part of an intended program of healthier living, and I am investing heavily in this. Instead, however, I use my savings to buy highly calorific foods which I consume to the point of endangering my physical well-being. I then regret this choice bitterly and resolve to start saving immediately for another break, to eat less, and exercise more.

In this case I am acting irrationally in the economic sense: having *invested* heavily in one course of action, I opt for another that is inconsistent with it by investing heavily in that too (Ross *et al.*, 2008). Thus, simply to eat to the point of incurring ill-health is not in itself irrational from an economic standpoint even if it leads to my early demise. By doing so, I may be a source of bewilderment to others, including economists, but I am not being economically irrational. I am simply expressing my preference. It is the striving to avoid or cut down on junk food, the resolution to take control of my life, the planning of scenarios that do not entail over-indulgence, and the initial steps toward avoidance, followed by a lapse into not moderate eating but bingeing that is the evidence of my irrationality. If I continue to invest considerable resources in both the forswearing of such food *and* in its consumption so that a recursive sequence of behaviors becomes a characteristic pattern of choice to the extent that aspects of my life such as job, family, and home are threatened or lost, then I am said to be addicted to this wayward diet. Economic rationality is simply consistency: for inconsistency to count as addiction we rely on more than a single perverse behavior; the attribution of addiction requires a molar perspective. Economic irrationality gives a strong clue to addiction and forms an essential – to some, sufficient – component of its definition.

Temporal discounting in context

This section is intended to locate temporal discounting in the contexts of evolutionary history, neurophysiology, cognition, and environmental contingencies. In addition, it expands upon the concept of executive function in order to account for the capacity to overrule the automatic tendencies of stimulus-induced, impulsive behavior.

Unpredictable futures and temporal discounting

That temporal discounting has a discernible neurophysiological substrate (e.g., Winstanley, 2010; Redish and Kurth-Nelson, 2010) strengthens the view that the capacity to discount may have evolutionary origins (Rogers, 1994). But the human tendency both to discount as a result of impulsivity and to contain this tendency by exercising self-control is in practice traceable to the effects of broad patterns of reinforcement contingencies acting within changing human societies. Hence, the tendency toward temporal discounting may have been acquired by the ancestors of modern consumers during Pleistocene times; temporal discounting may even be a cognitive module which represents an adaption to the conditions encountered at that time which had to be overcome in order to optimize fitness rates.

Bickel and Marsch (2000) draw attention to a pattern of environmental influence during and since the Pleistocene that is consistent with a modifiable tendency toward temporal discounting. Before the development of agriculture some 13,000 years ago, temporal horizons would likely have been very short. These circumstances, in the predominantly hunter-gatherer economy, wholly favored the immediate consumption of food as and when it became available. The opportunistic capture of wild animals, seasonal harvesting of wild berries and fruits, none of which were stored against future need and imposed no costs of production, would be behaviorally and economically optimal. The future could be and was almost totally discounted. The advent of agrarian cultivation and animal husbandry was an indication that temporal horizons had already shifted toward a greater concern for and ability to manage the future and hence a lower rate of temporal discounting.

Reasons cited by Bickel and Marsch (2000) for the transition to agriculture include the low availability of wild food and consequent increased costs of hunting and gathering; the greater availability of domesticable wild plants which could thrive in a wider range of habitats as a result of climate change, coupled with shorter harvesting periods and reduced costs of organized cultivation; the cumulative development of horticultural and agricultural technologies; and an increasing population density once the trend toward agriculture had begun. The advent of writing would have had a catalytic effect on the progress of organized cultivation:

> This analysis suggests that a consideration of long-term outcomes or, in other words, the development of a long temporal horizon results from the decreased availability of resources supporting short temporal horizons and increased availability of resources supporting long temporal horizons.... [T]hinking of the future does not come naturally to us unless it is the most attractive option (i.e., less costly) relative to other options.
>
> (Bickel and Marsch, 2000, p. 350)

These considerations support the view that cognitive and behavioral change is intimately linked to local contingencies of reinforcement. The advent of agriculture was marked by a shift in the pattern of reinforcement as the means of attainment of utilitarian benefits improved as a result of natural and technological developments and as new means became available for performance feedback (informational reinforcement) in the form of status, power, and the observed leisure of others. Social changes would also make these considerations more salient in an increasingly affluent and stable society. The most we can actually say is that genetic change represents a guiding principle for behavioral change in the absence of countervailing environmental contingencies but as the pattern of reinforcement is modified it is the contingencies that are more immediately powerful in modifying behavior and sociotechnical practices.

Further extension of the temporal perspective adopted by our ancestors was promoted, according to Bickel and Marsch (2000), by the transition from paganism to Christianity. They argue, however, that, more recently, social and cultural influences have reshaped Western societies in the direction of a shorter term temporal purview. In support of this they draw attention to the tendency in contemporary, affluent societies for consumers to receive immediate gratification and leisure which are in turn made available by the availability of low-cost reinforcers which can be delivered and consumed immediately. In addition, they cite changes in community and family structures which have removed forces that hitherto inhibited consumption. These changes promote a discernible redirection of temporal perspective toward the short term and the concomitant expansion of extreme consumer behaviors such as drug dependence, pathological gambling, and other forms of addiction.

A recurring implication is that changes in environmental contingencies are responsible for these transitions in the predominant patterns of consumer choice. But such changes in the factors likely to influence operant behavior are not sufficient to explain changes in the tendency to discount the future. Neurobiology and cognition also play a part in the explanation. Moreover, there is support for this idea from the cognitive archeology of the sapient revolution (e.g., Coolidge and Wynn, 2009).

The sapient paradox

The emergence in France some 40,000 years ago of a transition from the Middle to the Upper Paleolithic which accompanied the emergence there of *Homo sapiens* was marked by the advent of behaviors reinforced by significant utilitarian benefits. These included the construction of tools that incorporated blades, standardization in the production of stone tools which were also of a wider variety and complexity, and by faster technological change and regionally based specialization. Informational reinforcement was to the fore in promoting behaviors based on personal adornments such as the wearing of beads and pendants, and representational art in the form of carvings and cave paintings. Both functional and symbolic outcomes were embedded in the carving of antler, bone and ivory, and economic and organizational change within social systems (Mellars, 1991; Renfrew, 2007, p. 80).

These "fairly modest and localized" developments in France and a small number of other societies stand in marked contrast to the Neolithic or agricultural revolution much more widely encountered in western Asia, Europe, and beyond. Again, as highlighted by Renfrew (2007, pp. 82–83), these Middle to

Upper Paleolithic changes include, in the case of utilitarian benefits, food *pro-duction* rather than *gathering* via the cultivation of such crops as wheat, lentils, and flax. The scale and efficiency of horticultural production of this kind was accomplished by the innovative use of tools such as querns and grindstones. Certain animals like sheep, goats, cattle, and pigs were intensively produced and their bones incorporated into the artifactual usages noted above. The erection of mud, brick, and timber dwellings permitted settled habituation on which the evolution of more complex social organization would depend. Fire was increasingly employed in the parching of grains and the baking of bread, and the production of pottery-based vessels for domestic use was accompanied by the informationally reinforcing generation of clay models of animals and human beings. The capacity for potting was expedited by and contributed to more settled living. Sustained pottery production benefits from a more sedentary lifestyle, and the sheer volume of purposes to which pottery can be put encourages settlement. Pottery not only facilitates the cooking and serving of food; it is also a means of storage, often when pots are buried in the ground for later recovery. Pots function as gifts and pottery as ornaments, and are of course a convenient basis for trade through barter (de Waal, 2011). Tool production and use became more sophisticated with the advent of axes and other specialized technologies. What would now be referred to as supply-chain or logistics management was pioneered (e.g., in the procurement from afar of obsidian). The use of informational reinforcement to control behavior became apparent in the production of shrines for religious practices, and in the planned and organized allocation of the dead through funeral practices which on occasion involved the construction of tombs and other monuments. The decoration of pottery reflected informational reinforcement as well insofar as it embodied ethnic or status distinctions.

These extensive changes are characteristic of agricultural revolutions generally and constitute serious behavioral discontinuities between social systems based on hunter-gatherer subsistence and those founded upon sedentary lifestyles sustained by agricultural production. *Homo sapiens* and other early hominids subsisted, as hunter-gatherers, on vegetation, fruit, game, and carrion as they occurred naturally and exhibited nomadic lifestyles, having no need of long-term domestic sites like villages. Gupta (2004) cites climatic amelioration, which facilitated increases in both food availability and the size of the human population, as one of the factors that encouraged *Homo sapiens* to adopt a sedentary mode and take up the deliberate cultivation of foodstuffs. The "sapient paradox" to which Renfrew draws attention consists in the tardiness of these behavioral innovations and the emergence of the functional and symbolic outcomes to which they contributed, even though the cognitive capacity to produce them was in place. Thanks to radiometric analysis and DNA sequencing, it is now apparent that the human genotype was in place some 100,000 years ago. While the changes that led to the formation of the genome were of course primarily genetic, Renfrew (2007) argues that changes in human behavior since that time must be due to non-genetic processes. Although human cognitive capacities had increased dramatically by some 100,000 years ago, it was not until about 10,000 years ago that the human revolution consequent upon that huge mental endowment became apparent in the development of agriculture and sedentary civilization.

> If the arrival of the new species, *Homo sapiens*, with its higher level of cognitive capacity, its new kinds of behaviour, its sophisticated use of language, its enhanced self-consciousness, was so significant, why did it take so long for these really impressive innovations, seen in the accompanying agricultural revolution, to come about?
>
> (Renfrew, 2007, p. 84)

A possible answer appears through consideration of when the human revolution occurred and where. In our terms, manifestation of the potential tied up in the human revolution relied on the contingencies of reinforcement. The emerging consensus among archeologists is that the human revolution which was the result of genetic change occurred gradually in sub-Saharan Africa and was apparent about 150,000 years ago (Mellars *et al.*, 2007). Although the natural selection of *Homo sapiens* may have been arrested 100,000 years ago, however, neurophysiological development may still be expected to take place as a result of the ontogenetic effects of operant behavior on neuronal plasticity (Box 2.2). Cognitive development may also be expected to occur during the period extending from the human revolution to the massive changes in behavior patterns marked by the adoption of a sedentary civilization and symbolic reasoning. The sapient revolution seems to have consisted in the expansion of the executive functions.

Box 2.2 Neuronal plasticity

The brain is not fixed but changes in response, first, to experience, and second, to the action of *neuromodulators*. A neuromodulator is a particular kind of neurotransmitter, which influences the release of neurotransmitters at synapses and the extent to which postsynaptic neurons respond to the chemical signals they present. The same chemical may act as a neurotransmitter at one synapse and as a neuromodulator at others, regulating the flow or reception of other neurotransmitters. The effect is to "fine-tune" the brain's response to environmental events, as well as to "rewire" the brain over time, perhaps thereby aiding the storing of memories (O'Shea *et al.*, 2013). The environmental events include reinforcing and punishing stimuli, while memory embodies consumers' learning histories.

"Hebbian learning" refers to the strengthening of a synapse as a result of simultaneous activity in the presynaptic and postsynaptic areas. As long as both a synapse and a postsynaptic neuron are active simultaneously, the synapse will be strengthened in the sense that it is more likely to be the location of such activity in the future. *Long-term potentiation* (LTP) is an increase in the efficiency of synaptic transmission. It requires activity in order to occur and it may underlie learning. It is associated with a preceding period of intense synaptic activity and a subsequent (postsynaptic) depolarization. It is a component of Hebbian learning, since only those synapses capable of engendering LTP are known as "Hebbian." It is interesting to note in retrospect that Hebb's original surmise had no basis in the physiological knowledge of the time he published his book on this topic (Hebb, 1949). However, the discovery of LTP and its neural basis gave Hebbian learning an extensional basis by providing a mechanism for *synaptic plasticity*.

Two factors are required to produce LTP: an *excitatory input* and *postsynaptic depolarization*. The receptor, NMDA, is the key to this. *N*-methyl-*D*-aspartate is a doubly gated receptor found on the dendritic spines of postsynaptic neurons that exhibit LTP. The principal excitatory neurotransmitter in the hippocampus is glutamate which can bind with both NMDA and non-NMDA receptors. The specific role of MNDA in the induction of LTP is as follows. MNDA receptors are usually blocked by magnesium ions (Mg^{2+}) which are ejected from the NMDA receptors only when glutamate binds to them so that the membrane is depolarized. NMDA differs from other receptors in being voltage-dependent (gated), as a result of extracellular magnesium ions, as well as sensitive to the transmitter. Mg^{2+} is ejected only when both of these conditions are met and as a result calcium (Ca^{2+}) is able to enter the cell. The introduction of Ca^{2+} by way of the MNDA receptor assists the formation of LTP, since it is an intercellular messenger whose signal alters the enzyme activities that are responsible for the strength of the synapse. Central to the whole process is the requirement, mentioned above, that both the glutamate transmitter is present in the synaptic cleft and the level of depolarization in the postsynaptic neuron reach a critical level. The resultant capacity of the NMDA channel to act as a "coincidence detector" is an integral part of Hebbian learning which requires the temporal concurrence of appropriate presynaptic and postsynaptic events.

Why this is so is still a matter of debate and there are several hypotheses that may explain it. LTP may raise the sensitivity of postsynaptic non-MNDA glutamate receptors and thereby induce a greater release of presynaptic glutamate. (These AMPA receptors may be present within the neuron and move to the surface upon the occupation of MNDA receptors; their presence at the surface may then increase the receptivity of the postsynaptic membrane to glutamate, leading to LTP.) Alternatively, the dendritic spines themselves may undergo physical change so that EPSPs are more effective to the dendrites. A third possibility is that a message from the postsynaptic to the presynaptic level may cause an increase in the efficiency of the release of presynaptic neurotransmitter release.

LTP may remain for days or weeks; Toates (2011) suggests that it may persist for a lifetime as the basis of encoded memory. While MNDA is required for the induction of LTP, it is not relevant to its maintenance. NMDA receptors are chemically blocked when 2-amino-5-phosphonopentanoate (AP5) is introduced to CA1 neurons. This has the effect of inhibiting LTP induction. However, AP5 has no effect on LTP that has been previously established in the cells in question: the maintenance of LTP appears, therefore, to rely on non-MNDA receptors. As calcium enters the postsynaptic neuron in the course of the induction of LTP (the result of the unblocking of the MNDA receptors: see above), kinases are released. Kinases are enzymes that are both intracellular and calcium-dependent and have two functions relevant to the maintenance of LTP. First, some of them modify the AMPA receptors so that the AMPA channel can accommodate the flow of a larger number of ions; second, other kinases govern the rate at which new AMPA receptors become embedded in the membrane of the postsynaptic neuron.

A conceptual and practical difficulty arises, however, with this account of the role of presynaptic factors in the maintenance of LTP. The MNDA receptors that play a part in the induction of LTP are located in the postsynaptic neuron. Somehow the presynaptic neuron must be activated in order to increase the amount of glutamate it provides. How is it "instructed" to do so? The logic of the explanation given requires that a retrograde messenger be generated at the postsynaptic level which conveys the requisite information to the presynaptic neuron. But chemical synapses are unidirectional: a neurotransmitter travels from the presynaptic terminal to the postsynaptic membrane to communicate information. The resolution of this problem lies in the creation of a biochemical pathway, activated by the entry of calcium via the NMDA receptor, in which arachidonic acid is introduced into the synaptic cleft. A second such pathway, activated in the same way, includes the passage of nitrous oxide through the postsynaptic membrane. After their release, these messengers, which are capable of permeating the postsynaptic membrane, reach the presynaptic terminal. Both pre- and postsynaptic processes appear, therefore, to be implicated in the maintenance of LTP, but just how they work together to achieve this remains unknown.

Executive functions

Executive functions and prefrontal cortex

Barkley (2001, 2012) approaches the evolutionary psychology of temporal discounting versus self-regulation by considering the operations and effects of the executive functions (EFs) defined as a means of self-regulation that was an evolutionary adaptation within group-living species. The evolutionary development of the prefrontal cortex (PFC) permitted individuals to exercise greater control of their impulsive reactions to environmental events that would otherwise lead to the enactment of conditioned responses acquired in a learning history of classical or operant conditioning. EFs are concerned with the cognitive control of behavior, the ability to coordinate thought and actions and direct them toward the achievement of goals (Miller and Wallis, 2009, p. 99). Such executive control is in opposition to automatic brain functioning. It is acquired through a process of learning, though there are neurophysiological substrates for it. Another way of expressing their effects is to say that they enable individuals to "take charge of their actions and direct them toward unseen aims" (Miller and Wallis, 2009, p. 104). The most important aspect of this is the possibility of a change in temporal perspective that the EFs afford. As Barkley (2001, p. 1) puts it, "The EFs serve to shift the control of behavior from the immediate context, social others, and the temporal now to self-regulation by internal representations regarding the hypothetical social future" (Ardila, 2008; Jurado and Rosselli, 2007; Lyon and Krasnegor, 1996; Vohs and Baumeister, 2013). Barkley (2012) further considers the role of EFs in evolution by discussing them as extended phenotypes, a theme that is beyond the scope of the present project. The role of EFs in giving the individual pause to consider hypothetical future behaviors and their consequences clearly plays a central role in the interactions and relative balance of the decision systems that are at the heart of the CNDS model.

There are generally thought to be two levels of brain processing involved in these automatic and executive sources of control. In bottom-up processing, sensory inputs lead automatically to behavioral outputs that are consistent both with natural selection in the organism's speciational phylogenetic history and ontogenetic learning. This input–output loop which leads to the uninhibited achievement of short-term goals is assured unless the executive system intervenes to ensure that longer term goals are met. The prefrontal cortex (PFC) seems especially implicated in this executive processing. Note that this statement and the evidence on which it is based does not lead to the conclusion that PFC and executive function are identical. As Barkley (2012) is at pains to emphasize, the PFC and executive functions belong to distinct levels of explanation: the PFC is neurophysiological and belongs at the sub-personal level, while executive functions are cognitive and belong at the personal level of intentional discourse. (Banich (2009) draws attention to the wide range of definitions and mechanisms involved in explicating this topic fully.)

While damage to PFC does not impair sensory functioning, it can make normal social and economic life impossible. As Miller and Wallis (2009, p. 100) put it, "Despite the superficial appearance of normality, PFC damage devastates a person's life," typically leading to social breakdown and an inability to consider the consequences of their behaviors. These authors detail the resulting behavioral inflexibility in terms of five areas of cognitive deficit: *inhibition*, where behavior takes on a stimulus-bound character in the sense that the individual has no problem responding to immediate stimuli but becomes behaviorally fixated on maintaining specific actions in the presence of given stimuli to the extent that the behavior pattern is described as perseveration; *planning*, where following PFC damage the individual finds it difficult to organize behavior toward achieving a goal; *evaluation of consequences*, where goal-directed behavior requires an ability to compare alternative courses of action in terms of their likely outcomes and to select the one that is most likely to lead to the fulfillment of one's aims; however, damage to PFC leads to an inability to select the behavior that has the best chance of fulfilling goals. Inability to do this has severe implications for rationality; *working memory* (WM), where the inability to plan and evaluate following PFC damage may be the result of lack of knowledge of one's goals through loss of the short-term memory buffer on which cognition depends (Hofmann *et al.*, 2013). PFC functioning enables WM to provide a store of short-term information re goals and tasks; *the learning and use of rules*, where PFC is essential in top-down processing (i.e., when internal states and intentions guide behavior). Note that it is essential also for the ascription of intentionality, especially higher order intentionality, in mind-reading, theory of mind, and other aspects of predicting and responding appropriately to the behavior of others (Dunbar, 2014). In social situations such as these we rely on pre-formed models of action and its outcomes. PFC is also needed in order that behavior may be guided by abstract higher level rules. The capacity to call upon and if necessary formulate abstract rules is especially crucial in the case of innovative behavior. The general consensus among psychologists is that EFs are relevant to the solution of what Simon (1977) referred to as "nonpro-grammed decisions," those for which no response routine has been (or possibly can be) established. Banich (2009, p. 89), for instance, emphasizes that they are "the set of abilities required to effortfully guide behavior toward a goal, especially in nonroutine situations."

The nature of executive functions

What precisely are executive functions? Barkley describes them as "composed of the major classes of behavior toward oneself used in self-regulation" (2012, p. 4). One of these behaviors is response inhibition which ensures that a response to a stimulus can be delayed and that, once begun, responses can be interrupted. Barkley argues that it is not just the response that must be delayed: it is the decision, too. The prepotent response is that "for which immediate reinforcement is available within a particular context or which has been previously associated with that response in that context" (2012, p. 4). Positive and negative reinforcement must be taken into account since, while some impulsive behavior produces immediate reward, others serve to avoid or escape from aversive stimulation. Such activity, typified within the current discussion by selecting a LLR over a SSR, requires some sort of internal capacity to sense the future,

> to construct hypothetical futures, particularly for social consequences ... the weighing of alternative responses and their temporally proximal and distal outcomes – a calculation of risk/benefit ratios over time. Some neuropsychological mechanism must have evolved that permitted this relatively rapid construction of hypothetical social futures while simultaneously engaging in a temporally discounting economic analysis of immediate versus delayed outcomes.
>
> (Barkley, 2012, p. 5; see also Denckla, 1996; Banich, 2009)

Executive functions evolved as an adaptation to the problem of taking past occurrences into account and anticipating future events, including the consequences of current actions within social contexts. The executive function system consists of four executive functions: nonverbal working memory – sensing to the self; verbal working memory – internalization of speech;

self-regulation of affect/motivation/arousal – affective and motivational properties or valences (somatic markers: Damasio, 1994) which are associated with mentally representations of verbal and visual information to oneself; and reconstitution – covert self-directed play involving analysis and synthesis of sensory-motor and symbolic information.

The importance of motivation and emotion

Barkley (2012) is adamant that motivation and emotion be included in the understanding of executive functions. While what he calls the "cool" brain networks dealing with such capabilities as working memory, planning, problem-solving, and foresight are sufficient to cope with the "what, where, and when" of goal-directed behavior, "the 'hub' EF brain network ... provides the 'why' or basis for choosing to pursue that goal in the first place and the motivation that will be needed to get there" (Barley, 2012, p. 26; see also Blair and Ursache, 2013).

PFC and executive function: different levels of exposition

It is important to reiterate Barkley's argument that we maintain a strict distinction between the executive functions (EFs) themselves, which are cognitive constructs, and the brain regions such as the PFC which instantiate them (Barkley, 2012; Koob *et al.*, 2013). At the least, we are speaking in two different ways about the phenomena of behavioral control and it is important to keep them separate since, as we have noted, they enter into quite different modes of explanation. Barkley (2012) points out the tendency to conflate different levels of analysis when speaking of executive functions. "One is the neuropsychological level including thought (cognition), emotion, and verbal or motor action (behavior); the other is the neuroanatomical level including the localization of those neuropsychological functions to specific regions of the brain and their physiological action" (Barkley, 2012, p. 1). These levels of analysis correspond, respectively, to the personal level of exposition and the sub-personal level of exposition as defined in Chapter 1. EFs must be defined "separately and specifically at the psychological level without reference to the neurological level being an essential part of that definition" (Barkley, 2012, p. 2).

The nature of executive functioning is the

> internalization of sensory-motor action, self-speech, and emotion/motivation along with the internalization of play (reconstitution) [to] provide an exceptionally powerful set of mind tools that greatly facilitate adaptive functioning. In a sense, these executive functions permit the private simulation of actions within specific settings that can be tested out mentally for their probable consequences (somatic markers) before a response is selected for eventual execution.
> (Barkley, 2001, p. 9; cf. McIlvane *et al.*, 1996; Hayes *et al.*, 1996)

Reasons for believing the EFs to be adaptive follow on from the necessary properties of adaptations: universality, complexity, improbability, and functional design, all of which are characteristic of the executive functions.

Adaptation must do something useful for the organism: "A major purpose of the executive system is self-control, given that the executive functions are types of self-directed behavior humans use to self-regulate their social conduct for future ends" (Barkley, 2001, p. 13; see also Barkley, 1996a, 1996b). Barkley argues further that the executive functions evolved in order to facilitate reciprocal altruism or social exchange. This adaptation evolved because of the social niche and lifestyle in which humanity found itself: "the problem or problems to be solved by the EF/SR system were of a social nature" (Barkley, 2001, p. 14): i.e., group hunting by males, development of working memory, private sensing and speaking to the self, and need for inhibition. Barkley suggests five major activities for which inhibition may be required: reciprocal altruism (delayed social exchange) and formation of social coalitions, imitation, tool use, mimetic skill and communication, and self-defense and innovation against social manipulation.

The adaptive problems that each executive function addresses may be defined through consideration of the ancestral environment in which human mental processes evolved, what Tooby and Cosmides (1992) refer to as the *environment of ancestral adaptation*. Some features of that environment which impinge upon human problem-solving and behavioral regulation may persist today: for example, "despite marked changes in culture and technology, humans still live as groups that involve non-kin with whom they engage in reciprocal altruism or social exchange" (Barkley, 2001, p. 13). Barkley considers that the principal extra-individual agents which would pose problems that would require solution through the development of an executive function are other people who compose the social arrangements in which individuals lived and worked. In particular, the need for executive function development arose from competition with other people. The common thread appears to be social exchange and imitation through vicarious learning. This will necessarily involve inhibiting prepotent (immediate self-interested) responses, hindsight and foresight (working memory), and temporal discounting of the behavioral consequences that derive from bargaining and subsequent reciprocal exchange. The approach Barkley suggests has advantages in its ability to engage research at the neurophysiological level which is not possible through vaguer notions that the executive functions involve planning and decision functions devoid of any understanding of the adaptive framework that may have led to their development.

The neurophysiological basis of impulsivity and executive function

Miller and Wallis (2009) propose a neuropsychologically based depiction of this dual-process idea (Figure 2.2). Sensory cues are responsible for triggering the routines that have become established to the point of being automatic,

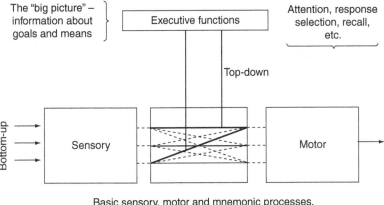

The "big picture" – information about goals and means

Executive functions

Attention, response selection, recall, etc.

Top-down

Bottom-up

Sensory

Motor

Basic sensory, motor and mnemonic processes, well-established habits and skills

Figure 2.2 Two levels of cognitive processes.

presumably through behavioral conditioning. The environmental stimuli responsible for this shaping of automatic behavior would control the organism completely were it not for the knowledge of goals and means imposed by top-down processing. These executive functions overcome the tendency of the organism to be governed by environmental evocations of the emotions, thoughts, and reflexive behaviors that have become associated with the environmental stimuli. Such behavior appears disinhibited and impulsive because it is enacted without consideration of future consequences. Such behavior would, moreover, tend toward inflexibility by dint of its being stimulus-bound (Miller and Wallis, 2009, p. 103).

Miller and Wallis (2009) also advance a neurobiological pathway to account for the acquisition by the PFC of the capacity to control the higher level cognitive functions involved in the regulation of behavior in the face of environmental programming. The first stage is the impingement of signals generated via reinforcement learning on the PFC circuitry: reinforced operant behavior is accompanied by the production of signals that associate PFC functioning with aspects of the stimulus field (the setting in which the behavior takes place), the nature of the behavioral response enacted, and the reinforcing and punishing consequences that are its outcomes. Responding repeatedly in these circumstances is capable of generating strong PFC representations of the contingencies of reinforcement that maintain such behavior. The second stage in the argument is to account for these signals and the actions of dopaminergic neurons of the midbrain (Box 2.3). In the course of learning through the repeated performance of behavioral responses, reinforcers initially activate the dopaminergic neurons themselves, but subsequently the stimuli that predict the reinforcers, rather than the reinforcers themselves, come to activate the dopaminergic neurons. Should an expected reward not appear, the rate of firing of the dopaminergic neurons is reduced. The discrepancy between the expectation of reinforcement and its non-appearance, coded by the dopaminergic neurons' activity, is known as the *reward prediction error* and is instrumental in the organism's subsequent ability to direct its actions more effectively toward the achievement of reinforcement (Miller and Wallis, 2009, pp. 103–104; Wagner and Heatherton, 2013). For discussion of the possible development of executive function and working memory and their role in general and fluid intelligence and reasoning, planning, and modeling capabilities, see Coolidge and Wynn (2005, 2009). Some interesting considerations with respect to Neanderthal cognition may be found in Wynn and Coolidge (2004).

Box 2.3 Incentive salience: the role of dopamine in reinforcement and reward

The precise role of dopamine in reinforcement and reward is still open to question. In spite of early indications that dopamine provided the chemical basis for reinforcement by generating pleasure (Berns, 2005), that hypothesis is now much less prevalent. Few researchers propose a causal role for dopamine in learning, limiting themselves to the idea that dopamine release codes the learning that occurs (Berridge, 2007, p. 399). Nor is it generally thought that dopamine synapses are the sole location of learning, though they do constitute a part of the neurophysiological chain involved in learning (Berridge, 2007, p. 399).

The first hypothesis examined by Berridge (2007) is that dopamine exerts a generally motivating influence upon behavior, being responsible for arousal, movement, and activity. This is an unexceptional theory: dopamine certainly has an activation-sensorimotor effect, but this explanation is limited in that it does not increase our understanding of why rewards are pleasing and sought after, or how they engender addiction and compulsion. The second idea he considers, namely the hedonia hypothesis, is a more sophisticated attempt to link the effects of neurotransmitters to reinforcement through the assumption that it is the chemical responsible for pleasant or unpleasant reactions to the consequences of behavior through the transformation of sensory inputs into hedonic experience (Wise, 1980). The central plank of the hedonia hypothesis is that dopamine is key to the sensitivity of behavior to its contingent effects by virtue of its capacity to convert the receipt of reinforcers and punishers into the positive and negative emotions that are the ultimate outcomes of behavior. There is evidence for this hypothesis from research that has investigated the blocking of dopamine via antagonist drugs which appears to reduce the hedonic impact of rewards ("anhedonia"). Individuals report pleasure when dopamine is released into the ventral striatum (e.g., when palatable foods are presented). But there are difficulties with this seemingly straightforward hypothesis.

Berridge (2007) argues that this hypothesis is not empirically supported, basing his conclusion on more sophisticated measures of dopamine's unique capacity to elicit *liking* responses than verbal reports. Another method draws upon the neurophysiological correlates of dopamine release which give clues to the brain regions implicated in liking. Facial reactions to stimuli, for instance, indicate that sweet tastes elicit tongue protrusion while bitter tastes elicit gapes, the former associated with particular areas of Nacc and ventral palladium in which the activation of *opioids* correlates with positive responses. (Opioids are chemicals produced in the body which have similar effects to the active ingredient of opium, morphine. Opiates, externally administered drugs such as heroin and morphine, activate *mu* receptors which mediate their pleasurable effects.) The hedonic impacts of sweet and savory stimuli are coded in the limbic forebrain areas. However, there is evidence that hedonic impact is not reduced when dopaminergic release in the forebrain is impaired (Berridge *et al.*, 1989). Destruction of all but 1 percent of dopamine in both the nucleus accumbens and the neostriatum has been found not to influence hedonic reactions to sweet tastes (Berridge and Robinson, 1998). Moreover, the finding that full prediction of juice rewards as a result of learning eventuates in monkeys' dopamine neurons ceasing to fire shows that any continuing hedonic consequences of the juice reward cannot be said to be mediated dopaminergically (Schultz, 2006; Schultz *et al.*, 1997).

We have noted already the consensus that dopamine release is not a cause of but codes learning. The reward learning hypothesis, which is the third that Berridge considers, proposes that by influencing neuronal plasticity, dopamine signals affect synaptic effectiveness, notably in the neostriatum and Nacc. This suggests a mechanism for the "stamping in" of S–S or S–R links that promote habit formation. Reward prediction errors (RPEs: Box 4.2) identified in work by Schultz and colleagues, and subsequently replicated by others suggest a role for dopaminergic as well as other neurons of the limbic system in the anticipation of reward as conditioned stimuli (CS) come to predict subsequent rewarding unconditioned stimuli (UCSs). This apparently occurs via the coding of response prediction errors. Berridge raises the chicken–egg question of whether dopamine transition leading to RPEs causes the rest of the brain to learn or whether learning more generally in the brain results in dopamine release. He argues that the evidence does not support the view that dopamine neurotransmission between the neurons of limbic structures including the Nacc and striatum is directly involved in the formation of novel S–S or S–R associations, whether these are posited to act as teaching signals or in the stamping-in of reinforcers.

The final hypothesis Berridge (2007) considers is that of incentive salience (Berridge and Robinson, 1993), which will assume importance in Chapter 3, in the context of situational influences on consumer choice. Berridge and Robinson (1993, 1995) propose that the release of dopamine is not responsible for the pleasurable consequences of consumption but for the arousal of anticipation of those consequences. The dopamine reward system thus evokes inordinately strong *wanting* that accompanies drug use rather than the addict's *liking* the effect of drug administration. This is the basis of incentive salience. Drugs like cocaine become effectual by blocking the presynaptic reuptake of dopamine and thereby induce the over-availability of this neurotransmitter. Hence, drug users are sensitized to the effect of the drug (Box 5.1). When the antecedent stimuli that compose the consumer behavior setting, and which have become associated with drug administration in the process of classical or operant conditioning, are encountered, therefore, the onset of dopamine production is transformed into intense, perhaps even compulsive drug craving. Addiction so caused persists well after the addict abstains, increasing the possibility of post-withdrawal relapse.

The propensity of the mesocorticolimbic dopamine system (Box 3.2) to be activated by drugs of abuse has the effect of imbuing the stimuli that compose the behavior setting in which the drugs are obtained and administered with what Robinson and Berridge (1993) call "incentive salience," namely the tendency of particular environmental stimuli to come to the attention of the individual who is thereby motivated to respond to them, to acquire and use them. Hence, the activity of the mesolimbic dopamine system may be said to induce goal-directed behavior, behavior involved in acquiring and consuming stimuli such as drugs or opportunities to engage in sex or gambling which in the process become *wanted* (McKim and Hancock, 2013, p. 119). The dopaminergic system is therefore involved in arousal and *wanting* but is not implicated in the individual's *liking* these stimuli such as the hedonic effects of a drug. Liking or pleasure is mediated, rather, by opioids, endocannabinoids, and the inhibitory neurotransmitter GABA.

These considerations are borne out by Winstanley's (2010) discussion of research on the neurophysiological basis of temporal discounting and executive control in which she draws particular attention to the role of the *nucleus accumbens* (NAcc), the *prefrontal cortex* (PFC), and the *anterior cingulate cortex* (ACC). The Nacc can be divided into two parts which are anatomically separate: the core and the shell. The NACcore (NAcc) is implicated in facilitating the role of CRs to shape behavior. Lesions of the NAcc block acquisition of autoshaped responses and impair Pavlovian-instrumental transfer (PIT). Rats that have undergone excitotoxic lesions to the NAcc rapidly increase the extent to which they select SS over LL in a delay-discounting task. (*Excitotoxic* indicates the process whereby neurons are injured/killed by excessive neurotransmitter stimulation.) PFC contributes to a number of higher level cognitive processes, including "monitoring internal resources, strategy development, detection of causal contingencies between events" (Winstanley, 2010, p. 103). PFC mediates delay-discounting judgments. Two areas in particular are implicated in goal-directed behavioral processes: the medial PFC (mPFC) as exemplified by the prelimbic and anterior cingulate regions, and the ventral PFC, including the OFC and agranular insula. Damage to the ACC increases premature or impulsive responses on a five-choice serial reaction time (5CRT) task, and also increases behavioral disinhibition. Animals with damaged ACC make more responses to the unrewarded stimulus in an autoshaping procedure (Box 2.4).

Box 2.4 Autoshaping

The procedure involved in autoshaping is as follows (Brown and Jenkins, 1968). A hungry pigeon was exposed to a disc which was then played for about eight seconds in every minute. Several seconds later, food was made available for four seconds, even though the bird had not emitted any response upon which the delivery of the food was contingent. In a short time, the pigeon began to peck at the disc whenever it was illuminated. Since the delivery of food was still not contingent upon this behavior, it was seen as enigmatic. Birds in general emit pecking responses whenever food is available; we can interpret the food as an unconditioned stimulus (US) that elicits the pecking behavior. The disc in Brown and Jenkins's experiment becomes a conditioned stimulus (CS) because of the pairing of the disc with the food. The conditioning procedure is known as *autoshaping*, the implication being that the birds had shaped their own behavior. From our point of view, it is of interest to note that radical behaviorists can interpret this behavior within the operant paradigm if they care to do so (see Skinner, 1983). Pecking the illuminated key will be followed at some point by a food reward and this may be seen as an operant process, were it not for the fact that the reception of the reward is entirely adventitious: there is no contingency of operant reinforcement in place. Even if one takes a molar view of behavior and argues that the relationship between responses and reinforcers is entirely reliant upon their correlation rather than their contiguity or contingency, it is not possible to make an operant interpretation of the behavior in the absence of any relationship other than a temporal accident between response and reinforcer. This is borne out by an ingenious experiment conducted by Williams and Williams (1969), who retained some features of Brown and Jenkins's study but added one of their own: pecking the key thwarted the food delivery. The reinforcement schedule in operation is known as an *omission- training schedule* (Bolles, 1979). The key pecking of the pigeons in this experiment was maintained and in some cases relentlessly. As the name given to this phenomenon by Williams and Williams, "negative automaintenance," suggests, these findings must be regarded as disappointing for radical behaviorists. Note also the subtitle of their paper: "Sustained pecking despite contingent non-reinforcement": the birds' behavior was maintained not just in the absence of reinforcement but despite the fact that the behavior in question foiled the presentation of food that was freely available in the absence of the behavior!

Temporal discounting as adaptation to environmental contingencies

The thesis that the tendency to discount steeply may have declined with the advent of settlement and agriculture is supported by a number of lines of inquiry; the picture is complicated, however, by the possibility that urbanization has been accompanied by a renewal of the tendency toward steeper discounting. The predictability and stability of the environment seems to be a determinant of these trends in the valuation of future events.

Winterhalter (2007) points out that the results of decision-making occur with varying degrees of unpredictably and that delay may engender temporal discounting, and cites the evidence that among the Mikea of Madagascar discounting rates of foragers are significantly higher than those of farmers (Tucker, 2006). More generally, animals' reproduction strategies vary with the resource abundance, benignity, and stability of the environment: where these factors are comparatively high, the strategy is described as "slow"; where it is comparatively low, as "fast" (Ellis *et al.*, 2009; Kaplan and Gangestad, 2005; van der Wal *et al.*, 2015).

Van der Wal *et al.* (2015) cite evidence that the structure of the environment is related to the rate at which animals discount the future: discount rates are higher, for instance, when food is relatively scarce and the ages of those giving birth are lower where mortality rates are higher. In addition, they argue that manmade environments increase discounting rates compared with natural environments. The former, typified by urban landscapes, are novel, inherently unstable in ways that promote interpersonal competition for food and mates, and social status, whereas rural environments are "intrinsically rewarding and enjoyable," characterized by predictability and plentiful resources. Children whose homes are in or near natural environments show greater capacity to delay consummatory acts, inhibit impulsivity, and concentrate. Simply being exposed to natural events such as plant growth has been shown to influence consumer behavior toward greater self-control. Environmental awareness is generated by exposure to natural scenes.

Van der Wal *et al.* (2015) tested the hypothesis that people who have been exposed to scenes of natural landscapes will exhibit lower discounting rates compared with those who are exposed to urban landscapes. They proposed that the effect would be mediated by an increase in self-control or greater valuation of future events, or both. Their research included two laboratory experiments and a field experiment. In the initial experiment, participants, randomly allocated to either the natural or urban environment conditions, were presented with photographic stimuli representing one or other of the environments, supplemented with auditory accompaniment to encourage immersion in the environment in question, followed by completion of a temporal discounting task. The second experiment was designed to elicit the possible mediators of the differential temporal discounting between the natural and urban environmental groups: variations in self-control, future valuation, or both. Apart from a control condition aimed at identifying such differences, and a different temporal discounting task, the procedure was unchanged from the earlier study. The conclusion was that personal psychologies of self-control and mood did not affect discounting rates, though concern for the future did. The field experiment required participants to walk through a natural or urban locale; at the mean, the rate of temporal discounting was 10 percent lower for participants in the natural condition as opposed to the urban condition.

Overall, these authors conclude that exposure to natural landscapes is associated with a decrease in temporal discounting and greater concern about future events; people presented with natural rather than urbanized environments are more likely to prefer LLRs to SSRs, to the extent that, compared with participants who were exposed to urban landscapes, those exposed to natural landscapes exhibited a 10 to 16 percent lower rate of discounting. Exposure to natural environments expands people's time horizons, while exposure to urban environments narrows them, at least immediately after exposure; no evidence of such differences emerged from information about participants having been brought up in or currently inhabiting one or other context (van Wal *et al.*, 2015).

3   Consumption and addiction

If music be the food of love, play on;
Give me excess of it, that, surfeiting,
The appetite may sicken, and so die.

William Shakespeare, *Twelfth Night*

The Continuum of Consumer Choice

In light of the discussion of temporal discounting in earlier chapters, consumer behaviors may be arrayed on a continuum ranging from the most routine (e.g., everyday brand selection) to the most extreme (e.g., life-disrupting episodes of addiction). One task of consumer psychology is to explain the pattern of consumer behavior exhibited across this range (Figure 3.1), and one hypothesis is that positioning on the continuum is determined by the degree of self-control versus impulsivity exhibited in the behavior.

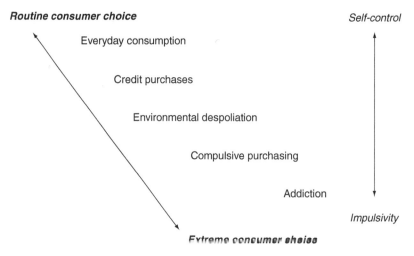

Figure 3.1 The Continuum of Consumer Choice I: from self-control to impulsivity.

The various consumer behaviors that comprise this Continuum of Consumer Choice differ from one another in terms of the extent to which consumers practice temporal discounting. Preference for a larger reward that appears later (LLR) over a smaller but more immediate reward (SSR) is depicted in terms of self-control, whereas preference for a SSR over a LLR is described as impulsivity. Routine consumption, typified by the everyday purchasing of familiar brands of nondurables such as foods, does not involve discounting and is generally within the consumer's capacity to practice self-control. Even less frequent consumer choices like occasional gambling can fall into this category. Although many such purchases are described as "impulsive" in the sense of being unplanned, they are not characterized by the kind of impulsiveness that results from the temporal discounting which is a feature of more extreme consumer behavior. Buying a new brand of cookies to try does not disrupt consumer behavior by requiring raising extra funds; having an extra glass of wine with one's restaurant dinner does not signal the onset of alcoholism; and buying a more expensive coffee-table book as a special gift does not spell financial ruin. The consequences of these behaviors may be accommodated easily within the consumer's normal pattern of conduct even if they require small savings to be made elsewhere.

Less routine and more impulsive in the temporal discounting sense is the purchase of durables like cars and houses that cause many consumers to incur debt which may impose costs far beyond those paid by the person who does not require a mortgage or credit terms. Yet the temporally closer option of buying sooner rather than saving up before buying is selected, even though the costs of the former are known in advance. A degree of impulsivity is apparent also in consumer behavior that leads to environmental despoliation: the current benefits of (over-)consuming can be temporally separated, indeed encapsulated, from the longer term damage inflicted upon the ecological system. Compulsive purchasing borders on addiction (Faber and Vohs, 2013; Müller and Mitchell, 2011); the indisputable addictions of problem gambling, problem drinking, or overeating to the point of obesity involve discounting the future at a very high rate.

While all consumer behavior is delineated fundamentally in terms of the reinforcement patterns which shape and maintain it, addictive behavior generally entails, as has been said, the pursuit of *immediate* reward at the expense of longer term, less favorable, or even deleterious outcomes, or perhaps missing out on later-appearing benefits. Moreover, as noted, addiction is typically accompanied by the expression of a strong desire to cease from or at least control consumption, followed by a lapse, further resolution, relapse, and so on (Ainslie, 1992).

It is probable that none of the consumer behaviors depicted in the Continuum of Consumer Choice avoids preference reversal totally, though in some cases it is far more trivial than others. Routine consumption rarely entails major shifts in preference; its vagaries are generally confined to temporary brand switching, sometimes amounting to unplanned purchasing, but at any rate unemotional. Buying on credit terms may, however, lead to regret, accompanied by a resolve to save up before purchasing in future, though financial circumstances may then necessitate a new round of installment buying. This need not become a compulsion let alone an addiction but it represents nevertheless a mode of consumer behavior that is governed by temporal discounting. Environmental despoliation may or may not entail preference reversal: some people may regret the damage they cause the environment through littering, unnecessary use of limited energy resources and water, and the generation of pollutants as in some forms of transportation. But it is generally the case that during any given period people are committed to one course of action, overconsumption or environmental protection; they may perhaps switch from one behavior pattern to the other but are unlikely to be constantly involved in mental conflict about their behavior for very long (Foxall, 2015c). Compulsive buying may well involve preference reversal, and addiction almost certainly does (Ridgway *et al.* 2008).

The Behavioral Perspective Model (BPM)

Consumer behavior is a function of two sources of reinforcement: *utilitarian*, which refers to the functional benefits of purchasing, owning, and using a product or service; and *informational*, which consists in the social consequences of these activities, the social honor, prestige, and status that others confer upon the owners and consumers of certain economic goods and services. An example of utilitarian reinforcement is the ability to discover what time it is from a wristwatch: almost any watch will provide this basic functional service. But some brands of watch provide something more: they confer status (within a particular social group) and may attract honor and prestige. This is so even if the small faces of some cocktail watches make telling the time by them difficult for some people who nevertheless wear them on social occasions. This is the *informational reinforcement* provided by the watch. It has an additional dimension insofar as an individual may accord him- or herself the honor and prestige that go with such goods, namely *self-esteem*. In short, utilitarian reinforcement is mediated by the product/service itself and consists in what it *does* in functional terms, while informational reinforcement is mediated by other people and oneself and consists in performance feedback on what one is doing and, crucially, how well one is doing it, according to social convention. Clearly, informational reinforcement differs from social group to social group: what confers high status in one social context (e.g., driving a luxury car in certain aspirational groups) may evoke low status in another (e.g., among those who value cars with a low carbon footprint).

Few goods embody only one source of reward but there are some, depending on the context in which they are provided. Thus, a person who is lost in the desert and experiencing extreme thirst is unlikely to inquire of a proffered glass of water, "Is it *Perrier*?" and a wedding ring is predominantly a symbol of one's (marital) status. In fact, almost all economic goods provide both utilitarian and informational reinforcement in varying combinations. This combination defines the *pattern of reinforcement* responsible for shaping and maintaining consumer choice, and Table 3.1 shows the four patterns and their associated classes of consumer behavior. Although this is a hypothetical proposal, it has been supported by considerable empirical research. Consumer behavior is also met by aversive consequences which are also either utilitarian or informational. There are, for instance, opportunity costs associated with all consumption: for everything we buy on a fixed budget we may have to forgo something else that would be desirable, as when a meal in a fine restaurant means a trip to the theater has to be postponed. Or a close friend or relative may not approve of our new hat or foreign holiday. If we buy these items less frequently the aversive consequences are termed *punishers*. Often, however, we behave in ways that help us to avoid or escape from aversive outcomes. Taking aspirin may help us to escape a headache, while taking a passport avoids embarrassment at the border. Escape and avoidance are *negatively* reinforced behaviors but they are still reinforced rather than punished: we are more likely to do them again when circumstances require. This summary of the BPM research program concentrates on patterns of positive reinforcement, since these are what primarily explain observed patterns of consumer choice. As we turn to addiction, however, the role of aversive stimuli – in punishment, escape, and avoidance – will loom larger.

Pattern of reinforcement involves consequential stimuli, those that follow a response and influence the rate at which similar responses are subsequently performed. Behavior may also be understood in terms of the stimulus field that precedes behavior, the *consumer behavior setting* and *learning history* which interact to form the *consumer situation*.

The consumer behavior setting is composed, first, of the discriminative stimuli in the presence of which the individual "discriminates" his or her behavior by performing only those responses that have previously been reinforced in similar circumstances. A consumer buying the ingredients for a meal that will form the basis of a dinner party for his or her boss may concentrate on acquiring those products and brands that have proved pleasing on previous occasions; he or she may be equally assiduous in avoiding products and brands that have not turned out so well or of which he or she has no knowledge. Second, the consumer behavior setting contains stimuli that enhance the relationship between the appropriate behavior and its reinforcement. An example

Table 3.1 Patterns of reinforcement and operant classes of consumer behavior

	Low utilitarian reinforcement	High utilitarian reinforcement
Low informational reinforcement	MAINTENANCE	HEDONISM
High informational reinforcement	ACCUMULATION	ACCOMPLISHMENT

Source: Foxall (1990/2004).

of such a *motivating operation* (MO; i.e. a prebehavioral stimulus that enhances the response-reinforcer relationship) is the prestigious brand name of the wine one plans to serve. What turns otherwise neutral stimuli into discriminative stimuli and motivating operations that induce or inhibit particular behaviors is the consumer's *learning history*, his or her previous behaviors in similar contexts, and the reinforcing or punishing consequences they have engendered. Learning history imbues the stimuli with significance, priming the physical and social elements of the setting to become stimuli that influence the rate of behavior.

Together, the consumer behavior setting and the consumer's learning history intersect to locate his or her behavior: they provide, respectively, the temporal and the spatial contexts for consumer choice. This location is the *consumer situation* which is the immediate precursor of consumer behavior.

Consumer behavior settings may be described further in terms of their capacity to induce (or deflect) particular behaviors. A setting in which many behaviors are possible is described as relatively *open*. Shopping in a large supermarket affords the opportunity to buy many products and many brands within each product category. In everyday terms, the consumer has a vast array of choices available and the specifics of what he or she actually purchases on any occasion can be difficult to predict. Shopping in a filling station forecourt shop or a high street convenience store means being confronted with fewer choices as the range of products and brands stocked is much smaller. Such an outlet is a relatively *closed* setting. Other closed settings ("relative" being understood rather than tediously repeated) are gymnasia, dentists' surgeries, sports being played by tightly defined rules, and playing roulette in a formal casino; in each case the behavior pattern for the consumer is quite tightly controlled and, although he or she *can* of course leave at any time, doing so becomes less probable given the physical and social arrangement of the setting. Open settings include attending a party, being on a resort vacation, cooking and consuming a meal at home, and having a quiet drink with friends; within the broad limits imposed by the social and physical surroundings, it is possible in these circumstances to engage in numerous types of behavior, to switch apparently randomly from one activity to another, to prepare, serve, and eat whatever ingredients one pleases, and to talk of whatever matters arise in conversation. Putting together the scope of the consumer behavior setting defined in terms of a continuum of *closed* to *open* settings with the pattern of reinforcement and classes of consumer behavior defined in Table 3.1 arrives at the eight *contingency categories* shown in Figure 3.2.

The summative Behavioral Perspective Model can now be constructed and is shown in Figure 3.3.

Verbal behavior and rule governance

Radical behaviorist explanation rested for many years on the view that behavior was a function of its observable, measurable consequences. Even recognition of the importance of language was met with an analysis of "verbal

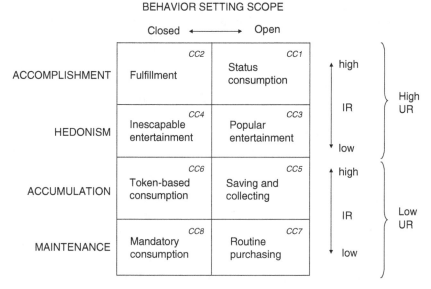

Figure 3.2 The BPM Contingency Matrix.

behavior" in terms of the reinforcing stimuli upon which it was contingent. However, while the behavior of nonhuman animals continues to be analyzed as "contingency-shaped" – that is, molded by direct contact with its reinforcing and punishing outcomes – human behavior is often explained by reference to verbal control. In this case, the stimuli that influence behavior are not encountered directly but through being specified in a verbal statement (Skinner, 1969). Technical skills are generally learned via the provision of instructions rather than by so-called "trial and error," which would be far less efficient and possibly hazardous to health and well-being (Bandura, 1986).

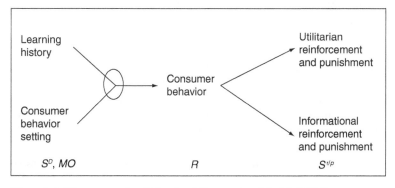

Figure 3.3 The summative Behavioral Perspective Model (BPM).

Verbal behavior is social: Skinner (1957) actually defined verbal behavior as behavior that is reinforced via other persons. In other words, the controlling consequences of such behavior are to be found in its social milieu rather than in the physical environment. As a result of our learning in childhood, which is what the others (parents and teachers) say is reliably connected to the consequences of behaving in a particular way, we are more likely to act upon their instructions and upon the instructions of other adults. Such instructed or rule-governed behavior – that which stems from the verbal activity of a speaker – may be understood as a response to a verbal discriminative stimulus which, through training, has come to take the place of the contingencies themselves. The rule states the elements of the three-term contingency in verbal form. For example, an advertisement might declare: using *Zing!* toothpaste (the response to a discriminative stimulus in the form of the brand name) will make your teeth whiter (the reinforcer). In this case, the entire message may be seen as a complex discriminative stimulus that sets the occasion for the recommended purchase use of the toothpaste in question. Another view is that verbal rules are motivating operations that enhance the value of a reinforcer; for example, an advertisement might contain a phrase such as "Taste the difference?!" which has the effect of making the whole three-term contingency it employs that much more salient to the consumer.

Three broad kinds of rules have been proposed based on the functions they perform in influencing behavior (Zettle and Hayes, 1982). The first kind of rule-governed behavior is *tracking*, which is an instructed behavior that comes under the control of the physical environment. A *track* is therefore a rule that denotes how the physical environment is arranged. Thus, in answer to a query how to get to the Guggenheim I may be told, "Turn left at the next intersection, then left again at the bank, and finally make a right at the lights. You'll see the museum on your left." By tracking the physical environment according to this rule, I will arrive where I plan to be; the tracking is therefore part of the verbal behavior of the listener, even though he or she may not have uttered it, because it is behavior under the control of verbal stimuli. This kind of rule-governed behavior has something in common with utilitarian reinforcement, since its outcomes are usually functional, mediated by physical products or by services; at their most abstract, the reinforcers in question are commodities to which the consumer gains legal title.

The second rule-governed behavior is *pliance*, which is behavior controlled by consequences that the speaker controls (or claims to control). The rule, a *ply*, presents the interpersonal consequences of compliance or noncompliance. A partygoer might be informed that his or her partner will disapprove of their drinking too much alcohol: the spoken or understood instruction "Don't over-indulge or no more parties!" is the ply. Advertisements frequently incorporate plys which suggest that social approval is contingent upon buying or using certain goods such as a high-status car. Pliance involves informational reinforcement, since the outcomes are socially mediated. Since most economic goods and services entail both utilitarian and informational reinforcement, any verbal behavior in the form of rules that motivates them makes appeals to a *pattern of reinforcement*.

The third kind of rule is the *augmental*, a strongly motivating observation that emphatically describes how a behavior will be reinforced or avoid punishment. An email which reminds us that if we book "just one more trip" with our favorite airline we will be eligible for a free night in a luxurious destination hotel constitutes an augmental. Insofar as it alters the relationship between the behavior and its reinforcer, notably by enhancing the value of the latter, its action resembles that of a motivating operation. Augmentals may reflect utilitarian and/or informational reinforcement.

Two lessons are apparent from this discussion. First, instructed behavior is always subject to two sets of contingencies: the social consequences that maintain the rule following and the natural contingencies that eventually take over if the instruction is effective. This is especially evident in the case of pliance (e.g., when a teacher suggests to her student that he go to the store for a certain book, she implies that his doing so will result in her giving her personal approval, a social or informational reinforce). In addition, the student obtains a useful book, a form of utilitarian reinforcement. The student's behavior in going to the store and purchasing the book is rule-governed insofar as it reflects the interpersonal regard shown by the teacher; it is also contingency-shaped in that it comes under the control of road layout, a physical store, and a book. The radical behaviorist assumes that rule-governed behavior provides just as much an extensional explanation as the three-term contingency demonstrable in the closed setting of an operant experiment in which a discriminative stimulus, S^D, response, R, and a reinforcer, S', are physically and unambiguously demonstrable with intersubjective agreement.

Second, what radical behaviorists call "private events" may assume a role in formulating and responding to rules. Contrary to popular belief, radical behaviorism actually embraces thinking and feeling as part of its subject matter. An individual may reflect on the contingencies in operation (as in the experiment mentioned above where it is necessary to choose between two sources of a reward) and conclude that the way to proceed is by enacting this or that behavior. A consumer may make his or her own rules based on a personal interpretation of experience and the information and instructions provided by elements in the promotions mix. Such personal rule formulation in the process of decision-making is especially prevalent when the individual lacks an appropriate learning history, or suitable socially provided rules (other-rules) for behavior in, say, a novel behavior setting.

Empirical evidence: behavioral economics of consumer choice

A large volume of empirical research which has had the dual purposes of testing the predictive capacity of the BPM and of elucidating the nature of consumer choice by viewing it through the lens of behavior analysis has been inspired by the model. This work has increasingly incorporated techniques pioneered in behavior analysis and, especially, behavioral economics (Hursh, 1984; Hursh and Roma, in press; Foxall, 2015a) in order to investigate behavior in the non-intentional terms that are the hallmark of operant psychology and experimental economics. Defining economic choice as the allocation of behavior within a framework of costs and benefits (Staddon, 1980), this perspective adopted matching and maximization techniques to the study of consumers' brand and product choices (Fagerstrøm *et al.*, 2011; Foxall, 1999b; Foxall and James, 2002, 2003; Foxall and Schrezenmaier, 2003; Wells and Foxall, 2013; Curry *et al.*, 2010).

Experimental research based on testing predictions and applications suggested by the BPM has involved both food retailing and offline and online marketing (Foxall and Sigurdsson, 2013; Sigurdsson *et al.*, 2011, 2013a, b, 2015). An important facet of this research has been the use of field experiments, typically in retail organizations which allow the full force of the marketing mix to be investigated in its effect on consumer behavior. Sigurdsson *et al.* (2013), for instance, tested the BPM in the context of Norwegian retailing with an econometric analysis of the effects of the pattern of reinforcement specified in the model. The predictability of each individual predictor (utilitarian, informational, and pricing) was tested and compared with multiple regression models, based on all three predictors, and with previous findings. This was done based on the analysis of buying behavior of brands for 10 different product categories. Results revealed that informational level was the best individual predictor for consumer buying behavior, but the combination of the three behavioral consequential predictors together (relying on the BPM) tended to give the best prediction.

Matching and maximization

Since the pioneering analysis of the relevance of Herrnstein's (1961, 1970, 1997) work to marketing and consumer research (Foxall, 1999a, 1999b), our investigations have demonstrated that this field of behavioral economics provides insights into the psychological measures of standard microeconomic variables such as product and brand choice, substitutability, complementarity, and independence (Foxall, 1999a, 1999b; Foxall and James, 2002, 2003; Foxall and Schrezenmaier, 2003; Foxall *et al.*, 2004, 2010a, b; Romero *et al.*, 2006; Wells and Foxall, 2012) which also serve to define product categories, subcategories, and brands (Foxall *et al.*, 2010a, 2010b). In a significant development, Oliveira-Castro *et al.* (2010) integrated matching with the BPM variables of utilitarian and informational reinforcement as well as price (Sigurdsson and Foxall, 2015; Bui Huynh and Foxall, 2015).

Price elasticity of demand

Further behavioral economics research has involved the operational measurement of utilitarian and informational reinforcement and the estimation of price elasticity of demand coefficients (Box 3.1) for brands featuring varying combinations of these elements of reward (Foxall *et al.*, 2004, 2007, 2010a, 2010b; Oliveira-Castro *et al.*, 2005, 2008). This work underpins the BPM approach by showing that consumer demand is a function not only of price but of the pattern of reinforcement delivered by goods. Of particular interest is the empirical research which demonstrates that changes in consumer behavior, measured as elasticity of demand for fast-moving nondurables, is a function of the pattern of utilitarian and informational reinforcement (Foxall *et al.*, 2004, 2013; Oliveira-Castro *et al.*, 2011; Yan *et al.*, 2012a, 2012b). For reviews see Oliveira-Castro and Foxall (2015), Yan and Foxall (2015), and Rogers *et al.* (2015).

Box 3.1 Price elasticity of demand

Price elasticity of demand is a measure of the responsiveness of the quantity of a good that consumers demand to changes in its price (see, e.g., Kagel *et al.*, 1995). Alternatively, we may state it as the responsiveness of *consumption* to a change in price. Expressed as a simple linear relationship, price elasticity of demand is

$$\text{Log } Q = b_0 + \log b_1 p$$

where Q is the quantity demanded of a commodity or reinforcer, b_1 is the slope of the demand curve that represents the elasticity of demand, and b_0 is the intercept.

Elasticity coefficients (b_1) are interpreted broadly in three ways. If $b_1 = 1$ we have unitary elasticity, meaning that a 1 percent increase in price results in a 1 percent decrease in quantity demanded. This coincidence is not unknown but is comparatively rare. More common is $b_1 < 1$, which represents inelastic demand: a 1 percent increase in price reduces quantity demanded but by less than 1 percent. The term "inelastic" does not imply that there is no relationship between a change in price and the quantity demanded: only that the change in quantity is less, proportionally, than the increase in price. This is in fact a very common occurrence for everyday consumer goods. Such goods are necessities, the primary reinforcers that are biologically determined and essential for individual survival and biological fitness. If a 1 percent increase in price reduces quantity demanded by more than 1 percent, demand is said to be elastic. This is commonly found in the case of luxuries, secondary reinforcers which are socially determined.

For details of other techniques employed in our research to calculate elasticity coefficients, see Oliveira-Castro and Foxall (2015), and Yan and Foxall (2015).

Consumers' utility functions

Consumers' utility functions demonstrate that consumers maximize measurable combinations of these goods: Oliveira-Castro *et al.* (2015a, b) show that consumers maximize selected combinations of utilitarian reinforcement and informational reinforcement. They employed the Cobb-Douglas utility function on account of its analytical tractability, associated to simple well-behaved indifference curves, which is among the most commonly used in economics (Voorneveld, 2008).

For the current context, the function is:

$$U_{(x_1,x_2)} = x_1^a x_2^b \tag{9}$$

where U is the total amount of utility obtained by consumption of x_1 and x_2, x_1 is the quantity of utilitarian reinforcement consumed, x_2 is the quantity of informational reinforcement consumed, and a and b are empirically determined parameters such that $a + b = 1$. The implication is that consumers maximize the utility that derives from particular combinations of utilitarian and informational reinforcement subject to the constraint imposed by their budget for the goods in question.

Summing up these results of empirical research in Consumer Behavior Analysis enables us to make some sense of consumer behavior as it actually occurs in many markets. Both rational choice theory which posits a utility-maximizing economic agent and matching theory predict similar behavior when reinforcers are arranged on ratio schedules as in the case of prices: the consumer has to make a fixed number of responses (payments of 1, 1p or 1c, etc.) in order to receive the reward. The expectation of both theories is that in this case the consumer will allocate her responses (budget) exclusively to the behavior that produces the product or brand that requires the fewer or fewest responses to obtain the reward. Consumers tend to make their purchases among the brands in a product category not in a totally brand-loyal fashion but so that the subset of tried-and-tested brands that constitute their consideration set are all selected over a sequence of shopping trips. (Each brand *does* have a clientele of sole purchasers who are 100 percent brand loyal but these are a rather small minority.) Consumers' consideration sets tend to provide utilitarian and informational reinforcement of similar levels, so a given consumer might purchase only premium brands, paying a considerably higher price almost habitually than would be required if she purchased the least expensive brand available, even though this was broadly similar in terms of its physical and functional features (i.e., its utilitarian reinforcement) to any other available brand. The consumer's behavior is explicable if she is thought of as obtaining both utilitarian and informational reinforcement in some optimal combination. Even so, most premium brand purchasers, like other consumers, tend to maximize by selecting the least expensive of the brands in the consideration set. Matching behavior and Consumer Behavior Analysis elucidate consumers' observed purchase patterns by their respective assumptions that consumers select the more/most advantageous brand or product at any choice point (on any given shopping occasion) and emphasizing the bifurcation of reinforcement into its utilitarian and informational elements: if consumers' choices maximize the reinforcement they receive and yet they do not exclusively (or even ever) purchase the cheapest available items, they must be maximizing something other than utilitarian reinforcement alone. We now have evidence that they in fact maximize a combination of both utilitarian and informational reinforcement (Oliveira-Castro *et al.*, 2015b).

Operant reinforcement and emotion

Linking emotion and contingency

The centrality of emotion in understanding reinforcement is nicely juxtaposed by Berridge and Kringelbach (2015, p. 646) with its role as the servo-mechanism of compulsion: "In a sense, pleasure can be thought of as evolution's boldest trick, serving to motivate an individual to pursue rewards necessary for fitness, yet in modern environments of abundance, also inducing maladaptive pursuits such as addictions." Rolls's (1999) theory of emotion proposes that the way in which the brain facilitates the reward and punishment of behaviors through the generation of emotions provides a key to understanding the neuropsychology of behavior. Brain systems involved in motivation and emotion transfer reward and punishment signals to the systems that produce action; the action systems tend to maximize the reward signals so obtained, switching behavior from the attainment of one reward to that of another following any reduction in the reward value of the former and as the possibility of punishment increases.

The automaticity of the rapid interaction of operant and Pavlovian conditioning which is emphasized by Rolls's theory may account for behavior in two ways. The emotion feeling may function as an internal discriminative stimulus to increase the probability of the behavior that produced it being reprised; it is also possible that the emotion feeling is the ultimate reward of the behavior in question and that, by definition, it performs a reinforcing role (Foxall, 2011). Either way, the effects of basic emotions on subsequent responding are immediate and uninfluenced by reflection at the cognitive level. Hence, Rolls's theory links emotion and contingency: "emotions are states produced by instrumental reinforcing stimuli" (Rolls, 1999, p. 61). The theory maintains, moreover, that the primary (biological) *goals* of behavior, rather than specific behaviors, are influenced by the genes which "selfishly" (Dawkins, 1976) regulate what will act as reinforcers and punishers in order to promote their own survival through the biological fitness of the organisms that are their vehicles. This theory accords with the view that the evolution of emotions was enhanced because of their causal effectiveness in bringing about particular behaviors and behavioral change (Toronchuk and Ellis, 2013).

Secondary goals, involving reinforcers that are learned in the process of conditioning (e.g., consuming a particular brand of baked beans rather than simply ingesting food), are indirectly determined in part by the genetic selection of ultimately rewarding emotional feelings. By enabling the comparative *evaluation* of reinforcers and punishers, the brain interfaces sensory inputs and action outputs: behavior is thus the outcome of the procedure in which the brain *computes* the values of sensory stimuli and selects between reinforcers and ways of avoiding punishers. The behaviors on which reinforcers and punishers act are motivational and emotional behaviors: motivational behaviors usually result from intracranial stimulation whereas emotional behaviors have their origins in stimuli that originate outside the brain. Sensory processing, that which relies on the identification of reinforcing and punishing stimuli via the sense modalities, enables the appropriate decoding and representation of the reward value of reinforcers once they have been identified.

Emotion and operant contingencies

Mehrabian and Russell's (1974) scales for the measurement of *pleasure, arousal*, and *dominance* suggest that these emotions can each be associated with particular structural variables of the BPM. Hence, situations hypothesized to be higher in utilitarian reinforcement will be marked by higher levels of reported pleasure; those hypothesized to be higher in informational reinforcement, by higher levels of reported arousal; and those hypothesized to be marked by openness will be higher in reported dominance. By emphasizing the satisfaction and pleasure which consumers are likely to receive from certain purchase and consumption environments, as well as the usefulness of this emotion in indicating the presence of positively reinforcing behavioral outcomes that will eventuate in enhanced survival potential and biological fitness, *pleasure* is redolent of utilitarian reinforcement. Pleasure, therefore, should be expected to be a disproportionately encountered response to consumer situations which result in utilitarian (functional) consequences. This does not mean that it will be exclusively the emotional response reported for such consumer situations: each consumer situation is defined in terms of relative contributions from utilitarian and informational reinforcement and consumer behavior-setting scope. But situations that are defined as relatively high in utilitarian reinforcement should produce relatively high pleasure reactions.

Inasmuch as it is defined primarily in terms of performance feedback, informational reinforcement may be expected to co-occur with reactions of *arousal* which is often associated with the identification of discrepancies between current and indicated performance. To illustrate, road markings that indicate one's excess speed, for instance, are presumably intended to embody such feedback and to engender perceptual responses that bring drivers' behavior into line with socially accepted norms. Mehrabian and Russell (1974) define a measure of the information rate of environments, scores upon which correlate significantly with arousal scores; this idea of information rate provides an indication of the variation from norms present in environmental stimuli such as noise, crowdedness, temperature, lighting, and social interaction rates, and thus includes the criteria of informational reinforcement without being coterminous with it. The expectation, therefore, is that consumer situations that are relatively high in informational reinforcement will be those for which reports of arousal are also disproportionately high. Open consumer behavior settings are by definition those in which the consumer has relatively large numbers of behavioral options (sources of reinforcement) and hence those in which he or she may be predicted to experience a higher degree of dominance than in closed settings in which behavioral choices are severely limited, perhaps to a single option. In the former, the consumer is more likely to be a determinant of the range of options available (through choice of store, time of shopping, lack of external compulsion), whereas in the latter, agents other than the consumer are likely to arrange these matters. It is probable, therefore, that consumer situations that are relatively open will engender higher feelings of dominance than those that are relatively closed.

Eight studies have consistently shown that pleasure scores are higher for consumer situations marked by higher utilitarian reinforcement; arousal scores, for consumer situations marked by higher informational reinforcement; and dominance scores, for situations marked by greater openness (Foxall, 1997b; Foxall and Yani-de-Soriano, 2005; Yani-de-Soriano *et al.*, 2013). The hypothesized patterns of emotional reaction to consumer situations defined in terms of the structural variables of the BPM shown in Figure 3.4 are also those identified by these empirical studies (Foxall, 2011; Foxall *et al.*, 2012).

Emotion and operant and respondent conditioning

Figure 3.5 develops the BPM framework in light of these relationships between behavioral contingencies and emotional feelings. In this figure,

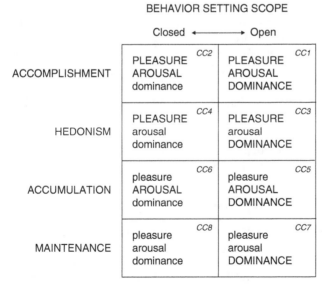

Figure 3.4 The BPM Emotional Contingency Matrix.

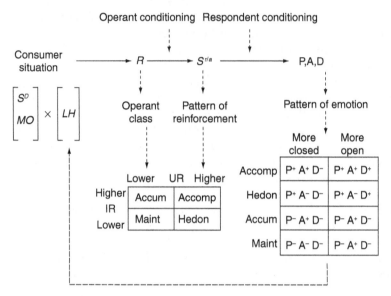

Figure 3.5 Behavioral contingencies and patterns of emotion.

Rolls's (2014) argument that emotions are states elicited by operant reinforcers is made explicit, and the classification of consumer behaviors and patterns of emotion identified in our empirical research (*see* Figure 3.5) is shown. In summary, the reinforcing and aversive consequences ($S^{r/a}$) of the individual's behavior (R) act as CSs which elicit the emotions of pleasure (P), arousal (A), and dominance (D) in various combinations depending on the contingencies of reinforcement. These patterns of emotion are retained, possibly as somatic markers, and influence the effective learning history that interacts with the stimuli composing the current consumer behavior setting to generate the consumer situation that is the immediate precursor of further behavior. The next question that arises is how the felt emotions of pleasure, arousal, and dominance come to modify learning history so that their impact may be expressed in the probability of further responding of a similar nature if appropriate consumer situations arise. A strong possibility is suggested by Damasio's (1994) somatic marker hypothesis.

The somatic marker hypothesis

The somatic marker hypothesis (SMH: Damasio, 1994) is one of two neurobehavioral decision theories that are especially relevant to the explanation of akratic and addictive behavior. The other, the competing neurobehavioral decision systems (CNDS) model, is discussed in Chapter 4. The principal strength of the SMH which makes it relevant in the present context of consumption stems from its treatment of emotions and feelings in linking neurophysiological responses to the operant behaviors that produced them and, through their role in manifesting consumers' learning histories, to the likelihood of their repeating the same and similar behaviors.

Damasio's (1994) *somatic marker hypothesis* (SMH) is a model of decision-making systems which emphasizes the role of emotion and feelings, downplaying economic considerations. Decision-making reflects the marker signals laid down in bioregulatory systems by conscious and non-conscious emotion and feeling; hence, Bechara and Damasio (2005; Bechara *et al.*, 2000) argue that in dealing with decision-making, economic theory ignores emotion. Economics is exclusively concerned with "rational Bayesian maximization of expected utility, as if humans were equipped with unlimited knowledge, time, and information processing power." They point, by contrast, to neural evidence which shows that "sound and rational" decision-making requires antecedent accurate emotional processing (Bechara and Damasio, 2005, p. 336; Phelps and Sokol-Hessner, 2012).

Damasio's (1994) hypothesis is the outcome of brain lesion studies in which damage to the ventromedial prefrontal cortex (vmPFC) was found to be associated with behaving in ways that were personally harmful, especially insofar as they contributed to injuring the social and financial status of the individual and their social relationships (see also Luria, 1966). Although many aspects of these patients' intellectual functioning such as long-term memory were unimpaired, they were notably disadvantaged with respect to learning from experience and responding appropriately to emotional situations. Moreover, their general emotional level was described as "flat." Damasio's observation on these findings was that "the primary dysfunction of patients with vmPFC damage was an inability to use emotions in decision making, particularly decision making in the personal, financial and moral realms" (Naqvi *et al.*, 2006, p. 261). The behavioral tendencies, notably the assumption of high-risk activities, observed in patients suffering impairment to the orbital frontal cortex, from Gage onward, represent emotional rather than cognitive deficits. They stem from an inability to elicit appropriate emotional signals, somatic markers, rather than dysfunctional intellectual capacities (Damasio, 1994). In this inheres the central point of the title and theme of Damasio's 1994 book, *Descartes' Error*. While the Cartesian assertion of a conflict between higher order cognition and emotion would support an interpretation that identified deficits in the former as the causal element in these patients' new behavior pattern, the SMH adverts to the possibility that emotional deficits actually account for it.

Thus was born the central assumption of the somatic marker hypothesis that "emotions play a role in guiding decisions, especially in situation in which the outcomes of one's choices, in terms of reward and punishment, are uncertain" (Naqvi *et al.*, 2006, p. 261; Bechara, 2011). Of relevance here is the finding that the vmPFC may be implicated in activity of the parasympathetic nervous system (PNS), which in contrast to the sympathetic nervous system (SNS) is involved in the explorative monitoring of the environment, the discovery of novelty, and social functioning broadly conceived (Eisenberger and Cole, 2012; Goldberg, 2002). This is corroborative of Damasio's hypothesis.

Inherent in the somatic marker hypothesis is the attempt to describe not only the separate functions of the brain regions involved in emotional processing but also the interconnections between them (Haber, 2009). The starting point is operant behavior, particularly the mechanisms of reinforcement learning (Daw, 2013; Daw and Tobler, 2013). Specific behaviors eventuate in rewards as a result of which the amygdala triggers emotional/bodily states. These states are then associated via a learning process to the behaviors that brought them about by means of mental representations. As each behavioral alternative is subsequently deliberated upon in the course of decision-making, the somatic state corresponding to it is re-enacted by the vmPFC. After being brought to mind in the course of decision-making the somatic states are represented in the brain by sensory processes in two ways. First, emotional states are related to cortical activation (e.g., insular cortex) in the form of *conscious* "gut feelings" of desire or aversion that are mentally attributed to the behavioral options as they are considered. Second, there is an *unconscious* mapping of the somatic states at the subcortical level (e.g., in the mesolimbic dopaminergic system (see Box 3.2)); in this case, individuals choose the more beneficial option without knowingly feeling the desire for it or the aversiveness of a less beneficial alternative (Ross et al., 2008; Di Chiara, 2002; Robbins and Everitt, 2002; Tobler and Kobayashi, 2009).

Box 3.2 The mesocorticolimbic system

A particularly important relationship between the midbrain and the forebrain is represented by the mesocorticolimbic system which is responsive to the sensation of rewards (Figure 3.6). DAergic cells are found within the mesencephalon (midbrain) in the pars compacta of the substantia nigra (SNc) and the ventral area (VTA). Some of these cells project axons that innervate the stratum, the central nucleus of the amygdala, and the dorsal nucleus accumbens (dNAcc) which are parts of the forebrain (which consists of the diencephalon and the telencephalon). The structure of dopaminergic neurons that accomplishes this is known as the mesolimbic pathway [VTA→NAcc]. Belonging to the evolutionarily old limbic system, the amygdala is primarily concerned in human beings with the processing of emotion, the thalamus with the transmission of sensory information, the hypothalamus aids in the maintenance of the homeostatic by governing the internal economy of the body, and the hippocampus with memory. The hedonia thesis holds dopamine to be implicated in the hedonic evaluation of rewards but more recent evidence suggests that it is more concerned with preparation for their receipt. The role of dopamine in motivation, arousal, and the prediction of the timing of rewards now seems more probable than its being the "pleasure chemical," a position it has ceded to the opioids. Dopamine influences the motivational value of rewards based on calculations of their being greater or less than, or the same as, they are expected to be.

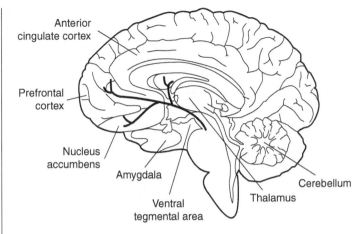

Figure 3.6 Mesolimbocortical pathway.

The mesolimbic dopaminergic system comprises the midbrain ventral tegmental area (VTA) and its projections to the nucleus accumbens (NAcc), and to the limbic system of the forebrain, primarily the amygdala and the hippocampus. The mesocortial system is implicated in the transmission of dopamine from the VTA to the frontal cortex. Together, these systems are known as the dopaminergic mesocorticolimbic system/pathway.

The essence of Damasio's (1994, 1999) work on emotion is his critique of Descartes's notion that reason and emotion are distinct regions of the mind and that emotion must be controlled by reason. The empirical findings of neuropsychology indicate otherwise: "work from my laboratory has shown that emotion is integral to the process of reasoning and decision making, for worse and for better" (Damasio, 1999, p. 41). That an excess of emotion may confound rational decision-making is a commonplace observation but Damasio has concentrated on clinical evidence of particular emotional shortfalls resulting from particular brain lesions and affecting the efficacy of problem-solving. He bases his conclusions on experience with patients who were entirely capable of making rational decisions until they suffered neurological injury to their prefrontal regions, notably in ventral and medial areas and to the right parietal area. The causes of such damage might be, for instance, a stroke, a tumor, or an accidental injury. The consequential deficits these patients suffered were primarily *emotional* and these losses reduced their capacity to decide rationally. The emotional deficits were selective but the result was always "a disturbance of the ability to decide advantageously in situations involving risk and conflict and a selective reduction of the ability to resonate emotionally in precisely those same situations while preserving the remainder of their emotional abilities" (Damasio, 1999, p. 41).

Damasio distinguishes *feeling*, which is a personal and subjective experience arising from *emotion*, which is a set of responses including those that are private, neurophysiological events, and those that are publicly observable. Emotions are biological phenomena, the outcome of evolution by natural selection, and as such they are centrally involved in the survival of individuals and their biological fitness. By providing initial and immediate reactions to particular situations, emotions help prepare the individual to respond appropriately. As such, emotions are intricately bound up with the events and behaviors that have previously resulted in reinforcing and punishing outcomes, pleasure and displeasure, approach and escape/avoidance, gain and loss (Damasio, 1999, pp. 54–55). Feelings are crucially important in learning the upshots of situational encounters and responses and employing them in the process of decision-making for further responding in similar situations. These considerations are fundamental to the somatic marker hypothesis.

The process of rational decision-making is typically represented as entailing the establishment of a goal, followed by a review of the available actions which could be undertaken to achieve it, and a comparative evaluation of these alternatives in light of their probable consequences vis-à-vis achievement of the goal (Bermúdez, 2009). Such problem-solving sometimes entails a detailed cost–benefit analysis (e.g., when an individual has to make a momentous decision, such as emigrating to another country or when a business organization is making investment plans). However, there are decision situations that call for a more rapid response than this if the individual is to survive: a police marksman may have to decide whether to pull the trigger without the luxury of such detailed contemplation of the alternative courses of action and their likely outcomes. Many of the choice points reached by animals also demand rapid fight-or-flight reactions in the face of life-threatening danger. The somatic marker hypothesis (SMH) is a theory of how these more imminent decisions are made. At its heart is the idea that "When the bad outcome connected with a given response comes into mind, however fleetingly, you experience an unpleasant gut feeling" (Damasio, 1994, p. 173).

Feelings of this kind are the result of previous operant behavior, the punishing (in this example) consequence of which was accompanied by an emotional reaction which is now represented in PFC and available to initiate this gut feeling which influences the current decision. Specifically, reinforcing and punishing stimuli eventuate in a related physiological-affective state, somatic markers, which are represented in the ventromedial prefrontal cortex (vmPFC). (We encountered this capacity of reinforcing and punishing outcomes of operant behavior to be registered in PFC in the account of the neurophysiological basis of executive functions advanced by Miller and Wallis (2009).) The recurrence of these emotional feelings in the course of decision-making may well influence cognitive appraisal and problem-solving. This does not mean that decision-making is entirely emotional: it does mean that there are limits to the cognitive control of decision processes, especially as a result of intellectual overload if too many potential future situations have to be compared and evaluated. It also means that the cognitive component of decision-making is amenable to modification and bias as a result of emotional feelings. A net somatic state is the result of the computation of positive and negative somatic markers and it is this which is the immediate precursor of decision-making and behavior. The complexities of decision-making are thus reduced as the potentially most beneficial course of behavior becomes apparent, not as a result of intellectual processes alone but also through the operation of an emotional learning history and its neurophysiological traces.

Damasio's hypothesis is derived, as we have noted, from observations of patients who have suffered damage to the relevant brain regions: the well-known case of Phineas Gage highlighted the fact that damage to the relevant areas of PFC could result in impairment in the ability to envision and evaluate future behavioral consequences, plan ahead, take the outcomes of previous behavior into consideration, or act responsibly in a social context where subtle cues normally guided behavior. Hence, impairment of PFC functioning may result in novel associations with people which the patient would previously have avoided, and deficits in the operation of executive functions. It may also manifest to a degree in the lack of empathy which is described as mild psychopathy or sociopathy. Such damage does not, however, affect normal sensory or intellectual functioning which relies on working memory, paying attention, or linguistic usage and comprehension.

Somatic markers may be activated to influence emotional responding, decision-making, and behavior in two ways: via direct experience of an appetitive or threatening stimulus – seeing a fresh cream gateau on the table or a vicious dog on the street – or via vicarious experience – just imagining the gateau or the animal. *Similar* approach behavior would accompany both the direct perception and the imagined food in the first example, while similar fight-or-flight reactions would be motivated in the second. Damasio (1994) terms these routes to the reactivation of somatic markers the "body-loop" and the "as-if body-loop," respectively. The responses inaugurated by the as-if loop are usually less strong than those which result from direct contact with the stimuli that originally instigated the somatic marker. All in all, somatic markers simplify decision procedures, obviating the need for comprehensive cost–benefit analysis by resolving behavioral consequences into the common currency of pleasure-displeasure (Cabanac, 2010).

A realistic conclusion which may be drawn from these considerations is that deficits in the functioning of PFC may result in a tendency to discount the future hyperbolically, and to do so steeply, vastly preferring SSRs over LLRs. The pursuit of short-term gain may take precedence over consciousness (through experience) of the deleterious consequences of, say, drug use. The emotional feelings, *somatic markers*, that would in most people bring about vividly unpleasant reactions to the idea of enacting a behavior pattern likely to bring about such outcomes, may therefore be absent in addicts. These negative somatic markers are the "alarm bells" that sound warnings to the contemplation of behaviors that have previously engendered aversive consequences. Their absence may be accompanied by accentuated influence of positive somatic markers so that they perform as "beacons of incentive" for behaviors with short-term pleasurable outcomes (Damasio, 1994, p. 174).

Damage to vmPFC has been shown to reduce the efficiency of decision-making. Individuals who are dependent on substances such as drugs and alcohol show a heightened tendency to make decisions leading to SSRs over LLRs. The advantage of somatic markers is that they enable rapid decision-making via a swift appraisal of alternative courses of behavior but this does not guarantee the rationality or advisability of the hastily acquired response. Such utility is a function of the reinforcing and punishing consequences of past behavior being qualitatively similar to those currently obtaining and thus likely to determine the wisdom or unwisdom of the selected behavior. The unconscious, unreflective mode of decision-making that the SMH implies may involve unawareness of the true consequences of behavior, a situation which can be partially or wholly overcome by the provision of information in the form of instructions. The capacity to receive, process, and act on such information requires, however, the cognitive abilities which we have described as executive functions.

Functions of emotion in decision-making

Fessler (2001, p. 191) argues that "emotions influence decision-making [by] the weighting of cost–benefit assessments" and this resonates sufficiently with the behavioral economic viewpoint we have adopted to make it an attractive starting point for linking emotion with decision. If we assume that economic behavior is that which works ultimately toward the maximization of inclusive fitness, there must be some mechanism for the evaluation of competing sources of reward that are simultaneously available.

Fessler's relating emotion to decision-making is instructive. The specific decisions that must be made can only be defined if the organism can "parse" stimuli so that they indicate the range of responses that have to be made, demarcating the probable outcomes of each response so that they can be evaluated and an optimal decision among the responses made. Fessler's argument that evolution is likely to have led to a mechanism for accomplishing these tasks reliably and rapidly and his citation of Barkow *et al.* (1990) in defense of this claim suggest adherence to a specific school of evolutionary psychology which we may not wish to embrace in its entirety. But his argument, that advanced organisms confronted with multifaceted environments (complex contingencies in our terms) achieve such parsing and prioritizing of their contexts via emotional reactions that embody previous experience, is plausible. The full range of functions performed by emotions that Fessler (2001) postulates in the process of decision-making are: (1) informing the individual of his status vis-à-vis his or her environment; (2) sustaining attention on stimuli; (3) promoting the retrieval of information from long- to short-term memory; (4) affecting "meta-decision-making" activities such as prioritization of decisions; (5) defining the scope of available decisions; (6) directing decision-making by virtue of their positive or aversive nature: note that emotions also promote the continuity of behavior across situations by evoking similar feelings from one to another; (7) influencing the comparative weighting of costs and benefits; and (8) interacting in the course of producing decisions. As he summarizes it: "Evolution appears to have patterned decision-making and hence behavior by shaping the eliciting conditions, cognitive consequences, action tendencies, hedonic values, and biasing effects of specific emotions."

But a reliable and rapid emotional system that can fulfill these requirements before an organism faced with a decision becomes victim to a predator must function very rapidly and reliably. The most reliable guide to a future environment is generally past experience of that or similar contexts. What links the past to current decisions about the future in Fessler's scheme is the experience of shame and/or pride which are emotional reactions to what we would call a learning history. Shame and pride are ascribed in particular social systems according to two forms of logic. In the first, (1) shame and pride register, (2) the fulfillment or violation of a social norm, (3) being aware of this, (4) noting another's awareness of this, (5) experiencing positive or negative affect from the other, and (6) experiencing a positive or aversive emotional reaction. In contrast to this six-point logic, there is a three-point logic which holds that (1) Ego assesses Other as more or less important than Ego, (2) Ego interacts with Other in a situation in which this discrepancy is salient for Ego, as a result of which (3) Ego experiences a pleasant or aversive emotional reaction. Whereas the six-point logic requires theory of mind on the part of Ego and other members of the social system (i.e., second order intentionality), the three-point logic views Other as simply a feature of the social environment, a S^D or *MO*, and is an extensional depiction of the situation. The three-point logic revolves around dominance and subordination (which relate to the scope of the consumer behavior setting); whereas subordination and submissiveness evoke the negative emotion of shame, dominance is more likely related to pride.

But even this is not sufficiently rapid for most decision-making. Fessler's thesis is that the key to this is the emotion of *self-esteem* which reflects the individual's experience to date of the consequences of behaving in particular ways (learning history, again). Self-esteem facilitates the estimation of current risks by indicating their future outcomes, thereby neatly complementing the thinking that underlies the BPM. Behavioral Perspective Theory has always proposed that the ultimate result of the performance feedback that is the essence of informational reinforcement is the self-esteem experienced by the individual as a result of being accorded social status by others or him- or herself. Now it is apparent also that self-esteem can be related to the emotions of pleasure and arousal to dominance in a single framework based on the BPM Emotional Contingency Matrix (Figure 3.4). Our key emotions of pleasure and arousal are closely, though not simply, related to Fessler's shame–pride reactions which bias assessments of risk and outcome in the course of enhancing what he calls "rank-striving" (which we understand as the search for dominance) and "approval-seeking" (informational reinforcement). The overarching emotional response, *self-esteem*, determines how often these emotions influence decision-making because self-esteem is "a mechanism that sums events to date" (in our terms, encapsulating learning history). Self-esteem thus modifies risk-taking in the light of future prospects (providing the content of the consumer situation which the BPM portrays as embodying the interaction of a learning history and a current predictive stimulation), a process in which serotonin is implicated.

In phylogenetic time, "this patterned attunement of cost–benefit assessments would have optimized fitness" (Fessler, 2001, p. 191). In our understanding this in terms of the BPM Contingency Matrix (Figure 3.7), shame equates with P^- A^- D^- (CC8), while pride is associated with P^+ A^+ D^+ (CC1).

What Fessler refers to as the "uber-emotions" of pride and shame may thus be related to the contingencies arranged by the BPM Contingency Matrix (Figure 3.2). The generation and sustenance of shame and pride as emotional states is closely related to learning history and its current perception: they are the outcomes of having violated or fulfilled social norms, being aware of this, noting another's awareness of it, consequently experiencing positive or negative affect, and experiencing an aversive or positive emotion. Alternatively, a shorter sequence is envisaged: the individual assesses another person as more or less important than him- or herself; interacts with the other in a situation in which he or she finds this discrepancy salient; and experiences an aversive or pleasurable emotional reaction. The first sequence requires theory of mind

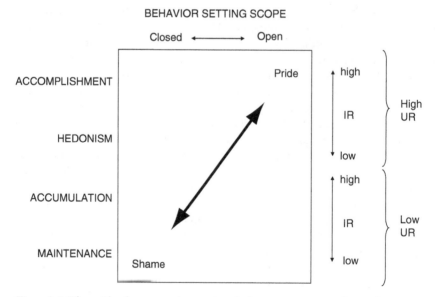

Figure 3.7 The pride–shame continuum in relation to operant contingencies.

(second order intentionality) while the first understands the other person as simply a feature of the social environment – an S^D or *MO*. This three-point logic, as Fessler refers to it, is thus closer to the extensional construal of the BPM than the intentional.

The course of addiction: a BPM interpretation

A key research question is why consumers differ so pronouncedly in susceptibility to the influences that bring about normal rewarding experiences (including physical acquisition of goods, social attention, and neurophysiological effects) and those that are implicated in addictions. Why do the majority of consumers never think of hoarding the kinds of everyday products they purchase let alone indulging to excess in the consumption of nicotine and alcohol, other drugs, gambling, or additional sources of addiction? If presumably the same influences may be shown to be effective in each case – and this is suggested by the BPM and the work on affective and cognitive influences on choice that we have considered here – why do they serve to initiate and reinforce the consumption behaviors of different consumers so variously? We know that the behavior of routine purchasers is also marked by matching, by the choice of the least expensive item within their consideration sets. Why is their behavior then not more extreme? The BPM proposes a single set of causes that account for everyday consumer behavior under the control of self-regulation, impulsiveness, and compulsion. Figure 3.8 suggests how progression occurs among them, and how recovery might be conceptualized in terms of operant contingencies and their associated emotional responses.

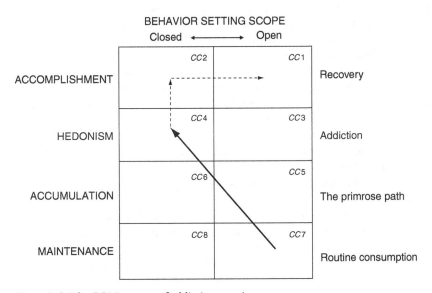

Figure 3.8 The BPM course of addiction matrix.

The inability of addicts to manage their behavior as do everyday consumers must be put down initially and locally to a breakdown of will (Ainslie, 2001), an abdication of executive function, and an inability to inhibit responses even when the consequences of such behavior in the past have been catastrophic and painful. It is the inability of the cognitive faculties to overcome the emotional imperatives that appears responsible for this breakdown. There may be neurophysiological reasons for this inability to cope with the executive requirements of moderate behavior. Some people appear unable to bundle future consequences of their behavior to compare them with current choices (Ross *et al.*, 2008). The broad modes of consumer choice shown by the Continuum of Consumer Choice (Figure 3.1) may be understood in terms of the pattern of reinforcement and the scope of the setting that maintains them (Foxall, 2007a, b). The first, *Routine Choice*, corresponds to the operant class, *Maintenance*, which is determined by relatively low levels of both utilitarian and informational reinforcement.

Such behavior, typified in open settings by routine grocery purchases, is characterized by matching but within a restricted framework compared with that found either in the operant laboratory or in the case of more impulsive consumers. Compared with most laboratory studies of matching which involve hungry nonhuman beings, reinforcement has a symbolic or informational element as well as an immediate utilitarian component; the overall pattern of reinforcement is central to consumers' price sensitivities, maximization takes place only within the consumer's consideration set, and there is a possibility of multibrand purchasing even on one shopping occasion (Foxall *et al.*, 2004).

In the case of grocery purchasing, the setting is open to the extent that multiple brands of each product are available as substitutes for one another, and many products are available which, while constituting independents and complements in the narrow sense, may also be substitutes on any particular occasion. Utilitarian reinforcement and informational reinforcement are both relatively low: the utility provided by food products is always important but the degree of substitutability among competing offerings is sufficient to ensure that no particular item is vital to life; informational reinforcement is important within the framework of the family/household and in terms of the buyer's self-esteem and perhaps among a few close friends, but does not have any broader connotations within the society. Most people, therefore, would receive very limited reward for hoarding, excess purchasing, or excess consumption: in fact, both behaviors are likely to lead to costs rather than benefits.

There is a degree of closure in the setting imposed by physiological considerations since there is a limit to what most people can and are willing to eat. In the case of more closed settings such as having to purchase a license in order to watch television, pay taxes, or fill out forms for a passport, these are negatively reinforced, unlikely to be repeated, and there is no kudos or material gain from performing them to excess. Melioration during this phase is scarcely an all-or-nothing process. The affluent consumer has a repertoire of substitutable brands the choice of any of which will satisfy his or her current need. Each product chosen is likely to add only somewhat marginally to the consumer's overall material and social welfare. The EFs are strongly to the fore insofar as emotional response is relatively low and the ability to control behavior through rational action is high.

The implication is that there is a progression from this routine buying behavior to behavior that can have a delayed deleterious effect upon the consumer and/or others in the form of unplanned purchasing which accounts for half of supermarket sales and a similar proportion of retail book sales, installment buying and credit card purchases, littering and related cases of environmental spoliation, all of which may be described in terms of melioration, the choice of whatever is less costly or more profitable over what might be more advantageous in the long term. This is an insidious progression. Unplanned brand or even product purchasing scarcely has profound consequences when it is pursued within the context of weekly supermarket shopping; installment buying is often affordable and taking the waiting out of wanting is often not morally ruinous; dropping the odd piece of litter does not spoil the commons irretrievably. It is when the harm for the individual or society passes a point of no return that worry sets in.

This does not mean that the behavior is halted: intertemporal choice is marked by the switching of preferences; first, from the resolve that one will act for one's own good and prosocially to indulgence in behavior that is harmful or painful; second, from this choice to regret for one's deviation and a strong desire to overcome it in future. It is only when these behaviors become so ingrained that the consumer has difficulty changing them that trouble is sensed. Prior to that point, even in the case of highly damaging activities that lead to addictions, the consumer may be said to be on the "primrose path" of pleasurable pursuits, entertaining no inkling of the ensuing loss of control of their behavior, believing that the longer term consequences of behavior are of little significance (as, of course, those of a single instance of the behavior in the early days may be), and coming gradually under the influence of the addictive substance or behavior in question (Herrnstein and Prelec, 1992). What begins as social drinking, the occasional flutter when out with co-workers, a monthly dining club, takes hold as the social rewards take second place to those mediated by the product or the practice itself.

The second stage, the *primrose path*, is dominated by the informational reinforcement that is mediated by other people: it is typified by the symbolic as well as functional results of eating and drinking, the use of drugs for leisure purposes with friends, gambling in organized places such as casino or bingo halls with a group of fellow players. The utilitarian reinforcement provided by the imbibed substance or the game is less important at this stage than the social intercourse made available by the situation (though it need not be lower than it would be in the case of Maintenance). The primrose path begins in the context of relatively open settings but the settings become progressively more closed as reinforcing reliance on the social approval of fellow revelers is overtaken by the addictive consequences of indulgence.

Why an individual moves from routine consumption to the primrose path is apparent if behavior is viewed as embedded in a network of contingencies that control the patterns of choice of which any particular response (say, drinking or abstaining from alcohol) is a part. Patterning is the key, according to Rachlin (1994, 2000a, 2000b), to both understanding and modifying behavior. The more long term a pattern of behavior has become, the more costly it is to the individual to interrupt it. The primrose path may be avoided if the individual were more aware of the consequences of getting into long-term patterns of choice; instead, it is single acts that loom large and whose immediate consequences are seen: the enjoyment of the chocolate éclair becomes the sole outcome of its ingestion.

Koob (2013) depicts addiction in terms of a three-stage cycle. Initially, drug administration is positively reinforced (i.e., the behaviors that lead to the ingestion of a drug occur more frequently because of the effects of the drug, particularly the subjectively experienced mood-enhancing ones). In this "*Binge/intoxication*" stage, which generally involves social interaction, drug use is acutely rewarded by the emotional effects of drug consumption.

Somewhere between the primrose path and addiction comes an initiation stage, perhaps marked by impulsiveness, a reaching out for the immediate rush of subjective pleasure provided by drug consumption rather than more conventional rewards. This may be inaugurated simply by socially influenced experimentation, perhaps during one's teens. By the onset of initiation the drug user has learned first hand the properties of the substance for him- or herself and is aware of what effect further ingestion will have upon his or her emotions and behavior.

Binge/intoxication (see also Koob *et al.*, 2014) is a phase that involves both utilitarian and informational reinforcement, the acute pleasures induced by ingestion of the drug as well as the social status gained by conforming to the norms of another individual or group who are already users. The brain region implicated in the processing of rewards, often known as the "reward system," is the *mesocorticolimbic dopamine system*, described above in Box 3.2. During the initiation of drug taking, the substance's capacity to generate acute reinforcement and positively rewarding affect has an intoxicating effect upon the individual. This alone may be relied upon to provide motivation to continue using the drug. But how is this commonsense observation underpinned by a neurophysiological mechanism? Generating motivated behavior necessitates a means of energizing activity and of ensuring that this behavior is goal-directed; a motivation system is, moreover, responsive to past behavior (McKim and Hancock, 2013, pp. 114–115).

The mechanism involves, therefore, both neurophysiological processes and operant contingencies. Incentive salience (Box 2.3) is a factor in the closure of the consumer behavior setting, since it results in individuals being attracted to the physical and social surroundings in which consumer behavior has been reinforced. In the majority of closed consumer behavior settings, even those represented by consciously undergoing dental surgery or using a complicated piece of machinery at the gym, one is able to leave at any time, but few do. The stimuli that compose the setting have acquired a salience in their own right. This is also true of the capacity of online gambling settings to capture the attention of the consumer and to maintain his or her behavior over long periods of time. Although the gambler is usually in his or her own home, apparently enjoying maximum discretion over their actions in this setting they seemingly control absolutely, their behavior may come under the control of the small screen as alternative patterns of behavior are discouraged and the stimuli that encourage continued play acquire increasing incentive salience. The arrangement of gambling machines in casinos and other commercial environments is similarly designed to close the setting by facilitating the dominance of a single pattern of behavior (Schüll, 2012).

In the second stage, which Koob (2013) depicts as "*Withdrawal/negative affect,*" the consumer moves from increasingly compulsive drug use to dependence, withdrawal, and prolonged abstinence. Withdrawal refers to deleterious consequences of ceasing to consume the drug. There is a strong likelihood of relapse in which seeking out and administering the drug are negatively reinforced: the drug is used primarily to remove the aversive effects of abstinence. Depending on individual differences in vulnerability to the drug, consumers are more or less likely to relapse into drug taking. Drug taking is now negatively reinforced: the effects are sought in order to stave off or escape from the unpleasant consequences of abstinence rather than for the highs it originally provided.

The third stage, namely "*Preoccupation/anticipation,*" is characterized by a craving for the drug. Although the cycle has been illustrated in terms of drug use, it describes the course of both substance and process addictions. The possibility of recovery is always present. Abstinence, even prolonged abstinence, is often a feature of the earlier phases of addiction, and is followed by withdrawal. This analysis is not pessimistic. The problem presented by immediate rewards of the ultimately less valuable option is capable of being overcome or ameliorated by embedding that response in a pattern of responses that are extended through time and whose effects may thus be compared with those of the single indulgence. This is Ainslie's (1992) concept of "bundling" future rewards (which we will encounter in detail in Chapter 4).

The path from sobriety to addiction may, therefore, be portrayed as that from *Maintenance in Open Settings* to *Hedonism in Closed Settings*; if recovery occurs, the sequence continues on to *Accomplishment in Closed and then Open Settings* (Figure 3.8). Maintenance in Open Settings (*CC7*) enables the behavior pattern of moderate consumption; moving from there into Accumulation (*CCs5* and 6) involves treading the primrose path: what matters is social approval, predominantly, and physical pleasure; second, the next stage is to Hedonism in Closed Settings (*CC4*) which involves gaining more hedonic rewards from consumption and less reinforcement by way of interpersonal reward, described by Rachlin (2000b) as characteristic of "the lonely addict" (Finkel and Fitzsimons, 2013; Fitzsimons and Finkel, 2013). The hedonic rewards are likely to consist increasingly in the assuaging of the deleterious effects of withdrawal symptoms (i.e., consumption is negatively reinforced). Finally, Accomplishment in Closed Settings (CC2) would involve the restoration of a more balanced pattern of reinforcement and more moderate behavior. This is consonant also with Rachlin's (2000b) idea of social discounting which proposes that the capacity to delay gratification is influenced by contingencies of reinforcement, notably those that are socially based and which (in our terms) eventuate effective in informational reinforcement (Kelley and White, 2011).

Implications for understanding addiction

Patterns of reinforcement

The pattern of reinforcement which consumers maximize consists in the combination of utilitarian and informational reinforcement that consumers obtain from particular behaviors; specifically, it comprises the amounts of each that are jointly maximized, as reflected in the consumer's utility function. In Figure 2.1 (hyperbolic discounting), the apparently irrational choice of SSR at t_1 over LLR at t_2 is elucidated by considering the pattern of both utilitarian and informational reinforcement obtained at t_1. The individual obtains not only the immediate functional benefits of more immediate consumption but the self-recognition that he or she has acted on his or her own volition to obtain them. He or she is in control and has the self-esteem that accrues to the person who can boldly make personal decisions and bear the consequences. The behavior is rather like that of the person who obtains conspicuous tattoos and body-piercings which may arouse curiosity and even revulsion in others. It resembles that of the speeding driver or noisy partygoer who knowingly disturbs others who are trying to sleep. Such behavior is a way of demonstrating what one is willing to do to establish one's individuality and autonomy. Whether or not the behavior of the person who selects SSR is witnessed, approved, or even condemned by others, all of which may function as informational reinforcers, he or she obtains the self-satisfaction of having made a decision and enacted a behavior despite the rules that specify alternative courses of action. There is something self-confirming in giving up a larger reward for a smaller, perhaps akin to the self- and social satisfactions that accrue to the conspicuous consumer, and this informational reinforcement is an important source of the utility obtained by the individual who behaves at t_1 rather than at t_2.

Now we cannot of course quantify this reinforcement in the manner that proved possible when we calculated the utility functions for consumers of fast-moving consumer goods. It is reasonable, nevertheless, to assume that extreme consumer behavior is motivated by similar broadly defined considerations as other modes of consumption and that consumers are maximizers of behavioral returns at all points of the Continuum of Consumer Choice. The idea that consumers are sub-optimizing by selecting SSR over LLR may therefore be erroneous, or at least an oversimplification: not only can we say that consumers who evince addictive behavior are maximizers; we can also propose what it is that they maximize, namely a particular pattern of utilitarian and informational reinforcement, even though we cannot quantify these benefits precisely. Economics would lead to the idea of sub-optimization, while consumer theory leads to the view that consumers maximize a combination of functional utility and social/personal utility.

Consumer situation

The relevance of learning history and the S^D and MO that comprise the consumer behavior setting (and which jointly compose the consumer situation) to addiction is illustrated by their promotion of incentive salience. The consumer behavior setting is composed of those S^D and MO that have previously been associated with obtaining and administering a drug or behaving in a particular way (e.g., gambling); the behavior comes under the control of these stimuli in the normal processes of learning. This applies to all modes of consumer behavior but other factors are at work in the case of substances and behaviors that are likely to lead to addictions. People and things associated with the drug and the behavior acquire incentive salience, and to encounter them anew is to be motivated to *want* to own and use drugs or take part in process-addictive behaviors. The individual's learning history is activated by the presence of situational stimuli which now become S^D or MO that control behavior by acting as directive stimuli and reinforce enhancers. The product- and person-mediated sources of utilitarian and informational reinforcement in the consumer behavior setting also engender the corresponding emotional responses of pleasure, arousal, and dominance and activate somatic markers that encourage the re-enactment of behaviors that have previously occurred in this kind of environment.

Taking Stock

This chapter has described the Behavioral Perspective Model as an extensional model of consumer choice, outlined the research that underpins it, and shown in essence how its variables are relevant to the analysis of addictive behavior. The remaining chapters build on and extend this treatment of addiction as consumer choice. In light of the methodology of Intentional Behaviorism described in the Introduction, we turn next to understanding the limitations of extensional explanation and the necessity of psychological explanation. Chapters 4 and 5 deal, respectively, with the intentional and cognitive interpretations that comprise psychological explanation.

4 Psychological explanation

Intentional interpretation

> Do not, as some ungracious pastors do,
> Show me the steep and thorny way to heaven,
> Whiles, like a puff'd and reckless libertine,
> Himself the primrose path of dalliance treads
> And recks not his own rede.
>
> William Shakespeare, *Hamlet*

Intentional interpretation

This chapter, together with Chapter 5, explores the psychological explanation of akrasia and addiction in light of the methodology of Intentional Behaviorism. It is concerned to demonstrate the necessity of a psychological explanation for the behaviors it reviews, and, in addressing the first stage of such an explanation, to propose a possible intentional interpretation for it. Chapter 5 provides the second stage, that of cognitive interpretation, suggesting a cognitive structure and accompanying functions that show how the intentionality proposed at the earlier stage of psychological explanation could be realized. The need for and shape of intentional interpretation are pursued in three contexts: the intertemporal valuation of rewards, the execution of picoeconomic strategies for overcoming akratic behavioral tendencies, and the cognitive distortions that arise in continued addictive behaviors exemplified by slot-machine gambling.

The first of these themes is fundamental to understanding the cognitive basis of addiction. It addresses the underlying feature of temporal discounting as well as the capacity to quit the cycle of preference reversal that addiction entails. This is the comparative evaluation of alternative and mutually exclusive reinforcers, and its inclusion is intended to illustrate the inability of a purely behaviorist depiction of such valuation to offer convincing stimulus-based referents for the operant explanation of the behavior. The way in which we understand the mechanisms required to evaluate outcomes that are distant in time will influence our approach to the explanation of addiction in general. This analysis raises the question of why some people escape from a behavior pattern which consists in the choice of immediate but inferior out-comes in favor of a new pattern characterized by patience and superior outcomes.

The second theme is derived from a sophisticated theory of akrasia and addiction, *picoeconomics* (Ainslie, 1992, 2001), which has both informed dis-cussion generally and inspired empirical research, and which explores in depth the interactions between competing short- and long-range interests in psy-chological and economic terms. The picoeconomic strategies that have been proposed for the overcoming of temptation, for substituting patience or self-control for impulsivity and rashness, shed light on the cognitive requirements of addiction theory.

The third theme is an example of pathological behavior which forms the basis of a widespread addiction, the so-called "near-miss" effect in slot-machine gambling (Schüll, 2012). Pathological gambling is well known to have similar neuronal substrates to those underlying substance addiction (Ross *et al.*, 2008, pp. 32–34). *Pathological gambling* (PG) is defined here as "A chronic inability to refrain from gambling to an extent that causes serious disruption to core life aspects such as career, health and family" (PG is also used to refer to pathological gamblers); *problem gamblers* are "people whose gambling behavior is at least a *nuisance* to them, and is so along the same dimensions as are used to operationalize PG," and *disordered gambling* (DG) "denotes the inclusive disjunction of the two ideas above, i.e., gamb-ling that is either PG or problem gambling" (see also Petry, 2005). Section 312.31 of the fifth edition of the *Diagnostic and Statistical Manual of Mental Disorders* (American Psychiatric Association, 2013) speaks of "gambling dis-order" rather than pathological gambling. Classifying PG as an addiction requires more than the observation that it is irrational or compulsive at the behavioral level. It requires a convincing degree of continuity of such gambling with substance addiction, especially in the face of serious and costly attempts to desist. Ross *et al.* (2008) argue that PG should be con-sidered a genuine addiction on biophysical grounds; indeed, they maintain, the paradigm case. This has been supported by research revealing a rela-tionship between PG and a deficiency of the mesolimbic dopaminergic reward system.

The psychological explanation of all three of these examples relies on the observation that psychological explanation which, by definition, entails representation, must also be capable of dealing with *mis*representation. This chapter begins, therefore, with a discussion of the model of psychological explanation that it employed. Then, for each of the cases, it describes the phenomenon of interest, discusses the limitations of an operant explanation for the behavior and establishes the need for its psychological explanation, and proposes an intentional interpretation of the behavior. Chapter 5 under-pins this intentional interpretation by examining the cognitive structure and functions necessary for its efficacy.

On psychological explanation

The nature of psychological explanation

Bermúdez (2003) proposes that the term *psychological explanation* be reserved for accounts of behavior that rely on internal representations. These ascribed representations may take the form of propositional attitudes or perceptual awareness. Psychologies such as behavior analysis take behavior as their sole focus, eschewing intentionality (and would perhaps be better characterized as "behaviorology" or "operancy."). Often, psychologists of either persuasion opt for one of these paradigms at the expense of abandoning the other. In the understanding of psychological explanation embraced by Intentional Behaviorism, however, the extensional level of exposition which behavioral psychology of this kind embodies is an essential first step in arriving at an intentional and cognitive interpretation. The theoretical minimalism upon which the Consumer Behavior Analysis research program has been founded is open to the possibility that psychological explanation will become necessary when extensional explanation by means of operant psychology has become exhausted. In order to clarify the approach to psychological explanation which I am taking, it is useful to compare it with the requirements for psychological explanation expounded by Bermúdez (2003; cf. Fodor, 1968).

Bermúdez notes, first, that psychological explanations are teleological: they explain behavior by reference to the desires and beliefs which the behavior either intends to fulfill or actually fulfills. Either way, the behavior is goal-directed in a manner that is not the case for mechanistically determined behavior. It follows − and this is the second characteristic of psychological explanations − that the behavior they seek to account for cannot be explained or predicted in terms of invariant responses to fixed stimuli. As an example of an invariant response, Bermúdez cites *innate releasing mechanisms* (the responses to which these lead are sometimes referred to as fixed action patterns) which, following Lea (1984), he notes (1) are always eventuated by particular stimuli, (2) are always topographically identical, (3) befall every member of the species presented with the appropriate stimulus conditions, (4) tend to be independent of the organism's learning history, (5) cannot be arrested or varied after their onset, and (6) serve a single function. Contra Bermúdez, I would argue that the point about behavior of this kind is that it is "innate, unlearned, and involuntary, and that it will occur even when it serves no function" (Dretske, 1988, p. 4). It *is* behavior but it is not − at least for the most part − learned behavior. It is firmly based in the phylogenetic development of the organism, and its occurrence and topography are only marginally if at all influenced in the course of the ontogenetic development of the organism. The prediction of the behavior of a member of the species in question is straightforward once the stimuli that inaugurate the sequence have been identified in the organism's presence. According to Bermúdez, psychological explanations are required only when such stimuli cannot be identified. But the process of "explanatory minimalism" which I am advocating involves more complex patterns of stimulation than those involved in innate releasing mechanisms. Classical and operant conditioning account for behavior without requiring so fixed a relationship between stimulus and response. Bermúdez (2005) accommodates this point, at least with respect to operancy.

Flexibility of conditioned behavior

First, both of these conditioning modes permit stimulus generalization and response generalization in which function is transferred from the stimulus or response involved in the original conditioning procedure. This alone permits a degree of flexibility absent in the operation of innate releasing mechanisms. It may be objected, of course, that both of these forms of conditioning may be understood only via psychological explanation, since the simple observation of stimuli and responses is inadequate to account for the complexities of information processing that must be involved. However, I take the more pragmatic approach that these styles of conditioning may be accorded either an extensional characterization (to the extent that they permit the prediction and control of behavior) or a psychological characterization (if this is required either for further prediction and control that is not available on the extensional assumption or a deeper explanation of the mechanisms involved in the procedures).

Second, operant conditioning belongs to the class of explanatory devices known as *selection-by-consequences* which also includes evolution by natural selection and cultural evolution (Skinner, 1981). The possibility arises in this evolutionary paradigm that the emission by the organism of "faulty" or inexact copies of responses are nevertheless reinforced and hence retained within the organism's behavioral repertoire. (Of course, it is possible to argue that operant conditioning is not explicable other than via psychological explanation; while this case can be made, however, my pragmatic criterion suggests that we should empirically exhaust radical behaviorism as a source of explanation before turning to psychological explanation.) Operant behavior is considerably more flexible than that produced by innate releasing mechanisms, but it still performs the function of allowing us to demarcate psychological from extensional explanation.

Bermúdez (2003, pp. 8–9) sums up the difference involved here as follows:

> The essence of a psychological explanation is that it explains behavior in terms of how the creature in question represents its environment rather than simply in terms of the stimuli that it detects. Psychological explanations involve appealing to representational states that function as intermediaries between sensory and behavioral output.

While I am in broad agreement with the first sentence, the second requires clarification. First, I do not necessarily think that psychological explanations provide *intervening* variables if that is what he implies. They may provide additional *interpretations* of behavior that do not need to be interposed between stimuli and responses. Second, I do not think particular observed behaviors are definitively classifiable once and for all as requiring either an extensional or an intentional explanation: rather it is the stance we take toward them that determines the explanation we attempt. Thus phenomena like stimulus and response generalization are not fixedly either mechanistic or psychological. Rather, to the extent that the operant paradigm allows us to predict and control behavior without resort to intentional phenomena, the behavior in question is "mechanistic"; when we require an intentional interpretation to make the behavior or certain aspects of it intelligible, however, we resort to an intentional stance and the behavior is viewed as intentional, requiring a psychological explanation. Third, rather than say that the representations used in psychological explanation are those which the creature uses, they are (following Dennett (1978) to a degree) the representations the investigator has to ascribe to the creature in order to make its behavior intelligible (and possibly to predict it).

Cognitive integration and misrepresentation

Bermúdez argues that the way this works is through *cognitive integration*, and this characteristic applies especially to behavior that may be portrayed as operant. "The behavior of organisms that are suitably flexible and plastic in their responses to the environment tends to be the result of complex interaction between internal states" (Bermúdez, 2003, p. 9; cf. Fodor, 1975, 2008). When we reach beyond the predict-and-control goals of extensional behavioral science to explain the why of patterns of behavior that display alternative responses to a given stimulus set, we seek an understanding of the flexibility they exhibit in the situational representations that guide their behavior. Psychological explanation assumes that animals' flexibility must derive in part from the plasticity of their internal representations which enable them to vary their responses to the environment. Past behavior will inform such representations, and the capacity to represent changing environments. Such representations also permit analogizing especially with respect to the comparison of current stimuli with those that have been responsible for past behavior, but we must plant our psychological explanations firmly on a sure rationale for the ascription of internal representations.

Bermúdez also notes that psychological explanation which relies on representations can also deal with misrepresentation. He specifically mentions tropistic and classically conditioned behavior as not requiring representational explanation because the responses involved are invariant so long as the organism has been exposed to the relevant stimuli. The local environment is sufficient to account for the behavior of an intact organism (i.e., one capable of recognizing the stimuli in question). "The need to appeal to how things are taken to be comes in only when the law-governed correlation between stimulus and response breaks down" (Bermúdez, 2003, p. 9). This, he notes, may arise in two contexts. First, the response may occur even when no stimulus is present; it is necessary in this case to argue that there is a representation of the stimulus which brings about the behavior. Second, the stimulus may be present and indeed registered by the individual but no appropriate response is forthcoming. The implication in this case is that the stimulus is inappropriately represented for it to bring about the requisite response. These examples of *misrepresentation* distinguish behavior which requires a psychological explanation from that which does not.

Intertemporal valuation

The nature of intertemporal valuation

The intertemporal valuation of reinforcers is fundamental to understanding akrasia and addiction, and many aspects of its discussion are also relevant to the other examples considered in this chapter. Preceding chapters have argued that, although there are many definitions of addiction, the essence of this extreme form of consumption is preference reversal based on temporal discounting (i.e., temporal devaluation): what appears initially to be an inferior option to one for which the consumer would have to wait longer becomes highly valued as its availability approaches. The irrationality of this behavior, at least its *economic* irrationality, lies in the contradiction between an individual investing heavily in a course of behavior only to sacrifice the results by adopting an inconsistent course of action. Although the hyperbolic discounting so exhibited may be behaviorally indexed in terms of preference reversal, its understanding requires the attribution of cognitive processes, since it depends on valuations of the outcomes of future behaviors that exist only as mental representations when the decision to opt for one or other of the rewards is made.

The initial expression of preference for a larger but later reward requires a verbal statement that necessarily entails intentionality. Preference reversal, in which the smaller-but-sooner-appearing reward becomes more highly valued, requires the ascription of a mental representation of the value of the larger-but-delayed reward (Ledgerwood and Trope, 2013). Addiction is not the only form of consumption that may be described in terms of preference reversal and temporal discounting but their appearance in an acute form in addictive consumption raises questions about the way in which cognition is employed to explain this pattern of behavior.

The behavior to be interpreted or explained is hyperbolic temporal discounting. The selection of SSR at time t_1 in Figure 2.1 is objectively observable behavior, as is any overt verbal behavior that accompanies or precedes it. This may, for instance, take the form of an initial stated preference for LLR which will become available at t_2. This may be followed by a stated revised preference for the SSR shortly before it becomes accessible. The difficulty for an operant explanation is that the greater magnitude of the reinforcer that will be available later should motivate the individual to show patience; instead, he or she takes what is clearly the less valuable of the two options. If rule governance is invoked as part of the operant explanation, then the actual behavior is also contrary to the rule voiced by the individual at the outset expressing a willingness to wait for the larger or better outcome. The problem is particularly evident in the case of over-indulgence in behaviors known to have deleterious effects upon health such as cigarette smoking, alcohol ingestion, or gluttony. The interpretation of the behavior that is intended to fit the observed facts is an intentional one, calling as it does upon the individual's *valuation* of the two rewards.

Although the other reward (the LLR) is by definition the greater reinforcer in objective terms, it is said to be discounted or devalued simply because it will not be available until a further period of time has elapsed. Hyperbolic temporal discounting reflects the individual valuing the LLR more highly than the SSR at the outset, t_0. As the time remaining to the accessibility of the SSR becomes short, however, the individual values the SSR very highly indeed. His or her valuation of the SSR exceeds that of the LLR at this point, often very substantially, with the result that he or she reverses his or her preferences and opts for the SSR. Speaking of the individual's valuation of the rewards may be based entirely on the observed behavioral phenomenon: the valuation may be said to *be* the behavior of selecting the SSR over the LLR at t_1. Or the valuation may be said to *be* the verbal behaviors emitted at the outset and immediately prior to t_1. However, the depiction of the individual's valuation of the alternatives in the form of hyperbolic discount curves (Figure 2.1; Ainslie, 1992) suggests that the valuation of the SSR becomes higher than that of the LLR at a point prior to t_1 (when the behavior of choosing the SSR occurs). At the point shown by the crossing of the curves in Figure 2.1, the individual's valuation of the SSR increases steeply, though his or her behavior has not changed. In the standard interpretation of the implications of hyperbolic discounting, therefore, we are assuming that valuation is an unobservable activity which is subsequently manifest in overt behavior at t_1; in other words, the assumption implicit in this interpretation of how the individual is valuing the two options is predicted on the theorist being able to discern how the individual values the items on the basis of inferences for which there is no overt stimulus-related or behavioral support. This can hardly be said to be a behaviorist account of the behavior (Box 4.1; Elster, 1999a).

Box 4.1 Intertemporal valuation as intentional

We have noted that a tendency to discount the future steeply is not in itself a definition of addiction but it is a recurring theme in definitions and is a sine qua non of understanding it. Preference reversal, reflecting hyperbolic discounting, is certainly a fundamental index of addictive behavior. It is itself a behavior or rather a discrepancy between verbal behavior ("I will select the LLR") and overt, observed behavior (the actual choice of the SSR). But as a behavioral datum, a behavioral criterion for the attribution of addiction, it is purely descriptive rather than explanatory. It is what is to be explained. Any neurophysiological correlates of preference reversal – more precisely, of verbal behavior at t_1 and choice behavior at t_2 – are similarly descriptive and do not explain the behavioral discrepancy.

These behavioral and neurophysiological descriptions might be explained in extensional language, where the truth value of statements relies on some form of correspondence theory: objects alluded to in the extensional statements and the relationships between them must actually exist and be demonstrable via interpersonal agreement on what is such an object and what counts as a relationship between objects in the statement: for example, the three-term contingency of radical behaviorism in which stimuli and behavior are juxtaposed in ways that can be confirmed or disconfirmed by experimental and quasi-experimental methods. However, when it comes to accounting for temporal discounting in extensional terms, it is not possible to fulfill these criteria by positing stimuli and responses and describing the relationships between them in terms of the three-term contingency. At t_1, the individual states a preference between the SSR and the LLR, neither of which actually exists at that point. The individual involved in expressing a preference at t_1 has only his or her or a third party's verbal behavior describing the opportunity to acquire the SSR at t_2 and the LLR at t_3. So too does the researcher who tries to explain this individual's behavior (i.e., his or her stating a preference for the LLR and then selecting the SSR). Moreover, the verbal behavior upon which the individual bases his or her selection process and his or her verbal expression of a preference (for the LLR) is itself intentional. It involves language *about* particular activities and their relationships. It is also intensional: it is possible (and seems more intellectually honest) to describe this behavior only in terms of that individual's desires and beliefs at t_1. These statements have the truth criteria peculiar to intentional language: non-substitutability of co-designatives, intensional inexistence, and non-existence.

We cannot explain the individual's behavior in terms of the discriminative and reinforcing stimuli of the radical behaviorist paradigm because we cannot identify the reinforcers to which his or her statement of preference at t_1 refers. The LLR does not exist as yet (or at least the opportunity to obtain and consumer it does not). We cannot say that past contingencies and learning history in which they are embodied explain current behavior. If Ego is a persistent chooser of the SSR even though he or she makes prior statements that he or she will choose LLR, his or her learning history will predict selection of the SSR again, not the LLR to which his or her verbal behavior at t_1 refers. Even if he or she draws upon a learning history of selecting the LLR to predict doing so again, the prediction rests on a mental image of prior choices. Consider the following scenarios.

A   If Ego has a consistent history of selecting the SSR at t_2 even though he or she always predicts at t_1 that he or she will select the LLR (at t_3), how is his or her verbal behavior at t_1 to be explained? There is no learning history for it. To say it is rule governed is an intentional explanation: it would be more candid to admit that only intentional knowledge may be had of Ego's behavior by saying that Ego has a desire (to obtain the LLR) and belief (that waiting patiently, forgoing the SSR, and acting appropriately when the LLR becomes available, will produce this). The SSR, LLR, and prescribed behavior can "exist" at t_1 nowhere other than in Ego's imagination. To say

Ego has been given a rule, "To maximize your returns, wait until t_3 before selecting a reward," is only to say that he or she must *think about* the contingencies between his or her behavior and their outcomes; if he or she responds by saying, "I will wait until the LLR becomes available at t_3 before selecting a reward," this is tantamount to saying that he or she desires the larger reward and believes that by waiting, he or she will secure it. Ego may utter these words simply to please another person at t_1 and receive their approval or avoid their disapprobation.

B   If Ego has a consistent history of selecting the LLR at t_3, this pattern of behavior is explained in the sense of being predictable on the basis of his or her learning history. In this case, Ego's verbal behavior at t_1, "I will wait until the LLR becomes available at t_3 before selecting a reward," may also be seen as a prediction based on his or her learning history. But this extensional account provides a limited explanation of Ego's behavior, since prediction is a very restricted goal. Simply knowing that Ego will not act until t_3 does not explain all aspects of his or her behavior. What form does his or her learning history take? How does it influence his or her (1) verbal behavior at t_1, (2) avoidance of the SSR at t_2, or (3) selection of the LLR at t_3? To account for this continuity of behavior we must assume memory processes, cognitive representation, and self-regulation via cognitive means. (Note that, as we will see in Chapter 5, the self-regulation inherent in using picoeconomic strategies to control one's future behavior requires cognitive explanation.)

C   If Ego has usually always been consistent in selecting the LLR at t_3 but on a given day chooses (for the first time) the SSR at t_2 instead, his or her behavior cannot be explained in terms of a learning history, or by the consequences of having selected the SSR previously, since this has never occurred. The behavior can only be explained in intentional language by reference to desires and beliefs. This does not mean there will not be some behavioral and neurophysiological correlates of this choice, but they do not explain the behavior; they simply circumscribe the intentional interpretation.

D   If Ego consistently selects the SSR at t_2 but on a given day chooses (for the first time) the LLR at t_3 instead, his or her behavior cannot be explained by his or her learning history, or by the consequences of having selected the LLR previously, since this has never been the case. The new behavior may be explained only intentionally: it must rely on desires, beliefs, emotions, and perceptions. If the individual has been given a rule (e.g., through an advertisement relying heavily on augmentals) this can only be understood in intentional terms. (To make an extensional interpretation of the rule, we would have to say that the vocal sounds or written images of the advertisement act as discriminative stimuli and motivating operations purely in the capacity of physical stimuli that have been previously paired with behavior. But that assumes a great deal about stimulus and responses generalization that is itself highly theoretical. Is this what radical behaviorists mean by rule-governed behavior?)

C and D represent precisely the kind of deviation from a pattern of behavior to which some behaviorists refer as deciding to switch to a new pattern of behavior. Such a change may be explained only in intentional language.

Behavioral continuity and discontinuity

Specifically, the aim is to explain the discontinuity in the addict's pattern of behavior when he or she (1) shifts from, say, substance abuse to abstinence, *or* (2) continues to pursue addictive behavior, even though its consequences are manifestly increasingly deleterious. In (1), *addiction–abstinence discontinuity*, there is a switch in behavior that cannot be attributed to the pattern of reinforcement that previously maintained behavior. The contingencies of reinforcement have not changed – they have not had time to do so. So why does the individual embark upon a new pattern of behavior? In (2), *addiction–aversion continuity*, there is a valuation of the object of addiction that is at variance with the facts of reinforcement. The contingencies change – gradually the consequences of behavior are becoming more aversive – yet the behavior is not punished.

How are we to explain these behaviors? One possibility is that in (1) there may be changes in neural activity: the impulsive system becomes relatively hypoactive, the PFC relatively hyperactive. This is at the heart of the CNDS model but this could also be as much the result of behavior change as a cause of it: at best we have correlative evidence. This is the impetus for an intentional interpretation. In (2) the aversive consequence serves to maintain and even increase the behavior that produces it. The only way to account for this is in terms of increasing incentive salience, progressively greater *wanting* and less *liking*. This is of course an intentional account.

A person is never presented with the stark choice between another drink now and a long life to come (or other actual benefits of abstinence), as though they were presently available alternatives, either of which could be chosen at once rather than the other. One of them – the benefits of abstinence – can be nothing other than a mental representation at the moment of decision. The whole discussion of this state of affairs is necessarily intentional.

One way of thinking of value is in terms of revealed preference: the consumer values the choices that are represented by his or her behavior and the value may be computed in terms of the opportunity cost of the enacted behavior. But from his or her point of view, that opportunity cost is a mental representation, a property of another mental representation, namely the alternative behavior he or she could have enacted. Economic valuing at the point of decision is always about something that may only be described as an intentional object. The valuing exists in thought and this thought is *about* something that does not yet exist and of which the consumer may have no reinforcement history. Although this mental valuation may not be identical to the one revealed in my actual behavioral preferences, at the time he or she is deciding it is a component of his or her decision processes. There can be no conception of preference reversal in the absence of such initial mental-level valuing. At t_1, he or she has to prefer b to a when all he or she knows of them is that they are mental representations. At t_2, he or she has to choose a over b when b is not in prospect until a further period of time has elapsed (t_3-t_2). At

t_2, b exists only as a mental representation. Anything he or she *says* at t_1 to the effect that they will select b over a is verbal behavior that is based on the mental representation of what each of these alternatives entails. Even if the consumer does have a reinforcement history of preferring b over a at t_1 and of actually selecting a at t_2, then a fresh decision on how to behave in future must rely only upon mental representations of past behavior and their outcomes.

Understanding the behavior of a person who "decides" to control his or her drinking by consuming only one drink at parties rather than a large number also relies on mental representation of a future state of affairs. It is immaterial whether this person has a learning history of doing similar things in the past (all manner of "deciding" followed by varying degrees of success). The point at which he or she "decides" to inaugurate a new behavior pattern indicates behavior that relies upon mental representation. This point of departure is important, even though a teleological behaviorist such as Rachlin (1994) would say that a decision has only been made when the person exhibits the new pattern of behavior over a sustained period. There is, however, still a point of inauguration of the new pattern of behavior and this has to be explained. The contingencies cannot explain it; nor can the person's neurophysiology. We have only intentional interpretation with which to frame an understanding. Even if the person has been warned by a doctor that the continuation of his or her current level of drinking will have severe effects on health and longevity, it is only a mental representation of future events that may account for an attempt to modify behavior. To say that the contingencies *have* been changed by the doctor's presentation of a rule for the patient's behavior is only to beg the question how this verbal account of contingencies never encountered by the patient can influence subsequent behavior without its elements being held as mental representations by the patient.

Revealed preference is appropriate to the extensional model of consumer choice: radical behaviorism has no other means of conceptualizing preference. But there are times when we must go beyond radical behaviorism's explanatory framework because we cannot identify the elements of the three-term contingency that are operative in a particular instance of observed behavior. We are then forced to depend on intentional interpretation. We have no alternative but to conceptualize preference as existing at a pre-behavioral level and we have no means of expressing this causative preference other than in intentional terms. The decision-making in terms of which we are forced to explain the behavior involves intentional language and the personal level of exposition. Acceptance of the theory of revealed preference does not obviate the theoretical commitment to "the representation of preferences in the heads of economic agents" (Rosenberg, 1992, p. 120). Although occurrences at this level may have neurophysiological correlates (revealed, for instance, as RPEs by neuroeconomics: Box 4.2), they are sub-personal events, the description of which cannot capture the essence of personal-level decision-making.

Box 4.2 Reward prediction errors

It has long been suspected, on the basis of experiments in which monkeys receive food rewards while the activity of their dopaminergic neurons in the VTA is recorded (Schultz, 1992), that dopaminergic neurons code reinforcement (Robbins and Everitt, 2002). As Watson and Platt (2008) point out, animal behavior is reinforced by the electrical stimulation of the dopaminergic neurons in the ventral tegmental area (VTA) in the reward circuit linking the midbrain with the central striatum and the PFC. They even show a preference for this source of reinforcement over primary reinforcers such as food and water. These dopaminergic neurons are responsive to such unpredicted primary reinforcers as well as to secondary stimuli, such as the sound stimuli produced by tones, that predict them (Schultz, 2000; Schultz and Dickinson, 2000). The response of these cells to food rewards which takes place in phasic bouts is transferred, following the establishment of predictive stimuli, to those stimuli: the dopaminergic neurons respond to the CS rather than to the reward. Moreover, should the reward not appear, the activity of the dopaminergic neuron (which is recorded at the level of the individual cell) is depressed precisely when the reward was predicted to occur. As Robbins and Everitt (2002, p. 174) point out, this is indicative that the dopaminergic activity is implicated in the establishment of an internal representation of the reward. In fact, the rate of firing of dopaminergic neurons codes both the magnitude and the probability of rewards (Watson and Platt, 2008).

Reward prediction error (RPE) is the difference between a reward actually obtained and that which was predicted or expected. A negative RPE results when the reward is predicted but not obtained; a positive RPE, when a reward is not expected but is nevertheless obtained (Schultz *et al.*, 1997). The reason why this subject has assumed such prominence in neuroeconomics is the possibility that RPEs may be reflected in dopaminergic neurons' firing rates. If so, the mechanism suggests an obvious linkage between neoclassical economics and neuroscience that is fundamental to the emerging discipline of neuroeconomics. In the present context, it adds to the explanatory power of operant psychology by proposing an underlying causal connexion (Glimcher, 2011).

While, in Pavlovian learning, the predictive significance of a signal (CS) for the arrival of a reinforcer is paramount, in operant learning, which is the principal paradigm we are using to interpret the behaviors of the marketing firm and its consumers, signals (S^Ds or MOs) influence the rate of repetition of a response that has previously led reliably to gaining the reinforcer (Daw, 2013; Daw and Tobler, 2013; Schultz and Dickinson, 2000). Associationism, which embraces both of these learning paradigms, argues that both involve the establishment of an association between the representations of either a signal (Pavlovian conditioning) or a response (operant conditioning) and the reinforcer. The procedure in which the association is formed requires that the reinforcer follow closely and reliably on the presentation of either the signal or the response, such that each repetition of the signal or response leading to the reinforcer strengthens the association (Schultz and Dickinson, 2000; see also Schultz, 2010).

The key determinant of whether a signal engenders learning, however, is not its simple presentation but its being unpredicted, novel, or surprising

(Di Chiara, 2002). The extent to which a stimulus is unpredicted is shown by means of a *prediction error* term ($\lambda-\Sigma V$), where λ is the strength of association with the reinforcer that predicts fully the occurrence of the reinforcer, and ΣV is the combined associative strength of all signals present on the learning episode in question. The prediction error ($\lambda-\Sigma V$) indicates the extent to which the appearance of the reinforcer is novel, surprising, unpredicted, or unexpected.

Schultz and Dickinson (2000) draw two conclusions from this which are relevant to the present discussion of bilateral contingency. The first concerns the evocation of emotions by the reinforcers and punishers resulting from operant learning, as posited by Rolls's (1999) theory of emotion. These authors define learning as acquiring predictions of outcomes whether these take the form of "reward, punishment, behavioral reactions, external stimuli, internal states" (p. 476). Internal states include emotions; hence, the reinforcing stimuli that evoke emotion feelings may also predict those feelings.

The second is Schultz and Dickinson's proposal of a sort of homeostatic principle by which behavioral outcomes that produce a mismatch (prediction error) between expected and actual reward alter subsequent behavior so as to reduce the gap between outcome and prediction. By explaining how behavior is modified in light of experience, this appears to be a mechanism for reinforcement. It explains how behavior is modified in light of experience. The process of behavior modification continues until the prediction error is zero, at which point the discrepancy between expected/predicted reinforcement and actual reinforcement is eliminated. The outcome occurs exactly as predicted. This process, in line with blocking, confines learning to stimuli that predict unexpected/surprising/novel events and eliminates learning with respect to redundant stimuli. This reasoning is very much in line with behavioral/operant learning and provides a neurophysiological explanation of learning. In instrumental or operant learning, the response manifests an expectation of reward; when the prediction is falsified by the occurrence of an unpredicted or not fully predicted reward (or a punisher), there is a reward prediction error which influences future predictions and behaviors. This, of course, is the essence of operant learning. RPEs thus influence reinforcers, punishers, external signals such as attention-inducing stimuli, and behavioral goals/targets.

Four points emerge from this analysis. First, rendering the behavior in question intelligible relies on a classic case of intentional interpretation. Second, the analysis is, nevertheless, that which many psychologists, including behaviorists, employ in accounting for hyperbolic discounting. Third, the behavior cannot be honestly justified on the basis of rule-governed behavior, since there is no evidence that meets behaviorist canons of scientific judgment on which to base this assertion; in any case, verbal rules are themselves intentional in character, since they are linguistic expressions that are necessarily *about* something other than themselves, and our *ascribing* them to an individual to explain his or her behavior is an act of intentional interpretation, Finally, it is therefore necessary to move beyond a radical behaviorist mode of explanation, which would require the observation of both stimuli and responses in order to explain the latter in terms of the former. It also seems more intellectually frank to couch our interpretation of what is happening in terms of the intentional concept of valuation rather than a quasi-operant "explanation" that deals in unobservables and confabulations of learning history. Nevertheless, we must look to the extensional sciences to *support* the interpretation, not in the sense that the valuation may be said to take place at the neurophysiological level, but such that the interpretation is *consistent with* what we know of our phylogenetic and ontogenetic histories and their implications for the influence of neurophysiology on behavior. The extensional sciences are also invaluable in circumscribing our intentional interpretation.

Limitations of behavioral interpretation

The need for a psychological explanation of the intertemporal valuation inherent in temporal discounting, and prerequisite to preference formation and reversal, is apparent from the misrepresentation of the objective probabilities involved. Although there is a rational appraisal of the rewards on offer at t_0 (see Figure 2.1), the SSR assumes greater valuation at t_1 simply because of its imminent availability: objectively, it remains inferior to the later-appearing LLR. Nothing about the LLR has changed since it was accorded a higher valuation than the SSR at t_0, except that the time to its availability has decreased (by $t_1 - t_0$). This alone ought to make it more attractive than it was earlier. Yet it is now accorded a much lower value than it was at t_0, and is perceived as less valuable even than the SSR. This implies an erroneous representation of both the SSR and the LLR at this later point. We might propose that, by selecting SSR at t_1, the consumer is rationally maximizing the combined utilitarian and informational reinforcement. The consumer would then be depicted as receiving self-esteem from being in charge, from having the power to choose SSR even though it is inferior. But this ascription to the individual of self-defined and self-accorded informational reinforcement is itself an intentional interpretation. It is tempting to conceptualize the feedback a consumer receives in the form of self-esteem or other private and subjective feelings, as "informational reinforcement," and this may be rationalized in terms of the BPM as an extensional construct. However, the ascription of self-esteem to another in order to account for his or her behavior is actually to offer an intentional interpretation. The inability to identify the stimulus conditions, of which the observed behavior (choice of SSR at t_1) would have to be a function if an operant explanation were to be justified, is simply covered up by the ascription of self-esteem. Given that we have no evidence of a reinforcing stimulus, "explaining" the behavior in terms of self-esteem is simply an example of inventing an explanatory fiction. If the selection of SSR at t_1 were accompanied by overt and objective informational reinforcement from others, in the form, say, of praise, then an extensional explanation of the behavior would be possible, since it would be feasible to predict and possibly control the chooser's behavior under these circumstances. The praise would provide the requisite stimulus conditions.

The behavior is a classic case of the first source of misrepresentation to which Bermúdez (2003) draws attention: namely the appearance of a behavior in the absence of the appropriate stimulus. The sole change in the stimulus conditions has been the passage of time from t_0 to t_1, but this cannot be a discriminative stimulus or motivating operation for selecting SSR. At what point has this elapse of time been trained as such a stimulus? And the limited passage of time from t_0 to t_1 is as much an indication that the LLR will be forgone as that the SSR is imminent. There has been no change in the stimulus conditions surrounding the LLR, apart from the already noted reduction in the time remaining until its availability – surely a plus – and yet it is now degraded simply because another reward is about to become available.

Picoeconomic strategies

The nature of picoeconomic interests

Matching research demonstrates that the value of a reinforcer is inversely proportional to its delay (i.e., as the delay becomes shorter, the value increases dramatically): this is the essence of hyperbolic discounting. The key difference between exponential and hyperbolic discounting is that in the former the LLR is always preferable to the SSR, regardless of time elapsed, whereas in the latter there is a period during which the SSR is so highly valued (because the time remaining to its possible realization is so short) that it is preferred to the LLR (Ainslie, 1992). This is clearly not because of its objective value which is by definition less than that which may be obtained through patience, but because the time remaining to its possible realization is now so short that it is preferred to the later but larger reward. Ainslie notes that these findings harmonize with Freud's observations that an infant behaves as if expecting immediate gratification but becomes, with experience, willing to wait for the longer term alternative. In other words, still paraphrasing Freud, if the pleasure principle is resisted, the outcome will be the exercise of the reality principle. In the terminology of behavioral psychology, the operants relevant to each of these principles are shaped by their respective outcomes. Ainslie argues that the two principles may be represented as two *interests*, each of which seems to employ devices that undermine the other. In discussing what these devices are, Ainslie (1992) gives a clue as to how we may speak of the operations of mental mechanisms and also how they are organized to produce phenomena in a cognitive account (i.e., one that conforms to the use of cognitive logic as we have defined it here).

Subsequent behavior that serves the longer rather than the shorter term interest is apparently rule governed rather than contingency shaped (Skinner, 1969). However, the "rules" exist only in the mind of the individual who may not have encountered the contingencies. It appears disingenuous to refer to them as rules in the extensional sense proffered by radical behaviorists. Such invocation of rule governance in the absence of empirical confirmation that the individual has previously performed rule-following behavior which has been reinforced is an explanatory fiction. Since we have no empirical indication of this kind it would more accurate to refer to the behavior as having been guided by appropriate beliefs. Such use of intentional language is an indication of the status of our explanation which may better, therefore, be referred to as interpretation.

Ainslie (1992) points out that interests arise in order to exploit rewards. They are the result, therefore, of, inter alia, different histories of reinforcement, exposure to distinct patterns of contingency. They carry out their exploitive deeds at particular periods and in light of the intrinsic limits to their mode of exploitation. The periods of time in question influence the behaviors favored by interests. The length of an interest's dominance influences how they defeat and are defeated by other interests and on whether the behaviors they engender have the subjective feel (affective quality) of being voluntary (Ainslie, 1992, pp. 96ff.). *Addictions* are temporarily preferred: they are marked by short-lived conscious preference followed by a time of regret. The reality of intertemporal bargaining between conflicting interests is brought home by Ross's (2012) further economic analysis of the peculiar social psychologies that might bind them into a continuing state of conflict characterized by recursive bouts of preference reversal.

Picoeconomic strategies of overcoming

The essence of Ainslie's system inheres in its treatment of the ways in which people behave in seeking to overcome their addictions. Four kinds of strategy may be employed in order to make the LLR more probable than the SSR.

Precommitment involves using external commitments to preclude the irrational choice: Ulysses binding himself to the mast prior to meeting the Sirens, the addict's ingestion of a substance that will induce physically unpleasant feelings such as nausea in the event of his or her imbibing alcohol or drugs, the student arranging that friends will take him or her to the library as an otherwise inescapable TV show begins, are all means of reducing the chance of opting for the SSR by manipulating the external physical environment. Two further strategies require internal commitment.

Control of attention restricts information processing with respect to the SSR, and is not dissimilar to Freud's ideas of suppression and repression, though in Ainslie's scheme the process may be conscious as well as unconscious (Rueda *et al.*, 2013). Taking a route home from the office that avoids bars or restaurants is one example; thinking about the car one can buy if one does not buy that package of cigarettes is another.

Preparation of emotion entails engineering the kind of avoidance or displacement through which one inhibits emotions usually associated with the SSR or to increase incompatible emotions. Reminding oneself of the health risks of, say, drinking to excess, imagining the angry reaction of others if one does so, day-dreaming about that new car that can be bought with money saved as a result of not over-indulging – all use cognitive control to refocus or escape from the emotional rewards of addiction.

The fourth strategy involves the formulation and implementation of personal rules and consists in making side bets with oneself about one's future behavior.

> *Public* side bets – of reputation, for instance, or good will – have long been known as ways you can commit yourself to behave.... What I'm describing are *personal* side bets, commitments made in your mind, where the stake is nothing but your credibility with yourself. They wouldn't be possible without hyperbolic discount curves, nor would they be of any use.
>
> (Ainslie, 2001, p. 94)

This aspect of the picoeconomic bargaining of competing short- and long-range interests provides an account of the operation of *willpower* in practice (Ainslie, 2001, 2007, 2010, 2011, 2013).

Most goals are achieved not in a single bout of decision-making and choice but via a progression of behaviors and their patterns of consequence which eventuate in the accomplishment of the desired change. The strategy of behavioral regulation by personal rules arises in the context of how an individual perceives the availability of the SSRs and LLRs he or she will encounter from the present moment onward. Each separate occurrence of such choices may, of course, be viewed as isolated in time and space from all the others; the akratic individual encounters each choice point as a unique incident, to be decided upon as it arises. It is easy in this approach to select the SSR because it will always, at the moment it occurs, have a higher value to the hyperbolic discounter than the LLR. Subsequent occasions offer no alternative to this simple decision rule: take the immediately higher value option as soon as it appears. The near-ubiquitous matching law underpins such behavior.

However, it is open to the individual to perceive choice at a grosser level of aggregation than the simple SSR-immediately/LLR-sometime incidence allows: he or she can frame the conflict in terms of that between a whole sequence of SSRs and a whole sequence of LLRs. This strategy permits the *bundling of rewards*, opening up the possibility of self-control. Taking a monadic point of view in which each decision point arises anew, the akratic consumer is likely to experience repeated preference reversals interspersed with regret. By viewing the choice as that between two streams of behaviors and their reinforcing and punishing outcomes, however, the consumer becomes open to the exercise of self-control. The choice becomes that of perceiving the entire sequence of future behavioral opportunities and conflicts as a single present choice between a bundle of LLRs and a competing bundle of SSRs. Looked at from this perspective, the sum of the LLRs is always greater than that of the SSRs (Figure 4.1). Decision-making thus requires advancing the SSRs and LLRs in time and in imagination (Ainslie, 2001; Elster, 2015, esp. ch. 15).

A key recognition here, to which Rachlin (2000a) also attaches considerable significance, is that one's current choice predicts one's future choices. If I wish to give up smoking, I may reason that one more cigarette will make no difference. Taking this "one last" cigarette is, however, predictive of my taking another later. Choosing the SSR now is not a discrete act in itself: it is something I observe myself doing. Viewing the resolution of my behavioral dilemma in favor of my short-range interest is something I interpret as increasing the likelihood of my making precisely the same decision next time the need to choose arises.

Ainslie argues that the form taken by the personal rules necessary to ensure this self-control is that of private side bets in which a person wagers future abstinence on the fact that he or she has just abstained. It is a matter of betting oneself that one will wait for the LLR not just on this occasion but again and again into the indefinite future until the goal is achieved. Viewing the accumulated reward sequences in this way means that the LLR is then *at all times* superior in value to the SSR, even when an SSR is immediately available: this prescription for consumer behavior is simply not open to the prediction of preference reversal. However, it is possible to forestall preference reversal by bundling together in mind a whole sequence of future behaviors which

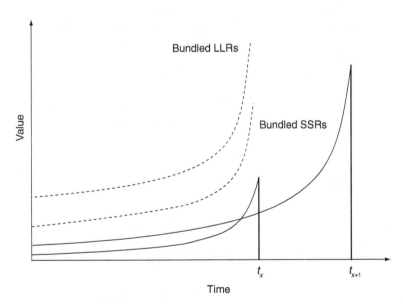

Figure 4.1 The principle of bundling.

eventuate in larger-but-later outcomes in order to compare the much larger cumulated reinforcement that would thereby be available with the cumulated outcomes of the corresponding sequence of smaller-but-sooner choices. In the process, the consumer may be portrayed as entering into a series of side bets with him- or herself to the effect that a single choice of a LLR now will predict his or her selecting the LLR on *every* occasion. This is akin to the consumer making a personal rule to select the LLR on the present occasion as a result of which the probability of him or her making a similar choice on subsequent occasions is strengthened (Ainslie, 1992; Rachlin, 2000a; Ross *et al.*, 2008). To stick to the rule is to win the bet. A lapse into the choice of an SSR is, however, detrimental to the individual's self-esteem, a movement toward the shame pole of the continuum shown in Figure 3.7. This capacity to move the future into the present through the disciplined use of imagination enables bundling to take place and the tendency toward hyperbolic discounting to be overcome.

Bundling, like the other strategies Ainslie discusses to circumvent akrasia, involves metacognition: not just the imagination of future consequences of behavior, but their amalgamation into a single amount, the comparison, at the point in time when none of these consequences has been delivered or experienced, of the sum total of SSRs as against the sum total of LLRs. It involves, crucially, the capacity to understand the relatedness of the first choice that will be made to the sequence of further choices that will become inevitable, the realization that the first choice is a sound predictor of later choices, and that by making a choice at t_1, either to take the SSR or defer gratification until the LLR becomes available, the individual is precommiting to a whole sequence of behaviors. These are no mean cognitive skills (Fishbach and Converse, 2013). These reflections require a rationality not measured by IQ tests. There may be observable behavioral acts or sequences of acts that are sufficient for the behaviorist to predict and perhaps control behavior, but confining our analysis to this sphere entails ignoring much of the story. It does not explain why an individual will continue to take drugs or gamble excessively, even though this has become an economically irrational lifestyle, or why an individual changes his or her behavior by selecting LLR over SSR. In other words, the behaviorist approach is unable to deal with aspects of the continuity and discontinuity of behavior and this is an important limitation of behaviorism; the explanation of behaviors such as these requires adoption of an intentional viewpoint.

Picoeconomics: the necessity of psychological explanation

In the case of the strategies for overcoming temptation presented by picoeconomics, namely precommitment, control of attention, preparation of emotion, and bundling, there is no misrepresentation of the contingencies in the senses mentioned by Bermúdez (2003); rather, there is an attempt to control their influence by means of mental manipulation leading to behavior change. Each strategy begins as a deliberate reframing of the contingencies as they are mentally represented. In precommitment, the individual resolves to ensure that the normally operating contingencies cannot exert their usual effect (e.g., by taking a drug that will engender nausea if alcohol is imbibed). Control of attention involves the selection of contingencies leading to a novel outcome: taking a route that avoids fast-food restaurants. Preparation of emotion is a matter of enhancing the effect of the longer term consequences of behavior in order to make them more effective: reminding oneself of the likely impact of smoking upon one's health and feelings of well-being. Bundling involves this mental redesign of the contingencies to a more obvious extent. It is the creation of a new contingency in which the aggregated outcomes of selecting a series of SSRs is brought into contact in imagination with the aggregated outcomes of selecting a series of LLRs. This is a misrepresentation of the contingencies as they would ordinarily be experienced.

Bermúdez (2003) is saying there is misrepresentation because the behavior of the individual is being determined by a misconstrual of the contingencies. In the first case the stimulus is not there, but the person behaves as if it were. In the second case the stimulus is there, but the person does not behave accordingly. At the personal level the significance of the environment is, literally, being ignored. This is misrepresentation of the environment at the personal level so it invites a cognitive explanation. In the picoeconomic strategies, the environment is being similarly ignored and we are substituting a mental representation to account for the behavior. Taking a drug to change one's experience of alcohol, finding a different route home, reminding oneself that the consequence of another piece of cake will be beyond dire, and amalgamating all the effects of your future behavior are the result of selecting the contingencies to which you will expose yourself. These are all misrepresentations or, better, reconstruals of the contingencies. The person is behaving in each case not on the actual construal of the contingencies as per the three-term contingency, but as he or she has imagined the consequences of behaving differently.

We can identify, then, three kinds of misrepresentation: (1) no stimulus → response; (2) stimulus → no response; and (3) mental reconstrual of the contingencies. In the last case the person determines the contingencies. We can only explain this behavior by ascribing to the individual the imaginative action of deliberately choosing the contingencies to which future behavior will be subject. This has implications for the conception of consumer *choice* we are adopting. It does not amount to free will but it defies any narrow conception of contingency control. This kind of reconstrual of the contingencies would draw upon the capacities of disengagement from present concerns and cognitive rehearsal of future behaviors and contingencies that currently exist only in the imagination such as Tomasello (2014) and Stanovich (2011) propose.

If the overcoming strategy is successful, we have to ask *why* the individual in question would change, since there has been no change in the contingencies. This is an instance of misrepresentation, and any behavior change must be attributed to a mental representation of the contingencies and an evaluation of their efficacy, necessitating an intentional interpretation.

Similarly, we must ascribe desires and beliefs (including perception) to the individual here, such that the person can either abstract from his or her experience or devise rules for his or her behavior.

Once again, it is impossible to explain the behavior in behaviorist terms, since the required stimulus field is not available and we must resort to an intentional interpretation/cognitive interpretation.

The "near-miss"

Almost there or also ran?

Almost everyone has bought a lottery or raffle ticket with a number that proved to be next in sequence to that which won. There is a strong tendency on these occasions to imagine that you came close to winning the jackpot and to curse your luck at missing out so narrowly. Only a moment's reflection is needed to realize that this is irrational: all numbers had an equal chance of being selected, and to be off target by one digit is no different from being off target by any other margin. It is clearly not the same as coming a close second or being runner-up in a contest. Yet the illusion can persist and it is not unusual to explain later to friends that you "almost won" rather than "decisively lost." We don't necessarily say this for effect; often, without giving it much thought, we genuinely believe it.

Similar emotions and thoughts may accompany scoring two identical icons in slot-machine gambling when three are needed for a win. Despite their actually being losses, these so-called "near-misses" can actually motivate additional play, even though, according to reinforcement theory, they should punish the gambling behavior. Yet the tendency of slot-machine gamblers whose scores closely approximate a winning combination to continue playing, and even to play with greater determination, is well documented (Skinner, 1953; Strickland and Grote, 1967; Reid, 1986; Griffiths, 1994; Kassinove and Schare, 2001; Côté *et al.*, 2003; Dixon and Belisle, 2015; Foxall and Sigurdsson, 2012). For the sake of decorum, I will henceforth refrain from inserting the term *near-miss* into inverted commas, but it is always to be understood as a commonplace designation rather than a coherent scientific concept.

Neurophysiological explanations

Attempts to explain this near-miss effect often point to neural functioning, since the same brain regions are recruited in the case of near-misses as are apparent for wins (predominantly the reward circuits of the midbrain dopaminergic system and the orbitofrontal cortex of the forebrain which they innervate), while outright losing recruits different neural areas (Chase and Clark, 2010; Habib and Dixon, 2010; Qi *et al.*, 2011). Clark *et al.*'s (2009) laboratory simulations of slot-machine gambling indicate that outright monetary wins and near-misses both activated identical striatal and insular circuitry. Near-misses recruit, as a stimulus to further gambling, the very reward circuitry that forms the neurophysiological basis of reinforcement.

Habib and Dixon (2010) explored neurophysiological and behavioral differences between PGs and nonPGs who experienced near-misses, expecting that PGs would view near-misses as closely allied to wins, while nonPGs would see them as more akin to losses. Their work identified a greater neurophysiological overlap between the win-like elements of near misses and the win network for pathological gamblers. They also identified neurophysiological win, near-miss, and loss networks that were (1) common to PGs and nonPGs, and (2) peculiar to each group as they experienced various gambling outcomes. The *win networks* were entirely discrete for the two groups: the exclusive win network of nonPGs incorporated the right superior temporal gyrus, while that of PGs focused on the uncus and posterior cingulated gyrus. Moreover, not only is a more extensive win network apparent for PGs but it also encompasses those brain regions responsible for emotion as well as midbrain elements that constitute the reward system. A common *loss* network was found for both groups, but each also showed a unique loss network. NonPGs recruited similar neurology for near-misses and for losses, while PGs' near-miss activations ovelapped with their wins. NonPGs also proved more realistic in judging the status of near-misses, seeing them as losses; by contrast, PGs see near-misses as more closely related to wins. Wins were more pleasant, positive, or rewarding for PGs irrespective of monetary gain. Finally, Chase and Clark (2010) integrate neurophysiological, operant, and cognitive explanations by pointing to the possibility that positive RPEs occur as gamblers foresee a win when the right-hand reel slows, and negative RPEs when its stopping reveals a no-win. Moreover, positive RPEs are especially associated with BOLD signals, suggesting a neural basis for gamblers' over-confident beliefs (Qi *et al.*, 2011; Winstanley *et al.*, 2011).

Although the neurophysiological evidence is based on correlation and cannot, therefore, of itself establish causality, it remains germane to the explanation of the near-miss phenomenon. It demonstrates, for instance, that the brain regions which provide the neurophysiological substrate of reinforcement are also involved in both outright wins and near-misses. Moreover, neurophysiological correlations with gambling behavior, and, in particular, responses to near-misses, differentiate PGs from nonPGs. The very fact that the brain circuitry relevant to accounting for reinforcement is implicated, however, means that the behavior in question has not been fully explained until it has also been related to patterns of reinforcement. However, the neurophysiological findings are not logically related to reinforcement and reward in this context. Explanation in terms of operancy does not fit, since the behavior is actually punished but does not diminish; interpretation in terms of informational reinforcement as a consequence of *not* winning is unconvincing; there is a misrepresentation arising from continued playing in the absence of prior *reinforcing stimuli* and in fact doing so in the presence of prior *punishing stimuli*. This is the first source of misrepresentation that Bermúdez speaks of: the appearance of the behavior in the absence of the apt stimulation; in fact, its enhancement. In Bermúdez's terms, the law-like correlation of stimulus and response has not been observed and we must interpret the behavior in terms of a mental misrepresentation on the part of the player.

There is a clear misrepresentation insofar as a reward in the form of the emotional consequence, namely *arousal*, appears in the absence of the appropriate prior behavior: the reward should be forthcoming as a result of the enactment of the appropriate behavior (gaining three identical icons on the gambling machine) which gives rise to the appropriate reinforcement (a payoff, usually financial, from the machine) which leads to the emotional reward (*pleasure, arousal, dominance*). The reward appears in the absence of the requisite behavior and its reinforcement. This is a variation on Bermúdez's first source of misrepresentation: a consequent stimulus (arousal) is forthcoming, and it does appear that this arousal is linked to the continuation of play, hence its status as a rewarding stimulus, but it is not produced by the enactment of the appropriate operant behavior (i.e., one which brings about a contingent reinforcer as a prelude to the appearance of the reward). There is a gap in the sequence required for explanation (i.e., behavior → reinforcement (physical) → reward (emotion)). Again, the conclusion is that the law-like correlation between the stimulus and the response has broken down: as a result, we must argue that there is a mental representation of both the behavior and the reinforcer that accounts for the appearance of the reward. This requires that the player mentally represent the behavior that achieves two identical icons as the necessary operant for what he or she mentally represents as a win, and that he or she represents the accompanying sights and sounds produced by the gambling machine as indicative of utilitarian reinforcers (rather than as informational punishers). The arousal felt after a near-miss must result from the *mental (mis)representation* of these auditory and visual stimuli as reinforcers. We have no way of explaining the continuity of the behavior other than to attribute it to the generation of arousal which is *interpreted* as a reinforcer by the player.

Operant explanation

The second source of explanation to be considered, therefore, attributes gamblers' persistence to environmental factors that would be expected to influence the rate of behavioral performance if it were conceptualized as operant (e.g., Hoon *et al.*, 2008). These include the primary and secondary schedules of reinforcement in effect when slot machines permit near-miss outcomes, and the temporal and spatial positioning of symbols indicating performance outcomes (e.g., prevalence of near-misses). This approach elucidates not only the influence that direct physical-situational factors, such as reinforcement schedule(s) and the design configuration of the gambling machine, exert upon playing, but also that of gamblers' verbalizations in the course of play which may guide their behavior. Research on these "self-rules," verbalizations of the apparent contingencies, may inform the search for cognitive distortions that influence gamblers' choices.

The near-miss phenomenon is puzzling for behaviorists who interpret monetary gains as reinforcers (consequential stimuli that increase the rate of responding) and their absence as punishers (that reduce it). Reinforcement contingencies do generally exert influence over machine gambling behavior. Haw (2008, 2009), for instance, reports that the effectiveness of variable ratio and random ratio schedules derives not from the average frequency of wins they engender, as is widely believed, but from the number of early wins and unreinforced trials. Moreover, the density of programmed near-misses may be more important in sustaining play than big wins (Kassinove and Schare, 2001). Ghezzi *et al.* (2006) examined the effects of win magnitude and near-miss frequency on persistence in a series of experiments in which near-miss effects took a variety of forms. The authors conclude that neither programmed nor obtained reinforcement rate controlled gambling behavior, concluding that behavior analysts should understand gambling in terms other than those of directly acting, contingency-driven outcomes.

The effectiveness of contextual factors in controlling gambling behavior apparently derives from their capacity to evoke arousal. Arousal may result from a surprise gambling outcome due to changing schedules of reward or symbolic features such as flashing lights and loud noises that accompany not only an obvious win or even a loss masquerading as a near-miss. Such symbolic reinforcement undoubtedly has neural correlates (though these have not been investigated in research seeking causes of the near-miss phenomenon) and counterparts in gamblers' verbal behavior that may indicate cognitive distortion. Hence, a behaviorist interpretation focuses in particular on the role of informational reinforcement of a subset of non-wins interpreted as near-misses, and the corresponding emotion of arousal in signaling performance feedback.

Interpretation in terms of informational reinforcement

Reviewing early research on the neurophysiology of problem gambling, Griffiths (1990a, 1990b, 1990c) draws attention to a potential neurophysiological substrate in PGs, the role of arousal in gambling, and the role of endorphins. Carlton and Manowitz (1987), for instance, reported that by comparison with controls PGs exhibited hemispheric activation deficits on verbal and nonverbal tasks similar to those found in some kinds of Attention Deficit/Hyperactivity Disorder involving inattention and impulsivity. PGs also tend to be deficient in serotonin, a neurotransmitter which inhibits control of inattention and impulsivity. In the context of a possible substrate for excessive gambling, Griffiths (1991) mentions Roy *et al.*'s (1988) finding that PGs showed "a significantly higher centrally produced fraction of cerebrospinal fluid level of

3-methoxy-4 hydroxyphenolglycol" which is believed to stimulate impulsive behavior and sensation seeking (Griffiths, 1990a, p. 349).

The role of arousal is sufficiently established in excessive gambling for the comment that excitement is the "gambler's drug" to have become a cliché (Brown, 1986, 1987). Also important from the point of view of relating neurophysiological and research on affect is that physiological measures of arousal correlate well with verbal reports of arousal as a subjective reaction (Mehrabian, 1980). Heart rate increases in the course of gambling and endorphins (endogenous morphine), which mimic the effect of opiates, mediate PG. His respondents' sole recreation was fruit (slot-)machine playing since nothing else stimulated them in the same way. They played especially when they reported being "depressed" or "feeling down," since the slot-machine gambling changed their mood to a "high" (during gambling), though this was followed by a "low" and, eventually, anger. They mentioned excitement, which is immediate, albeit short-lived, as the predominant reinforcer but winning money was also important. It is noteworthy that PGs differed from nonPGs in experiencing statistically significantly higher levels of excitement during gambling. These results support the findings of others with respect to arousal and endorphins (though the research was not specifically intended to elucidate any biological substrate). Griffiths speculated that arousal, as a major reinforcer, may produce endorphins leading to tolerance which leads to more gambling. Moreover, gamblers' representing their near-misses to themselves as near-wins might expand their arousal which might reinforce play. This is noteworthy as an early indication that cognitive distortion may have a neurophysiological basis.

A second theme is the role of visual slot-machine symbols and the audio effects as reinforcers of some kind, a conclusion that has been tentatively accepted, though sometimes without strong conviction by behaviorists and cognitivists alike. While monetary rewards perhaps remain the primary source of behavioral reinforcement, symbols are a secondary influence on behavioral continuity (Foxall, 2010a, 2011; Foxall and Sigurdsson, 2012). The BPM, as we saw in Chapter 3, proposes twin sources of motivation based on both the utilitarian or functional benefits (including the monetary rewards in gambling) of consumer behavior and its informational or symbolic consequences that provide performance feedback. That chapter noted that there is considerable evidence, first, for the role of symbolic reinforcement in maintaining non-compulsive consumer behavior; and second, for the capacity of symbolic reinforcement to engender arousal. But does it follow that the arousing accoutrements of failing to win in slot-machine gambling provide informational reinforcement and thereby stimulate further play? Let us examine this possibility.

According to the BPM, emotional states are a direct outcome of the reinforcement contingencies that define consumer situations (Foxall, 2011; Foxall and Yani-de-Soriano, 2011). During the *primrose path* phase, gambling is governed by informational (mostly social) more than utilitarian (monetary) results, and is often motivated through social drinking and organized gambling in public places. As reinforcing social approval is overtaken by the addictive consequences of monetary and symbolic consequences, the contexts become progressively more closed. Symbolic reinforcement occurs as a consequence of the PG's conditioning history. The critical aspect of this history involves a correspondence between the colors, lights, and sounds generated by gambling machines in response to so-called near-misses. These effects not only arbitrarily signal a reduction in time to reinforcement (Fantino and Logan, 1979), but are also correlated with aroused happiness to this performance feedback. This may be defined in terms of the facial expression or vocalization sometimes shown by PGs when "winning" (Dixon *et al.*, 2010; Green and Reid, 1996), or with the use of subjective rating scales (Foxall and Yani-de-Soriano, 2011; Foxall *et al.*, 2012), to provide a means of relating emotional responses to contingencies of reinforcement.

The import of interpreting these results in terms of informational reinforcement is that the outcomes of near-misses are in themselves as reinforcing as monetary gains; moreover, the efficacy of these symbolic reinforcers is enhanced by the arrangement of the paraphernalia of gambling, namely the ways in which slot-machines respond to play outcomes that are actually losses in similar fashion to those that are outright wins. We can now understand why the sights and sounds generated by gambling machines in response to so-called near-misses are as effective in promoting further gambling as the financial gains that follow unmistakable successes. It is perfectly comprehensible why the cognitive mediation of these rewards by gamblers results in their reporting that they are feeling lucky and want to continue playing. It is not a matter of loss being rewarding: a near-miss is as much a successful outcome in view of the symbolic meaning it has acquired in the course of a gambling history as it would be if every near-miss were marked by the receipt of money. The application of the consumer behavior model to gambling confirms what has been suspected: that the potency of slot-machine gambling as a potential contributor to personal and social disruption is not as likely to be meliorated by the manipulation of schedules of reinforcement that govern the payout rate to gamblers as by the control of the symbolic reinforcers that influence arousal and thereby promote continued playing.

Evaluation of the interpretation

The interpretation is plausible but cannot overcome the difficulty that the utilitarian reinforcers necessary to account convincingly in behaviorist terms for the behavior are generally absent. The status of the knowledge gained in the process of behavioral interpretation is likely to fall short of that required to reach the intersubjective agreement on which the plausibility of such an exercise rests. This does not mean that the effort of attempting such an interpretation should not be made; it does entail, however, employing the strictest standards of plausibility before such an interpretation is accepted. And it requires that an intentional interpretation of the behavior under investigation be generated for purposes of comparative evaluation. In this case, the interpretation does not overcome the basic problem of a radical behaviorist account, namely that of relating utilitarian reinforcers reliably to patterns of behavior. The parallel with the phenomenon of behaviorists' responses to autoshaping is clear, as is the necessity of an intentional interpretation.

This does not negate the principle of behavioral interpretation which has been applied to numerous aspects of consumer choice and marketing management (e.g., purchase and consumption, saving and investment, the adoption and diffusion of innovations, environmental conservation, and the marketing firm: Foxall, 2010a; Vella and Foxall, 2011; Vella, 2015). It does, however, caution against the uncritical acceptance of behavioral interpretations which fly in the face of fundamental implications of utilitarian reinforcers and punishers.

To "explain" the near-miss phenomenon in terms of informational reinforcement would require assuming that the behavior to be reinforced had become the achievement of two rather than three identical icons and that, while this would not yield utilitarian reinforcement in the form of financial gain, it would eventuate in a series of sounds and sights which, by engendering arousal, would maintain play. This seems a fanciful means by which to ensure that the operant framework is preserved intact. Moreover, it relies on a cognitive transformation, a misrepresentation of the contingencies by means of a symbolic reversal.

Intentional interpretation

This brings us to the third source of explanation, which invokes *cognitive distortion* to account for gamblers apparently judging near-misses to be indications that the probability of winning has been increased (Griffiths, 1994, 1995). The discussion of cognitive distortion has in fact already begun with the identification of the misrepresentation implicit in gamblers' near-miss-influenced behavior, but it is important not to overlook the significance of the findings of neurophysiological research that have also been discussed.

It is significant that, rather than overemphasize a biological basis for PG, Griffiths (1990a, 1995) concludes emphatically from his own research that both neurophysiological and cognitive factors play a part in excessive slot-machine gambling. In particular, persistent gambling entails cognitive bias: illusion of control, biased evaluations, notions of near-misses behaving as reinforcers rather than punishers (Reid, 1986; cf., however, Sundali *et al.*, 2012). This cognitive approach involves the attribution to gamblers of beliefs about the nature of the game, how it operates, and their own progress as players. Such a judgment may be relevant to the learning of a skill, but it is unjustified in the context of games that have probabilistic outcomes. But this instance of the "gambler's fallacy" is actually widespread, as is supported by the finding that regular gamblers perceive a greater degree of skill to be involved in slot-machine gambling than do non-regular gamblers, and that gamblers' perceived control is related to their gambling persistence (Clark *et al.*, 2009, 2012; Chase and Clark, 2010). An implication is that the treatment of problem gamblers should concentrate on the (re-)learning of cognitive judgments by means, inter alia, of cognitive behavior therapy.

A near-miss is not, of course, an outcome that *actually* "comes close to being successful," in Reid's (1986, p. 32) phrase: it is an outright failure that *may be interpreted* by the gambler as somehow approximating a win, an interpretation of events that somehow influences further behavior. Explanation of the subsequent patterns of playing in terms of cognitive distortion take as its key variable not the objectively observable similarity of the pattern of the symbols shown on the machine to those that denote a win but the interpretation put upon this by the gambler. The ascribed interpretation of this outcome and its behavioral after-effects in terms of "closeness" is the hallmark of an intentional explanation.

Cognitive distortion arises from several sources. Perhaps the best known of these, another form of the "gambler's fallacy," refers to the belief that a run of failures must be followed by several successes or one large win as a result of the "law of averages" by which sequential consequences are supposed to balance out. Similarly, a run of successes is expected to be followed by a number of failures. But this is not the only source of cognitive distortion based on a fallacy about the nature of risk. For instance, the interpretation of slot-machine players' tendency to be motivated by near- misses may also be traced to gamblers' illusion that their involvement in selecting the target icon increases their personal control over the outcome of the gamble (Dixon *et al.*, 2007).

A feeling of personal control also results from the belief mentioned above that playing slot-machines successfully reflects *skill* and that apparently coming close to winning indicates the acquisition of prowess. Some tasks such as sports performance, where there is a genuine probability that persistence will enhance expertise, are indeed improved through practice, but this is not the case in gambling where the probability of winning is reset on each trial (Langer, 1975). Slot-machine design nevertheless takes advantage of the illusion of control through skill by affording players the opportunity of "nudging" or "holding" their icons in order seemingly to influence the generation of a winning line (Schüll, 2012). Moreover, self-perception of one's level of skill is higher among PGs than among other gamblers, while irrational statements about win propensities occur more frequently among those who gamble more often (Griffiths, 1990a). Griffiths (1994) reports that irrational statements about win propensities are more frequent among more regular than other gamblers, though the incidence of irrational verbalizations was lower in his study of arcade gamblers than earlier research (Ladouceur *et al.*, 1988) encountered. Griffiths (1994) interprets his own research, nonetheless, as confirming the general trend of work on cognitive bias. Importantly, he found that regular gamblers were more likely than others to comprehend their behavior in terms of the acquisition of a skill.

In work based on a data-gathering technique that encourages respondents to think out loud by continually speaking as they gamble, some three-quarters of the statements about the operation of the game made by regular gamblers were erroneous (i.e., they expressed sentiments to the effect that the player was improving his or her performance, getting better at the game, and so on) (Ladouceur and Walker, 1996; Ladouceur *et al.*, 1988; Gaboury and Ladouceur, 1989; Walker, 1992). Even gamblers who showed during interviews that they were aware that chance alone was responsible for the outcomes of their games made these erroneous statements in the course of playing. While making erroneous statements is common to both frequent and infrequent players, they tend to increase with playing frequency. Griffiths (1994) reports this for slot-machine gamblers, and Baboushkin *et al.* (2001) report that potential PGs are more likely to make erroneous statements.

Near-miss, gambler's fallacy, and entrapment

Ariyabuddhiphongs and Phengphol (2008) establish the relative importance of near-miss, gambler's fallacy, and entrapment on gambling persistence; entrapment is a variation of the sunk-cost effect in which, having invested so much time and money in a pursuit, the individual feels the costs of quitting are insuperable, and hence persists. Their work shows that near-miss alone has a strong and significant effect on behavior; the other two variables are weak and non-significant. Nevertheless, it is plausible that the strong effect of near-misses on gambling motivation is strengthened by the other two variables.

Wohl and Enzle (2003) revealed that more important in gambling motivation than the incidence or magnitude of a gain or loss is the extent to which the gambler feels lucky. The subjective experience of luck is, in turn, influenced by whether a modest win ($10) is signified as the near-miss of a JACKPOT (delivering $70) or as the near-miss of being BANKRUPT. These signaled outcomes were hypothesized to reflect, respectively, upward or downward counterfactual thinking: as predicted, gamblers who are led to believe they have just escaped a large loss feel luckier than those who think they have narrowly avoided a large gain, and are more likely to continue gambling, possibly because their imagined luck engenders arousal. Self-perception of luck by a player led to believe that he or she has narrowly avoided a big loss eventuates in continued play; however, such self-perception is reduced in one who imagines that he or she has narrowly missed out on a large payout, who thereafter doubts his or her ability to win the jackpot (cf. Dixon and Schreiber, 2004).

Continued playing in the wake of a near-miss may be correlated with neurophysiological and environmental stimuli and may permit the prediction of the behavior, though they cannot explain it along radical behaviorist lines. The neurophysiological events are not being activated in response to an actual win; they cannot be generated by utilitarian operant reinforcement; if they have also accompanied genuine wins, they may function as learned (secondary) informational reinforcers; however, if they are not identical to the visual and auditory stimuli that accompany genuine wins it is difficult to explain their sustaining effect on behavior in exclusively operant terms. It is more probable that the behavior of the gambler must be understood in terms of his or her cognitive interpretation of the significance of these occurrences (similar considerations apply to the excessive playing of online games: see Karlsen, 2013).

Intentional interpretation: conclusion

The evidence on the near-miss effect suggests that an explanation of this phenomenon in terms of extensional behavioral science is not feasible and that a cognitive explanation must therefore be undertaken. Clearly, there is no indication of the sequence of responses and reinforcing stimuli that would be required for an account in terms of the three-term contingency. If, for whatever reason, the visual/auditory stimuli produced by the machine elicit positive emotional responses, it is still not possible to interpret the behavior as operant. For this to be the case, there would have to be a sequence in which positive reinforcement (which could be objectively ascertained and would take the form of cash wins) was followed by reported positive emotion; however, in gambling behavior that is under the control of near-misses, there is no reinforcement. Rather, there is a clear indication of failure which ought to constitute punishment (i.e., a behavioral outcome which leads to reported negative emotion and a reduction in the rate of play). Neither occurs: the reports of emotional response are positive and play continues, sometimes with added persistence.

The only alternative is to propose a cognitive explanation of this behavior, which relates to cognitive distortion (e.g., by invoking the gambler's fallacy, the fallacy of increasing skill, or the gambler's subjective interpretation of the stimuli as reinforcers/rewards). Such an interpretation is not consistent with the environmental contingencies that link the observed behavior of the gambler to the outcomes of his or her play. It could be that the stimuli (the sounds and sights provided by the machine, notably the indication that only two matching symbols have resulted from previous play) have acquired the power to elicit positive emotions through Pavlovian conditioning and that these stimulate further play, but this effect should diminish as the reinforcers (cash wins) fail to appear. If these stimuli are acting as informational reinforcers, why do they reinforce *losing*? Rather than reflecting feedback on the performance of the gambler, these stimuli bear only a negative relationship to the state of play. They may, nonetheless, be *interpreted by the gambler*, who has accepted one or other of the fallacies outlined above, as performance feedback of a kind. There is no way that an operant account of the near-miss phenomenon could cast them as sources of informational reinforcement, but a cognitive interpretation in terms of the gambler's mental misattribution of their significance may be adduced to account for his or her continued playing. The inability of extensional behavioral science to account for the behavior makes inevitable the behavior's interpretation in terms of processes of valuation that are ascribed to the gambler. The gambler is discounting the future by ignoring the punishments which his or her behavior is attracting, reinterpreting the stimuli including the display of two correct symbols as positive feedback when objectively they are signals of negative outcomes, of failure rather than success. In terms of temporal discounting, the player is valuing the symbols of a near-miss as indications that he or she is on the way to the LLR when in practice he or she is settling for a series of auditory and visual stimuli self-defined as SSRs.

The inevitability of psychological explanation

The requirement that the near-miss effect be the subject of psychological explanation is clear from the misrepresentation inherent within it. As we have seen, Bermúdez (2003) argues that misrepresentation may take two forms: the appearance of a response in the absence of the appropriate stimulation and the failure to enact the response despite the appearance of the stimulus. Either of these instances necessitates psychological explanation (Bermúdez, 2003). In the tendency of the near-miss to increase behavior we see the former. We can add a third kind of misrepresentation to the two that Bermúdez puts forward. The machine-based stimuli that consist in the sights and sounds provided by the machine to accompany the appearance of two but not three identical icons actually correlate with failure. The misrepresentation here is between an adventitious stimulus, albeit one that may have some relevance to a wholly different context, and the performance of an unrewarded response. To refer to them as informational reinforcers must be based entirely on their appearance when the player's performance results in utilitarian reinforcement (i.e., a genuine win of points or money); they would then be learned via classical conditioning as CSs that signal a win. Nevertheless, their effect requires the ascription of mental operations to the player insofar as he or she *interprets* or *perceives* them as rewards. They may be seen as socially mediated consequences of playing but they are not rewards in the normal sense: they are discriminative stimuli or perhaps more accurately motivating operations that engender further payment to stay at the machine. To designate them as rewards is clearly a misrepresentation.

One source of this behavior may be human beings' inability to calculate probabilities accurately or even to appreciate the nature of risk (Gigerenzer, 2002). This may give rise to the gambler's fallacy to the effect that a win must follow a run of losing outcomes. In light of this widespread inability, gamblers can be misled by the visual and auditory stimuli generated by slot machines in the event of a win, especially if these also accompany so-called near-misses. Clark (2010) also mentions the possibility raised by Wagenaar (1988) that these techniques increase the likelihood that players will remember wins more readily than failures and that they will as a result play all the more. We have also seen that the illusion of personal control over the starting point of games and the illusion that one is not losing but nearly winning can both exert influence on persistence in play that are based on misunderstanding of chance.

Let us sum up the question of cognitive distortion in slot-machine gambling as it relates to the bounds of behaviorism: the need to account for behavioral continuity/discontinuity, the need to forge an understanding of behavior at the personal level of exposition, and the need to delimit behavioral interpretation. The continuity, indeed enhanced continuity, of the behavior is not explicable in operant terms; this behavior in fact shows the most blatant disregard for the contingencies. The sole alternative is an intentional interpretation which ascribes beliefs to the player that are erroneous in view of the contingencies. Interpreting the behavior inherent in the near-miss phenomenon requires the ascription of desires and beliefs: we can account for this behavior only if we attribute severe misapprehension to the player, desires and beliefs that are at odds with the contingencies such as they are. It is not that there are no contingencies of reinforcement or that they cannot be known: rather, that the player's behavior is clearly not under contingency control and therefore we must attribute it to the player's subjective (mis)apprehension of them. The behaviorist can only resort to a nonempirical assertion that the behavior is under contingency control, even though it is not possible to demonstrate this in behaviorist terms. The intentional interpretation circumscribes such an account by making clear that the behavior must be under perceptual control and intentional control; however, these rest on distortions of the actual contingencies (to the extent that there are any). The cognitive distortions discussed for slot-machine gambling are found in other contexts of addictive behavior (e.g., MacKay and Hodgins, 2012). They do not necessarily involve the conscious or deliberate deception of others or oneself but they provide nonetheless a mask or a veil behind which to hide from the consequences of one's behavior.

A comprehensive explanation requires some aspects of reinforcement learning, neurophysiological processing, and cognitive distortion, though the latter is most clearly implicated as the immediate cause of the near-miss phenomenon. We have seen that the explanation of the increase in gambling propensity in the face of the failures presented as near-misses in terms of cognitive distortion is well supported by the evidence. We have also reviewed the evidence for a neurophysiological basis for the near-miss phenomenon which is indicative of differences in localized brain function between PGs and other gamblers. By treating the cognitive distortion and neurophysiological explanations in sequence, the impression may have been given that these sources of influence are self-contained alternatives. Clark (2010, p. 324) points out, however, that "Cognitive distortions must be instantiated at the neural level and individual differences in brain function or neurochemistry may plausibly influence one's susceptibility to developing erroneous beliefs about gambling." We have noted the neurophysiological reward system which processes reinforcers and is implicated in their capacity to influence the rate of similar behavior in similar situations. Acquiring money, which is a secondary, generalized reinforcer, activates the same brain regions as do primary reinforcers like food and drink, namely the ventral striatum and mPFC (Clark, 2010). We have also noted the role of the DAergic neurons of the mesolimbocortical system in responding to reinforcers, and the operation of RPEs and neuronal plasticity in increasing or inhibiting the likelihood of continued responding.

We have also reviewed the specific neuroanatomical and neurochemical responses to scoring wins, losses, and near-misses, and the manipulation of the illusion of control as well as that of the near-miss. Clark (2010) cites all of this in evidence of the thesis that gambling recruits a neurophysiological system which is sensitive to tracking improvements in skill. This system presumably underlies operant discrimination learning in which successful outcomes shape the particular responses that will be subsequently emitted in a goal-oriented setting; this is the procedure in which stimuli acquire their discriminative properties. Both nongamblers and gamblers evince similar neurochemical processes as they learn to discriminate their behavior on the basis of coming close to a preferred solution. The difficulty is that the near-miss effect is based on a cognitive distortion rather than the genuine learning of a skill. The "anomalous" (Clark, 2010, p. 327) recruitment of the neurophysiological reward system gives rise to further cognitive distortions such as the gambler's fallacy which encourage playing with an intensity that is not logically borne out in the objective circumstances relating patterns of behavior and patterns of reinforcement. Just as drugs of abuse may hijack neurophysiological systems concerned with the delivery of reinforcement and reward in ways significant for the well-being of the individual and ultimately his or her biological fitness (Box 2.1), so process addictions are capable of taking control of systems that evolve to fulfill similar ends through the acquisition of expertise in manipulating the physical environment.

5 Psychological explanation
Cognitive interpretation

I'll so offend, to make offence a skill,
Redeeming time when men think least I will.

William Shakespeare, *Henry IV, Part I*

Cognitive interpretation

The second stage in the construction of a psychological explanation is the "cashing out" or intellectual justification of the intentional interpretation ascribed to an idealized system, one that optimizes a performance which we can make more intelligible by presenting it in intentional terms. I should like to contrast the relationship between the stages of intentional interpretation and cognitive interpretation Intentional Behaviorism employs and those of Dennett's (1987) "three kinds of intentional psychology." Dennett's system is a sophisticated attempt to arrive at a cognitive explanation of behavior that includes sub-personal neuroscience as well as intentionality.

The first intentional psychology he considers, *folk psychology*, is abstract, meaning that the desires and beliefs it employs are not necessarily components of the "internal behavior-causing system" to which they are attributed. Beliefs are concepts like that of the center of gravity; the calculation-bound operations to which the concept leads are more akin to those involving a parallelogram of forces rather than cogs and levers. Folk psychology is therefore instrumentalist rather than realistic in the sense most realists would require, though Dennett (1987) maintains that human beings really have desires and beliefs just as they really possess centers of gravity and the Earth has an Equator. Folk psychology alludes to two kinds of construct which, following Reichenbach, Dennett terms *abstracta* which are "calculation-bound entities or logical constructs," and *illata* which are "posited theoretical entities" (Dennett, 1987, p. 53). Dennett proposes refining folk psychology by devising two further intentional theories, "one strictly abstract, idealizing, holistic, instrumentalistic – pure intentional systems theory – and the other a concrete, microtheoretic science of the actual realization of those intentional systems – what I will call sub-personal cognitive psychology" (SubPCP) (Dennett, 1987, p. 57).

Intentional Systems Theory (IST) is akin to decision theory and game theory: "similarly abstract, normative, and couched in intentional language" (Dennett, 1987, p. 58), though it uses the common terms *beliefs* and *desires* with a technical meaning. IST deals with the system as a whole, instrumentally, and is not concerned with how the system is structured to implement the mechanisms that realize the system's behavior. The purpose of this competence theory is to specify the intentionality the system ought to have, given its history and current position, and its test is the veracity of the predictions it produces of the system's behavior. But this is not enough: "there must be some way in which the internal processes of the system mirror the complexities of the intentional interpretation, or its success would be a miracle" (p. 60).

The brain may be regarded as a semantic engine, concerned with determining what stimulus inputs mean; but, at the neurophysiological level, the brain is no more than a syntactic engine, one that just distinguishes inputs according to their "structural, temporal, and physical features" and these inputs govern its operations. Dennett's big question is: How does the brain get semantic meaning from syntax? Syntax does not determine semantics; hence, we must conclude that the brain cannot do this. But according to Dennett it can "approximate" this impossible task by mimicking the behavior of the impossible object (the semantic engine). In doing so, it capitalizes on similarities between "structural regularities – of the environment and of it own internal states and operations – and semantic types" (Dennett, 1987, p. 61). An animal needs to *know* when it has finished feeding but it has to settle for a sensation in its throat and a stretched stomach to signal this, since these mechanical operations usually accompany its actual goal. The purpose of SubPCP is to formulate and evaluate models of how nature assembles these near-enough activities. Unlike the *abstracta* of IST, the *illata* that provide the elements of SubPCP can enter into testable scientific theories. SubPCP is a performance theory, one which shows how the *abstracta* of IST are instantiated.

While *abstracta* are calculation-bound, *illata* are concrete. In Dennett's examples, centers of gravity and the Equator are *abstracta*. They are not concrete; intentional states are *abstracta* but they are not *illata*: they do not literally inhabit people's heads. Atoms, electrons, and planets are *illata* however, namely entities that have a definite place in scientific theories. Moreover, in Dennett's sub-personal cognitive psychology, *illata* are "intentionally characterized" elements (especially of neurophysiological systems). While electrons are *illata*, Elton (2003) points out, the magnetic property we attribute to a piece of iron that has been magnetized is an *abstractum*: there is no magnetic state existing within the metal. All that exist in the piece of metal are atoms of iron: having a belief is like this.

The purpose of cognitive interpretation in Intentional Behaviorism is not to provide an account of the underlying neurophysiology that grounds the intentional account provided by IST but rendering that neurophysiology in "intentionally characterized" terms which transcend the personal and sub-personal levels of exposition and the languages of explanation appropriate to them. It is to elaborate the cognitive apparatus that would be necessary to bring about the intentionality of the intentional interpretation and to show how this cognitive structure and its functions are sustained by research in the extensional sciences of neurophysiology and operancy. This maintains the separation of the levels of exposition. It thereby entails that the cognitive interpretation is just as firmly located at the personal level as the intentional interpretation. Both of these interpretations are competence theories, though one grounds the other. The performance theories are those behavioral sciences and neurosciences which inhere in the super-personal and sub-personal levels of exposition, respectively.

Competing neurobehavioral decision systems

We encountered one example of neurobehavioral decision theory in Chapter 3, namely Damasio's somatic marker hypothesis, a sophisticated model that links behavior and its consequences to neurophysiology, emotion, and the probability of further behavior of a similar kind. In this chapter, a second strand of neurobehavioral decision theory is discussed, especially in relation to its capacity to encompass metacognitive control. This is the equally sophisticated *competing neurobehavioral decision systems* (CNDS) model, which proposes that the initially self-controlled and subsequently impulsive behaviors involved in preference reversal can be traced to neurophysiological and cognitive bases of competing decision systems. On this view, addiction results from hyperactivity of the limbic and paralimbic dopamine system (thought to be responsible for impulsive and emotional responding) and hypoactivity of the frontal lobes (thought to be responsible for the "executive" functions of foresight and planning).

The *competing neurobehavioral decision systems* (CNDS) *model* of Warren Bickel is perhaps the most developed and integrative version of a neurobehavioral decision theory. It is certainly the most explicit with respect to the role of temporal discounting as an index of neurophysiological imbalance (Bickel and Yi, 2008). This model also attracts attention for its incorporation of operant behavioral economics and neuroeconomics, and for its suggestions of applications for the treatment of addicts (Bickel *et al.*, 2007, 2011a). By emphasizing that imbalance between an individual's "impulsive" and "executive" systems is indexed by his or her rate of temporal discounting, the CNDS model promotes understanding of addiction as a "failure of temporal horizon," identifying the mainsprings of suboptimal behavior as the exaggeration of the reinforcing effects of the consequences of behavior and an inordinately strong desire for immediate satisfaction. In behavioral economics these are described in terms of the elasticity of demand for the reinforcer (following from its excessive valuation) and the discounting of future rewards over present consumption (reflecting impulsivity). The link between the two is presumably to be found in the neurophysiological effects of the reinforcer on behavior. Bickel and his colleagues argue that while these behaviors are inconsistent with rational choice theory they are consistent with behavioral economics of demand and discounting. Hence, they note that people who suffer from reinforcer pathologies make particular choices between commodities they consume and social behaviors where the latter result in less intense or delayed gratification (Bickel *et al.*, 2013).

In a nutshell, hyperactivity of the impulsive system, based on limbic and paralimbic brain regions, coupled with hypoactivity of the executive system, based in the prefrontal cortex, results in a tendency to discount the future steeply and to engage in addictive behavior (Bickel and Yi, 2008). A major premise of the model is therefore that the impulsive and executive systems must be in some respects antipodal and yet contribute in a complementary manner to the determination of the individual's temporal discounting behavior and valuation of currently and potentially available reinforcers. These have been concerns of the CNDS model's authors who also emphasize the role of metacognition (i.e., "cognition about cognition" or "thought about thought") in the regulation of inter-system connectivity (Jarmolowicz *et al.*, 2013). In attempting to clarify further the factors responsible for the achievement of relative balance between the impulsive and executive systems, this chapter explores further the antipodality of the model's component decision systems and, in particular, the nature and role of metacognition in their relationships.

However, straightforward as the idea appears, the CNDS model has two important potential implications for the resolution of the question of multiple selves. First, so long as it proves feasible to incorporate *cognitive* or decision-making contributors to the extent of an individual's temporal discounting tendency, it links to the capacity to regulate behavior through goal-setting and maintenance, social cognition (understanding why others behave as they do), and insight (taking one's own imperfections into account in judging behavioral outcomes). Second, the model's incorporation of operant behavioral economics and neuroeconomics (Bickel *et al.*, 2007a, 2011a, 2012a) facilitates its integration with the economic reasoning which underlies another significant contribution to the explanation of multiple selves and their interaction, namely *picoeconomics* (Ainslie, 1992, 2001; Foxall, 2014a, 2014b; Ross, 2012).

The impulsive system

The CNDS model differs in emphasis from Damasio's somatic marker hypothesis. Their underlying similarity inheres in an acknowledgment that separate functions are performed within the overall impulsive-executive system. But Bickel draws attention to the interconnected operations of the impulsive system and the executive system in the production of behavior (Bickel *et al.*, 2007a). The CNBDS hypothesis is open, moreover, to the incorporation of economic analysis in the form of behavioral economics and neuroeconomics (Bickel *et al.*, 2011c). Impulsive action, defined as the choice of a smaller but sooner reward (SSR) over a larger but later reward (LLR), is certainly associated with the overactivation of the older limbic and paralimbic areas, while the valuation and planning of future events and outcomes engages the relatively new (in evolutionary terms) PFC. However, it is the interaction of these areas, which are densely intermeshed, that generates overt behaviors. The CNBDS hypothesis thus stresses the continuity of the components of the neurophysiologically based decision system and Bickel's conception is therefore one of a continuum on which the impulsive and executive systems are arrayed theoretically as polar opponents (Porcelli and Delgado, 2009).

The impulsive system inheres in the amygdala and ventral striatum, a midbrain region concerned with the valence of immediate results of action, evinced in the increased distribution of dopamine during reinforcement learning, and is liable to become hyperactive as a result of "exaggerated processing of the incentive value of substance-related cues" (Bechara, 2005, p. 1459; see also Delgado and Tricomi, 2011; Walton et al., 2011; Dayan, 2012; Symmonds and Dolan, 2012). Drug-induced behaviors correlate with enhanced response in this region when the amygdala displays increased sensitization to reward (London et al., 2000; Bickel and Yi, 2008; Box 5.1). The receipt of positive reinforcers of all varieties causes the release of dopamine in the nucleus accumbens. This is true of both utilitarian reinforcers such as drugs of abuse, and the receipt of informational reinforcers such as social reward or self-esteem. It is also the case in the receipt of money, which has both utilitarian and informational aspects. In the case of a drug of abuse, such brain reward is acute. The effect of the drug in inculcating long-term potentiation at specific synapses is recorded in the hippocampus as the result of experience (memory). The amygdala is involved in the creation of a learned (conditioned) response to the stimuli that accompany the use of the drug. These accompanying stimuli may take the form of informationally based reinforcers and discriminative stimuli.

Box 5.1 Sensitization and tolerance

Sensitization refers to the increased effectiveness of a drug when it is used repeatedly. There are both quantitative and qualitative modes of sensitization: the increased effect may be a higher level of the subjective feeling associated with the substance (e.g., reported euphoria) or a novel kind of experience (such as hallucination). The opposite effect is *toleration,* in which the effects of drug administration reduce over time so that increasing amounts are required to generate the same result. Toleration is especially apparent in withdrawal symptoms that accompany abstention. The cause of tolerance, which is much more common than sensitization, may be the degradation of the neurotransmitter receptors with which the drug combines in order to produce its effect or the reduction in their number (Altman et al., 1996). Some substances can result in both effects at once. Sustained cocaine use, for instance, is likely to

induce qualitative changes in behavior such as loss of muscular control (sensitization) while the amount of the drug required to produce a "high" or "rush"
becomes progressively greater. The contemporaneous generation of quite separate drug effects and their differential neuropsychological implications account
for this combined experience.

Sensitization suggests the increased positive reinforcement of behavior that
leads to the ingestion of the drug; such behaviors are prevalent during the
binge/intoxication stage. Toleration also involves behaviors the consequences
of which lead to increased drug taking. Hence, they are still positive reinforcers: the individual is taking the drug in order to obtain the highs associated
with it. However, doing so means harder or more work.

Specifically, Bickel *et al.* (2012a) identify, in addition to trait impulsivity,
four kinds of state impulsivity: behavioral disinhibition, attentional deficit
impulsivity, reflection impulsivity, and impulsive choice. Trait impulsivity
is associated with mesolimbic OFC and correlates with medial PFC, pre-
genual anterior cingulate cortex (ACC), and ventrolateral prefrontal cortex;
venturesomeness (sensation-seeking) correlates with right lateral orbitofrontal cortex, subgenual anterior cingualate cortex, and left caudate nucleus
activations. The concept of trait impulsivity recognizes behavioral regularities that are cross-situationally resilient (DeYoung, 2013). Within this broad
construct, sensation-seeking or venturesomeness is widely known to be
related to a need to reach an optimum stimulation level (Zuckerman,
1994). Bickel *et al.* (2012a) associate it with sensitivity to reinforcement,
the theory of which has been extensively developed by Corr (2008b) and is
discussed in greater detail below. Of the four state impulsivities discussed
by Bickel *et al.* (2012a), behavioral disinhibition is associated with deficien-
cies in the anterior cingulate and prefrontal cortices, attentional deficit
impulsivity with impairments of caudate nuclei, anterior cingulate cortex,
and parietal cortical structures, and with strong activity in the insular
cortex; reflection impulsivity with impaired frontal lobe function; and
impulsive choice with increased activation in limbic and paralimbic regions
in the course of the selection of immediate rewards.

This latter condition is strongly predicted by reinforcement sensitivity
theory (McNaughton and Corr, 2004; Box 5.2). It is debatable whether the
state impulsivities mentioned here are anything other than the behavioral
manifestations of trait impulsivity in particular contexts. The four state impulsivities that Bickel *et al.* (2012a) note are probably outcomes of a general
tendency to act impulsively from which they are predictable. Behavioral disinhibition is the inability to arrest a pattern of behavior once it has started; it
is also evinced in acting prematurely with deleterious outcomes. Attentional
deficit impulsivity is failure to concentrate, to persevere with salient stimuli.
Again, the outcome is the adoption of risky behavioral modes with poor consequences. Reflection impulsivity is failure to gather sufficient information

before deciding and acting; inability to gauge an adequate measure of the situation leads to unrewarding behaviors. Impulsive choice is a behavioral preference for a smaller reward appearing sooner (SSR) over a later but larger reward (LLR) for which the individual must wait. All of these state impulsivities are actually behaviors, the outcomes of trait impulsivity. More relevant to the present discussion is *preference reversal* in which a longer term, more advantageous goal is preferred (e.g., verbally) at the outset only to decline dramatically in relative value as the delivery of the earlier, less advantageous reward becomes imminent.

The executive system

Bickel *et al.* (2012a) define executive functions as "behavior that is self-directed toward altering future outcomes" (p. 363; see also Barkley, 2012) and point out that executive functions are consensually associated with activity in the prefrontal cortex (PFC). The PFC is generally recognized as implicated in the integration of motivational information and subsequent decision-making (Watanabe *et al.*, 2009; see also Kennerley and Walton, 2011), exerting a supervisory function that governs the regulation of behavior (Bickel *et al.*, 2012a); hence its designation as a supervisory attentional system (SAS) (Shallice and Cooper, 2011).

The *executive system*, located in the prefrontal cortex, is normally associated with planning and foresight, and is implicated in the evaluation of rewards and their outcomes (Walton *et al.*, 2011; Dayan, 2012; Symmonds and Dolan, 2012), but is hypothesized to become hypoactive in the event of addiction; the absence of its moderating function is responsible for the exacerbation of the effects of the hyperactive dopaminergic reward pathway; this imbalance is then viewed as the cause of dysfunctional behavior (Bickel *et al.*, 2012a, 2013). In summary, the CNBDS hypothesis posits that drug seeking results from "amplified incentive value bestowed on drugs and drug-related cues (via reward processing by the amygdala) and impaired ability to inhibit behavior (due to frontal cortical dysfunction)" (Bickel and Yi, 2010, p. 2; Jentsch and Taylor, 1999; Rolls, 2009).

While some authors emphasize a single element of executive functions such as the attentional control of behavior or working memory or inhibition, others stress groups of elements: planning, working memory, attentional shifting or valuing future events, and emotional aspects of decision-making. Addiction may then be viewed as a breakdown in the operations of the executive functions or as impaired response inhibition leading to the increased salience of addiction-orientated cues. Bickel *et al.* (2012a) concentrate on Attention (Rueda *et al.*, 2013), Behavioral flexibility, Planning (Gollwitzer and Oettingen, 2013), Working memory (Hofmann *et al.*, 2013), Emotional activation and self-regulation (Carver and Scheier, 2013; Koole *et al.*, 2013; McRae *et al.*, 2013) which they group into three major categories: (1) *the cross-temporal organization of behavior* (CTOB) which is concerned with the awareness of the future consequences of current or contemplated behavior and therefore with planning for events that will occur later; (2) *emotional activation and self-regulation* (EASR) which involves the processing of emotion-related information and "initiating and maintaining goal-related responding"; and (3) *metacognition* which includes social cognition and insight, empathy, and theory of mind (ToM).

The cross-temporal organization of behavior comprises *attention* (closely related to the dorsolateral prefrontal cortex (dlPFC), *behavioral flexibility* (frontal gyrus activity); lesioning of PFC is well known to be associated with the diminution of behavioral flexibility (Damasio, 1994; Bechara, 2011), *behavioral inhibition* (the right inferior frontal cortex and insula are activated during behavioral inhibition which is also associated with reduced activity in the left dlPFC, the right frontal gyrus, right medial gyrus, left cingulate, left putamen, medial temporal, and inferior parietal cortex), *planning* (in which the dlPFC, the vmPFC, parietal cortex, and striatum are implicated), *valuing future events* (in the case of previewing and selecting immediate rewards: limbic and paralimbic regions; in the case of long-term decisions: prefrontal regions; McClure *et al.*, 2004); and *working memory* (dlPFC, vmPFC, dorsal cingulate, frontal poles, medial inferior parietal cortex, frontal gyrus, medial frontal gyrus, and precentral gyrus) (Bickel *et al.* 2012a, pp. 363–367). Working memory, defined by Nichols and Wilson (2015, p. 55) as "The capacity to simultaneously hold information in attention and manipulate it," is central to the exercise of executive function.

Emotion and activation self-regulation (EASR) concerned with the management of emotional responses is implemented in the medial PFC, lateral PFC, ACC, and OFC. *Metacognitive processes (MP)* involve recognition of one's own motivation and that of others which is implemented in the case of *insight* or self-awareness by the insula and ACC, and in the case of *social cognition* by the medial PFC, right superior temporal gyrus, left temporal parietal junction, left somatosensory cortex, and right dlPFC; moreover, *impaired social cognition* follows lesions to vmPFC (Damasio, 1994; Bechara, 2005; Bickel *et al.*, 2012a, pp. 367–368).

Behavioral economics of reinforcer pathology

Operant behavioral economics

The CNDS hypothesis is closely associated with behavioral economics and neuroeconomics, in terms of which the "reinforcer pathologies" that define addiction are explicated (Bickel and Johnson, 2003; Bickel and Marsch, 2001; Bickel and Vuchinich, 2000; Bickel *et al.*, 1999, 2010, 2011a, 2011b). Behavioral economics is frequently assumed to consist primarily in a repudiation of neoclassical microeconomics if not to constitute an outright attack on it. In fact, the term "behavioral economics" describes several subdisciplines which combine economics and psychology in different ways.

It is applied, for instance, to Simon's (1987) tempering of neoclassicism with the cognitive limitations of real world managers and consumers, as well as to Kahneman and Tversky's (1979) demonstrations of the boundaries of economic rationality. The complexity inherent in merely delimiting the field is apparent from the fact that these schools of behavioral economics are not discrete subdisciplines but approaches that overlap with and impinge critically upon one another. This antagonism toward neoclassical microeconomics is not embraced, however, by the brand of behavioral economics assumed by Bickel. The style of behavioral economics which Bickel employs is based on the fusion of basic neoclassical microeconomics with the experimental method of operant psychology, a school originated by Ainslie (2015), Hursh (1980, 1984; Hursh and Silberberg, 2008), Herrnstein (1997), and Rachlin (2000a), among others, which has found ready application in the investigation of addiction (Bickel and Vuchinich, 2000; Vuchinich and Heather, 2003).

There is in fact a natural affinity between operant psychology and microeconomic theory in that both consider behavior as the allocation of a limited number of responses among alternative sources of reward (Foxall, 2015a; Foxall and Sigurdsson, 2013). Robbins's well-known definition of economics as "the science which studies human behavior as a relationship between ends and scarce means which have alternative uses" (Robbins, 1935, p. 16) comes close to the perspective on behavior in which an organism (including nonhuman beings as well as human beings) allocate a fixed number of responses among alternatives (Staddon, 1980). Operant behavior is economic in the sense that it may be studied as the allocation of a limited number of responses to produce benefits and, at the same time, incur costs. This covers all that behavior analysts study as operant choice: we refer to reinforcing and aversive stimuli rather than to benefits and costs. But what makes the behavior economic is that we have limited resources to allocate over a seemingly unlimited range of opportunities. The benefits and costs relate ultimately to biological fitness and are seen most graphically in the acquisition of the primary reinforcers necessary for life. But, in any given culture, secondary reinforcers also play a central role in the relationship of individual conduct to biological fitness via economic choice. The view that operant behavior is economic is reflected in definitions of rewards or reinforcers found in biology and especially neuroscience which cast them as "stimuli for which an organism will work." At the same time, this supports the contention that choice is "behavior in the context of other behavior" and that it may be analyzed in economic terms.

The reinforcer pathologies, the analysis of which is central to the competing neurobehavioral decision systems hypothesis, involve (1) an excessively high preference for immediate acquisition or consumption of the reinforcer even when this is known to have longer term deleterious effects; and/or (2) an excessively high valuation of a commodity (i.e., a behavior, experience, or physical substance) (Bickel *et al.*, 2011a).

Overvaluation of immediacy

The extent to which a reinforcer affects the rate at which a response is enacted depends on how long the reinforcer is delayed following the occurrence of the behavior. Discounting the future follows a hyperbolic rather than an exponential pattern. Exponential discounting means, among other things, that the discounting takes place at a fixed rate per unit of time. It thus embodies the rational perspective on financial transactions followed by banks in their lending: a later but larger reward (LLR) is more highly valued than a sooner but smaller reward (SSR) at all times and the temptation to select the latter over the former is minimal. However, in hyperbolic discounting, the rate at which a commodity is discounted decreases with the time that has elapsed (Ainslie and Monterosso, 2003): while the LLR is valued more highly than the SSR in the beginning, when the latter becomes imminent it is valued much more highly to the extent that the individual is strongly tempted to take this immediate reward instead of that which is more delayed but ultimately more valuable. The branch of operant behavioral economics that deals with temporal discounting thus shows addiction to be "a constriction of temporal horizon" in which hyperbolic discounting provides a measure of the imbalance between impulsive and executive systems (Bickel *et al.*, 2006; Bickel and Yi, 2008).

Elasticity of demand

Another behavioral-economic construct, namely price elasticity of demand, has been used to evaluate the exaggerated demand for commodities like food, opportunities to gamble, and drugs which is another aspect of the reinforcer pathology that defines addiction. A large increase in the unit price of a commodity that results in a small decrease in consumption indicates that a high valuation is placed on the item. Addiction involves persistent consumption of a commodity even when its cost increases sharply; the inelasticity of demand in the face of price rises – that is, insensitivity of consumption to changes in the cost of acquiring it – is a central definitional element in the economic analysis of addiction (Becker and Murphy, 1988). Exaggerated valuation of a commodity emerges as a vital component of addiction that is capable of analysis in terms of operant behavioral economics but which may also be modeled by neuroeconomics. (For a critical discussion of the relevance of demand elasticity to rationality and addictive behavior, see Elster, 1999b.)

Neuroeconomics is intimately concerned with the economic valuation of reinforcers. An organism's survival and inclusive biological fitness is contingent upon the valuation it forms of the reinforcing consequences of its behavior (Schultz, 2000; Rolls, 2008). Neuroeconomics posits a counterpart of this evaluation in firing rates of neurons (Camerer *et al.*, 2005; Glimcher, 2004; Politser, 2008) which evolved so as to predict the reinforcing and punishing consequences of responses by making possible the comparison of expected rewards with those that have followed similar behavior previously performed in similar circumstances. As a result, the reinforcing outcomes of behavior become goals. Such evolutionarily and genetically selected reinforcers not only make appropriate approach behavior more probable; they also elicit emotional states that act as the ultimate rewarding effects of behavior which enhance its continuity (Schultz, 2000; Rolls, 2008). By maintaining operant responses, reinforcers control the rate at which learning occurs by facilitating calculation at the neuronal level of discrepancies between the predicted reward and that which has occurred in the learning history of the individual. Dopamine neurons' indexing variations between predicted rewards and actually occurring rewards comprise the "reward prediction error" or RPE which is a fundamental datum of neuroeconomics (Rolls, 2008). Hence, neuroeconomics maps "economic decisions straightforwardly into the neural substrates that produce those decisions" (Zak, 2004, p. 133; Schultz *et al.*, 2008; Montague and Berns, 2002).

The basic tenet of the competing neurobehavioral decision systems hypothesis of differential functioning of the limbic and paralimbic system on one hand and the prefrontal cortex on the other is supported by neuroeconomists' identification of two brain regions accounting for reward (Politser, 2008; Ross *et al.*, 2005). The striatum, located in the basal ganglia and incorporating the nucleus accumbens (NAcc), works with the hypothalamus, amygdala, and hippocampus, which have been collectively identified as the so-called "emotional center" of the brain. Adjacent to this are areas concerned with reward: the ventral tegmental area (VTA), the pars compacta of the substantia nigra (SNpc), and the anterior cingulate cortex. The brain region to which these belong is much older in evolutionary time than the second of the neurophysiological areas involved in the processing of reward. This is the PFC and, especially, the OFC which is particularly dedicated to processing reward. While dopamine is not the only neurotransmitter of significance to reward processing, its role is especially germane to the explanation of economic behavior. Reward signals are emitted by the VTA and SNpc which take the form of the emission of dopamine at rates that facilitate comparison with a baseline level, thus enabling an assessment of whether the reward matches, falls short of, or exceeds expectation. Since changes in dopamine release influence behavioral outputs, reward processing in the dopaminergic system entails learning.

Reinforcement pathologies also have implications for understanding the influences on consumption over the Continuum of Consumer Choice.

The Continuum of Consumer Choice revisited

Figure 5.1 depicts the Continuum of Consumer Choice in terms of differences between modes of consumer behavior stemming from price elasticity of demand and steepness of temporal discounting. Routine purchasing, exemplified by everyday brand selection, is lowest on both of these measures, while extreme consumption, exemplified by addiction, is highest. Other modes of consumption vary between these polar extremes.

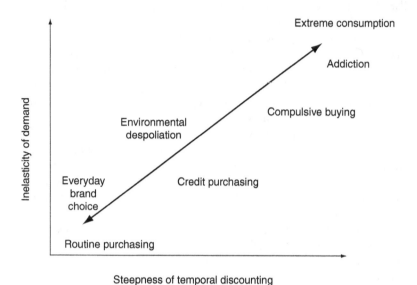

Figure 5.1 The Continuum of Consumer Choice II: the effects of reinforcement pathology.

Exploring the cognitive dimension

There are four reasons for thinking more formally about the place and function of a cognitive dimension within the CNDS model: (1) the tendency to conflate cognitive and neurophysiological terminologies; (2) the need to take emotion into account; (3) the "valuation" involved in temporal discounting is a mental construct which requires explanation in terms of cognitive representation and evaluation; and (4) the concern that the present dual process structure of the model may be inadequate to the task of accounting for the metacognitive processes involved in the exercise of self-control. None of these applies uniquely to the CNDS model; they simply suggest ways in which it may be further strengthened.

The CNDS hypothesis is described by Bickel and colleagues in neuroscientific, cognitive, and behavioral terms, without regard for the domains of explanation to which each of these categories belongs. For example, although they offer what purports to be a behavioral definition of executive function, they define several of its component parts in terms that are cognitive. Following Barkley (1997a, 1997b), they define executive functions as "classes of self-directed behavior to change one's future reinforcement" (Bickel *et al.*, 2012a, p. 362). But they list among those of its elements which suggest "cross-temporal organization of behavior" *attention, planning, valuing future events,* and *working memory.* These are clearly cognitive events. Similarly, among the elements that make up "emotional and activation self-regulation," they list "the processing of emotional information" and "initiating and maintaining goal-related responding." Finally, as elements of "metacognitive processes" they list "social cognition" or "theory of mind" and "insight." Following Daruna and Barnes (1993) and Winstanley *et al.* (2006), Bickel *et al.* (2012a) define impulsivity apparently behaviorally as "actions that appear prematurely expressed, unduly risky, poorly conceived, and result in undesirable consequences" (p. 362). They describe impulsivity, however, as comprising "trait impulsiveness" which is a structural personality variable in which they include sensation-seeking, attention-deficit impulsivity which manifests as a "diminished ability to persist" and which leads to risk-taking, and "reflection impulsivity" which is a "deficit in the tendency to gather and evaluate information before making a decision" (ibid.). All of these are intentional.

Barkley (2012), as noted, draws attention to a tendency among writers on *executive function* to conflate that term with the functions of the PFC and vice versa. He notes in particular a slippage of discourse involving two levels of analysis: the neuropsychological, to which he attributes emotion and cognition as well as behavior (including both verbal and motor activities); and the neuroanatomical, involving the localization of these functions to specific areas of the brain. This distinction is actually potentially confusing rather than enlightening but he clarifies:

> EF is a term describing psychological functions and thus belongs at the psychological level of analysis. If our understanding of EF is to advance, the concept of EF and its nature must be defined separately and specifically the psychological level without reference to the neurological level being an essential part of that definition.
>
> (Barkley, 2012, p. 2)

The definition of EF at the psychological level is an essential prelude to the identification of the brain areas involved in the generation of the emotions and thoughts that constitute EF (Denckla, 1996).

Before considering the cognitive requirements of neurobehavioral decision theory, we should be aware of the nature of the CNDS model and the extent to which it is already amenable to metacognitive explanation. After that, the possibility that picoeconomics can provide the required cognitive component may be assessed and the nature of the explanation of behavior provided by picoeconomics itself may also be assessed. Finally, the possibility that a more elaborate cognitive model is required in order to account for the intentional interpretation provided by picoeconomics may be presented.

The nature of metacognition

Metacognition denotes thinking about thinking or cognition about cognition, and is exemplified by our thinking through the plans we have made or reconsidering a decision. The term is often used as a synonym for theory-of-mind and is employed in studies of children's learning to ascribe intentionality to themselves and to others (e.g., Papaleontiou-Louca, 2008). Shea *et al.* (2014) apply metacognition to the operation of type 1 and type 2 systems (Kahneman, 2011; Evans, 2010) where the former are cognitive systems characterized by rapid, automatic responses while the latter feature slower, more deliberative reaction to events. In greater detail, Shea *et al.* (2014) distinguish system 1 metacognitive systems from system 2 metacognitive systems: the former function in the absence of working memory and are "typically fast, automatic, associative, effortless, and non-conscious" (Shea *et al.*, 2014, p. 186). By contrast, system 2 metacognitive systems rely on working memory and are "typically slower, serial, rule-based, more effortful, and conscious" (Shea *et al.*, 2014, pp. 186–187). The cognitive styles of S1 and S2 systems as they term them give rise to metacognitive analysis insofar as the two types of system act cognitively on more basic cognitive representations. Although Shea *et al.* (2014) are open to the possibility that S2 metacognitive processes are implicated in intra-personal behavior regulation (which is our interest here), their primary emphasis is on inter-personal, inter-agent cooperation. Moreover, they argue that S2 metacognitive systems enhance such cooperation by, first, distributing metacognitive representations for verbal communication; second, evaluating metacognitive representations to motivate appropriate action; and third, extricating metacognitive representations from weak metacognitive information. These functions are also necessary for intra-personal picoeconomic agents to reconcile their competing interests.

S2 systems also exert synchronic (enhancing the performance of multiple agents simultaneously engaged in a common task) and diachronic (influencing how other agents later think and act and so enhancing joint performance) supra-personal cognitive control (Shea *et al.*, 2014, p. 190). Economic modeling of the interests proposed by picoeconomics reaches similar conclusions (Ross, 2012). While economic models indicate the options available to the agent, system 2 metacognitive models suggest how choice (cooperation rather than conflict) would be exerted at an overarching cognitive level. Although supra-personal metacognition is compatible with intra-personal, inter-agent metacognition, it is not obvious that it is historically or logically prior to it; nor is intra-personal metacognition necessarily a side-effect. However, it is probable that cultural evolution played a dominant role in the development of S2 metacognition as a cognitive control mechanism that overcomes impulsiveness by engendering cooperation between short- and longer term interests. The modification of a temporal horizon from that predisposing toward impulsiveness to that in which consumption can be delayed is traceable to the transition from hunter-gathering to agriculture and more recent religiously based communities; hence from early hominins to modern human beings.

In the spirit of Intentional Behaviorism, we would only turn to metacognition as a source of explanation when the stimulus conditions needed to support a behaviorist explanation are not available. I would like to re-examine the three instances in which a metacognitive explanation is necessary in the contest of akratic and addictive behavior that were considered in Chapter 4. First, the process of intertemporal valuation of alternative courses of action requires that the individual engage in cognitive appraisal of *a representation of the STI* and its outcomes, of a cognitive appraisal of *a representation of the LRI* and its outcomes, and in the evaluative comparison of the two so that a decision as to how to behave may be reached. Second, picoeconomic strategizing requires decoupling to enable the mental rehearsal necessary for bundling and other strategies of overcoming to be undertaken. And third, the cognitive distortion apparent among slot-machine gamblers requires to be understood in terms of a form of psychological rationality which goes beyond that measured by IQ tests. The task at hand is to consider carefully the place and function of metacognition in neurobehavioral decision theory, which by its nature is constrained in its cognitive interpretations by considerations of neurophysiology and behavioral science.

Dual process antipodality

The CNDS model is an example of a dual process theory (i.e., one that builds on a substantial volume of social scientific argument that human cognition is characterized by two styles of processing) (Frankish and Evans, 2009). Type 1 processing is *autonomous:* its execution is *rapid* and *mandatory*, economizes on central processing capacity and higher level control systems, and employs *parallel* processing so that it avoids interfering with other cognitive operations. These characteristics illustrate the *computational ease* which makes type 1 processing the default processing mode: unless it its overridden, it will automatically generate responses to environmental conditions. Type 1 processing includes the regulation of behavior by the emotions, encapsulated modules that solve adaptive problems, implicit learning processes, and the automatic firing of overlearned associations. By comparison with the type 1 thinking that characterizes the *autonomous mind* (Stanovich, 2009a), type 2 processing is *slow* and makes *heavy computational demands*. It requires attention, which is costly, and is involved in conscious problem-solving, eventuating in behavior directed toward achieving long-range consequences.

Bases of antipodality in the CNDS model

The distinction between the impulsive and the executive systems, and that between their respective styles of processing, suggests at least two bases of evaluation and judgment that have opposing tendencies toward behavioral outcomes. This implies that the systems may be construed as antithetical in important respects that can be related to their interaction to produce particular observed behavior patterns. These antipodal tendencies of the impulsive and executive systems ought ideally to indicate why behavioral imbalance would result from the hyperactivity of one system simultaneously with the hypoactivity of the other, a possibility which Bickel *et al.* (2012b) have investigated. These authors propose eight executive functions relevant to the CNDS model: Attention, Inhibitory control, Valuing future events, Cognitive behavioral flexibility, Working memory, Planning, Emotional activation and self-regulation, and Metacognitive processes. The first four are categorized as concerned with the *cross-temporal organization of behavior* (CTOB). *Emotional activation and self-regulation* (EASR) comprise two elements: Processing of emotional information, and Initiating and maintaining goal-related responding, and *metacognition* (MC) which comprise two more: Social cognition (consisting in theory of mind, empathy) and Insight (or self-awareness). In addition, they propose as elements in the impulsive system two trait impulsivities: *Sensation-seeking* and *Sensitivity to reward*, and four state impulsivities: *Behavioral disinhibition, Attention-deficit impulsivity, Reflection impulsivity*, and *Impulsive choice* (preference for SSR over LLR). The impulsive and executive systems, delineated in terms of the components identified by Bickel *et al.* (2012a), are shown as interacting systems in Figure 5.2.

Bickel *et al.* (2012a) assess antipodality by reference to four criteria: definition, measurement, overlapping of clinical populations, and commonality of neural substrates of the elements of impulsivity and executive function that comprise the CNDS model. It emerges from their analysis that the four state impulsivities are definitionally antipodal to four of the executive functions. Attention-deficit impulsivity and attention are clearly opposites, while the definitions of behavioral inhibition and behavioral disinhibition contain common characteristics that set them apart. In addition, reflection impulsivity tends toward the opposite of planning. Finally, the selection of SSR over LLR is antipodal to the capacity to value future outcomes. Note that the four executive functions identified as having antipodal impulsivities all belong to the cross-temporal organization of behavior (CTOB) grouping.

The analysis of antipodality also reveals coterminous measures of impulsive system and executive system items in the case of attention-deficit impulsivity and attention, and for behavioral inhibition and behavioral disinhibition. Reflective impulsivity and planning are less similar in their measurement.

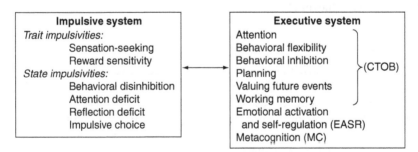

Figure 5.2 Competing neurobehavioral decision systems: a dual process model.

Finally, the delay discounting methods employed to measure impulsivity have recently come to be used in the measurement of executive functions. Note once more that these results establish CTOB as the seat of executive function which is the antipode to impulsivity.

The third source of evidence is the overlap of clinical populations whose members suffer from addiction and who show either hypoactive executive function or hyperactive impulsivity. Some substance users/abusers, for instance, demonstrate response inhibition deficits and excesses in behavioral disinhinbition. When the substance is alcohol, this tends to be accompanied by lack of attention on the one hand and exaggerated attention-deficit impulsivity on the other. Deficits in planning and high levels of reflection impulsivity are found in users of amphetamines, cigarettes, and opiates. Finally, addicts to alcohol, cigarettes, cocaine, and heroin display steeper discounting of delayed rewards more than controls do. Executive function deficits are also closely related to drug addiction.

Finally, in terms of the overlap in neural substrates of brain regions implicated variously in the functioning of the impulsive and executive systems, it is noteworthy that the insula and parts of the PFC are implicated in both behavioral disinhibition and behavioral inhibition. Moreover, since choice impulsivity and the valuation of future events are measured by means of delay discounting assignments they must recruit the same brain areas; they also cite the strongly emerging evidence that the limbic and paralimbic areas are implicated in immediate choice while parts of the PFC are implicated in the selection of delayed rewards (and therefore with the valuation of future events). Again, it is noteworthy that all of these executive functions belong to the CTOB category. There is, however, little evidence of any overlap between the neural substrates of reflection impulsivity and planning other than the observation that individuals with lesions to the frontal cortices exhibit high reflection impulsivity which supports the view that dlPF and dmPFC are concerned with planning. There is also a paucity of evidence for any neural overlap for attention and attention-deficit impulsivity. Nor is impulsivity antipodally related to working memory, EASR, or MC, even though impediments to these are found variously in addiction. Overall we may conclude that CTOB is antipodally related to the state impulsivities by evidence that they implicate similar neural substrates but that there is little evidence that the other elements employed in the categorization of executive functions shown in Figure 1.1 are similarly related to impulsivity. This does not constitute an original critique of the CNBDS model; indeed, the points made are all acknowledged by Bickel *et al.* (2012b). These authors specifically note that working memory answers no antipodal aspect of impulsivity and they draw attention to the lack of antipodal relationship between EASR and MC on one hand and impulsivity on the other. Such a relationship would be expected if EASR and MC belonged to executive functions. However, this examination of the findings suggests an alternative depiction of how the impulsive system and executive system are related.

Locating metacognition

Since the evidence for antipodality locates the competing activities of the impulsive and executive systems firmly within neurophysiological bases, the task remains of placing the decision-making or cognitive elements of CNDS, currently located in the executive system (Figure 5.2), for which no evidence of corresponding and antipodal functions within the impulsive system has been adduced. There are in fact good reasons for separating metacognition (MC) and emotional activation and goal regulation (EASR), in which these cognitive or decision-making functions inhere, from the neurophysiological dimensions that are demonstrably antipodal. Because both MC and EASR involve thought or feeling about thought or feeling, I shall refer to them collectively as *metacognition*, though they may not exclusively fulfill this role in explaining human behavior. The justification for treating these cognitive variables as involved in the explanation of behavior is as follows.

If the CNDS model were conceived of solely in terms of the neurophysiologically defined impulsive and executive systems that have been shown to be antipodal, then the individual's behavior manifested in a degree of temporal discounting peculiar to him or her would be the outcome of a sub-personal battle between opposing biological forces. Behavior would be starkly determined by innate neurophysiological capacities resulting from phylogenetic evolution, modified by a learning history that results in neural plasticity formed in a process of Hebbian or similar learning (Rolls, 2008). Behavior would be no more than contingency shaped, determined in its totality by contingencies of natural selection and operant conditioning. However, this would be to ignore the rule governance of behavior, the possibility of an influence of reflective thought on responding. By including MC and EASR in their model, Bickel *et al.* (2012a) take this into account. Their inability to find or suggest functions of the impulsive system that are antipodal to these cognitive functions, which in any case repose uneasily among the other elements of the executive system depicted in Figure 5.3, argues for their separate consideration. The resulting reconceptualization is shown in Figure 5.2, in which MC and EASR are shown separately from the executive system which contains only those elements that are demonstrably antipodal to elements of the impulsive system. The impulsive system retains *pro tem* the traits of impulsivities, sensation-seeking, and reward sensitivity that have no demonstrable correspondents in the executive system. Figure 5.3 indicates also the reliance of MC and EASR upon working memory.

The empirical outcome of the search for antipodality between impulsive and executive systems represented by Bickel *et al.*'s (2012a) research suggests the framework shown in Figure 5.3. But there is a theoretical imperative for the proposal that metacognition occupy a superordinate position to the competing impulsive and executive systems. If the conflict of these systems is to be resolved by means of "cognition about cognition" or "thinking about thinking," it follows that such metacognitive activity must take place in a

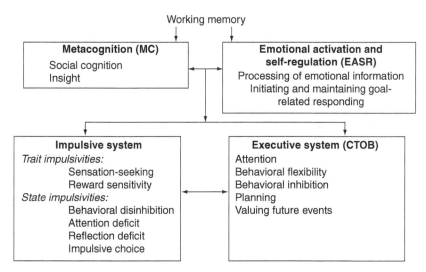

Figure 5.3 Separation of metacognition (MC) and emotional activation and self-regulation (EASR) from the executive system.

forum separate from the systems themselves: how else could such activity decide between the interests which these systems underpin? As a judge always sits apart from and acts independently of the advocates of plaintiff and defense, the realm of mediation, intercession, and arbitration in decision-making cannot be incorporated within either the short-range interest that tends toward immediate gratification or the long-range interest that seeks a wider echelon of optimization.

A tripartite theory

Recent theoretical developments in multi-process theory suggest that meta-cognitive processes such as MC and EASR are most appropriately positioned as superordinate to the interactions of impulsive and executive systems as well as other systems that influence their interrelationship (Stanovich, 2009a). That no antipodal relationship is evident between MC and EASR, on one hand, and components of the impulsive system, on the other, suggests that this possibility should at least be considered as a means of understanding more fully the import of the CNDS model.

The similarity of the type 1/type 2 dichotomy to that of the impulsive system/executive system distinction is readily apparent. But any conclusions about the structure of the CNDS model in terms of these different styles of processing should take account of Stanovich's proposal for a tri-process theory (Figure 5.4). In proposing such a structure, Stanovich (2009a) extends his earlier model both conceptually by adding a level of processing as well as by increasing

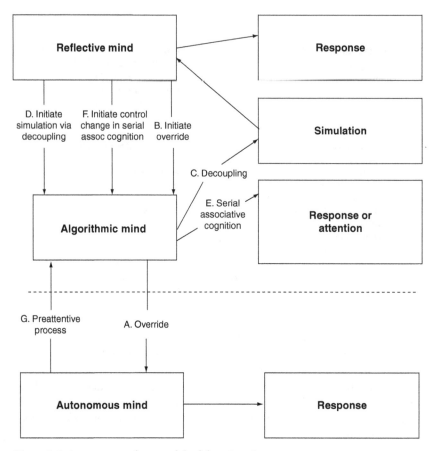

Figure 5.4 A more complete model of the tripartite structure.

the number of systems that comprise each level of processing. Thus, instead of a single Autonomous Mind, Stanovich (2009a) proposes "a *set* of systems in the brain that operate autonomously in response to their own triggering stimuli and are not under the control of the analytic processing system [i.e., system 2]" (p. 56). This heterogeneous set, to which he refers as The Autonomous Set of Systems (TASS), contains systems that are related in terms of their style of functioning (i.e., automaticity) rather than related by modularity. The proposed tri-process CNDS model incorporates two systems of Automatic Mind: the state-impulsive system comprising the state impulsivities, and the trait-impulsive system comprising sensation-seeking and reward/reinforcement sensitivity.

Type 2 processing is divisible into two sorts of operation, each characteristic of a "kind of mind" (Dennett, 1996). The *Algorithmic Mind* involves individual differences in fluid intelligence, that which is measured by IQ tests, while the *Reflective Mind* involves individual differences in rational thinking dispositions (and, presumably, in strength of self-regulation: Bauer and Baumeister, 2013; Rothbart *et al.*, 2013). Rationality is broader than intelligence, requiring well-formulated desires (goals), highly calibrated beliefs, and the ability to act on them in order to achieve the goals. It is, therefore, closely associated with the elements that Bickel *et al.* (2012a) position as components of the executive system which, in their analysis, found no corresponding antipodal response in the impulsive system.

The distinction between the two type 2 systems posited by the tri-process theory rests on several functional differences. The key function of the Reflective Mind is the inauguration of the call to begin cognitive simulation or hypothetical reasoning. The key operation of the Algorithmic Mind in this is the decoupling it carries out. Decoupling is cognitively demanding, assisted by language, which provides "the discrete representational medium that greatly enables hypotheticality to flourish as a culturally acquired mode of thought" (Stanovich, 2009a, p. 63). Hypothetical thought requires the representation of assumptions, for instance, and linguistic forms like conditionals readily allow for this. Decoupling abilities differ in their recursiveness and complexity. Decoupling makes it possible to distance oneself from the representations so that they can be reflected upon and improved. Decoupling is therefore the key function of Algorithmic Mind. It is clearly a system 2 operation in that its operation occurs serially and incurs high computational expense. The literature on executive function and working memory, he argues, supports the view that the main function of Algorithmic Mind is to achieve decoupling among representations while conducting cognitive simulation.

The cognitive control exerted by elements of the tri-processual model is justified as follows. System 2, representing Analytic Mind, contains two levels of functioning: the *algorithmic* level and the *reflective* level. TASS systems will function on a short-range basis unless this is overridden by the algorithmic system which gives precedence to the long-range goals of the analytical system. These latter reflect the goals of the person and the "epistemic thinking dispositions." But these goals and dispositions must arise at a level superior to that of the algorithmic system, namely in the reflective system "a level containing control states that regulate behavior at a high level of generality" (Stanovich, 2009a, p. 57). This distinction of analytical systems gives rise to a tripartite system of cognitive processing. The Algorithmic Mind and the Reflective Mind share properties (such as capacity-limited serial processing) that distinguish them from the Automatic Mind (Stanovich, 2009a, p. 58) But Algorithmic Mind and Reflective Mind may still be distinguished from one another, especially if we think in relation to the impulsive and executive systems. If these two systems are in conflict or competition, as the CNDS model proposes them to be, any adjudication between them that results in a compromise or balanced influence on behavior will have to be conducted at a superordinate level of processing. It must draw upon system goals and strategic procedures that are not the property of either of these systems but of a level of processing that is superior to both of them. This is Reflective Mind.

Stanovich (2009a) argues that measures of the executive functions actually draw upon elements of Algorithmic Mind rather than Reflective Mind. While the term "executive" seems superficially to suggest that these functions concern the highest level of mind, Reflective Mind, the tasks used by cognitive scientists to assess executive function actually test skills that result from Algorithmic Mind. Research in cognitive psychology in particular has been concerned with tasks that involve algorithmic level decoupling abilities: Stanovich mentions "stop signal paradigms, working memory paradigms, time sharing paradigms, inhibition paradigms" which are highly suggestive of the components of executive function that Bickel *et al.* (2012a) found to be antipodal to state impulsivities. Individual differences in Reflective Mind capabilities are barely involved in these tasks, if at all. Reflective Mind, especially with respect to its involvement in epistemic regulation and cognitive allocation, is involved in cognitive control at a level beyond that of the computational capacity to maintain decoupling. Stanovich argues, therefore, that the executive functions have been misnamed: they are essentially *supervisory processes*, he maintains, based on externally provided rules rather than internally inaugurated decision-making (2009a, p. 66). By contrast, Reflective Mind is involved in setting "the goal agenda" or in operating at the level of epistemic regulation which he defines as "directing the sequence of information pickup." Executive functions are not engaged in this kind of work.

While the executive system belongs to Algorithmic Mind, however, it does not constitute Algorithmic Mind exclusively. The executive system is fundamentally involved in the overriding of Automatic Mind but other functions of Algorithmic Mind such as the execution of decoupling are not carried out by the executive system. Similarly, the impulsive system is not the sole element of TASS; the trait impulsivities (sensation-seeking and reinforcement sensitivity) also belong to TASS and are involved in moderating the tendency toward impulsivity or self-control at the behavioral level. Hence, even the type 1/type 2 dichotomy recognizes a complexity which goes beyond that of the original CNDS model. However, Stanovich (2009a, 2009b, 2011; Stanovich *et al.*, 2012) argues for a further distinction, this time between the kinds of processing for which type 2 systems are severally responsible, which if accepted complicates the division between impulsive and executive systems made by the CNDS model. The interaction of type 1 and type 2 processing is evinced by the capacity of the second to prevent the automatic responses inherent in type 1 processing to engender impulsive behaviors that result in suboptimal outcomes. "Better" responses depend on type 2 *hypothetical reasoning* in which the individual builds models of the world and performs cognitive simulations on them. Stanovich *et al.* (2012, p. 787) comment, "When we reason hypothetically, we create temporary models of the world and test out actions (or alternate causes) in that simulated world," words reminiscent of Popper's observation that "our conjectures, our theories, die in our stead!" (Popper, 1959). In order to effect this cognitive functioning, type 2 processes can override those of type 1, interrupting and suppressing type 1 functioning and then substituting alternative responses. Moreover, in order to form simulations, it is necessary to *decouple* simulated models from the real world so that they can be manipulated independently. This initiation of decoupling secondary representations from the world and maintaining them while simulation occurs is a type 2 operation.

Having "taken TASS offline," Algorithmic Mind initiates decoupling which enables cognitive simulation to take place. The outcomes of this are reviewed by Reflective Mind which initiates change in serial associative cognition which influences Algorithmic Mind to develop a response. The initiation of serial associative cognition illustrates that while all hypothetical thinking involves Analytic Mind, not all the actions of Analytic Mind involve hypothetical thinking. Serial associative cognition is somewhat shallow thinking, "cognition that is not rapid and parallel such as TASS processes, but is nonetheless inflexibly locked into an associative mode that takes as its starting point a model of the world that is *given* to the subject" (Stanovich, 2009a, p. 68). Serial associative cognition "is serial and analytic ... in style, but it relies on a single focal model that triggers all subsequent thought" (p. 70). Hypothetical thinking constitutes a vital *reasoning* function. The reflective and algorithmic processes of Analytic Mind each have a key function within this process. Hypothetical thinking is closely related to the notion of TASS override. The analytic system must take TASS-initiated tendencies toward behavior offline and replace them with a more appropriate response. Such better responses come from cognitive simulation where they may be tested; only if they survive that test will they be adopted.

A tripartite neurobehavioral decision theory

It is feasible, therefore, to propose an augmented model by incorporating MC and EASR as components of a level of processing superordinate to those of the impulsive and executive systems (Figure 5.5). This figure depicts two type 1 impulsive or TASS systems: the first comprises the state impulsivities that Bickel *et al.* (2012a) showed to be antipodal to components of the executive system; the second is composed of the two trait impulsivities, namely sensation-seeking and reward sensitivity, that are not linked antipodally to elements of the executive system. They are shown here as exerting modifying influences on the relationship between the state impulsive system and the executive system. This key relationship is shown by the bold arrow. The executive system exerts type 2 influence on this relationship which is modified also by the action of the type 2 Reflective system which promotes balance between the State Impulsive system and the executive system. The type 2 systems draw upon Working Memory, another element ascribed to the executive system in the original CNDS model (Figure 5.2) which has no antipodal complement in the Impulsive system for their operations. For this reason, it is shown separately from the type 1 and type 2 systems in Figure 5.5. The relationship between the state impulsive system and the

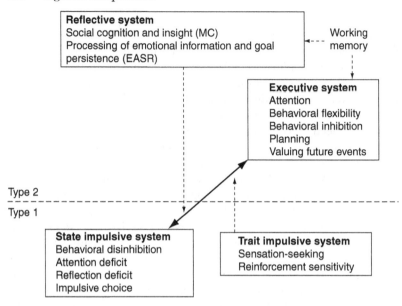

Figure 5.5 Metacognitive control of competing neurobehavioral decision systems.

executive system (bold arrow) is the immediate precursor of the degree of temporal discounting exhibited in the individual's behavior.

Individual differences in sensation–seeking and reward or reinforcement sensitivity, which may derive from the individual's neurophysiology and/or learning history, are posited as moderating the relationship between the impulsive and executive systems. Sensation–seeking is understood by Zuckerman (1979, 1994) as a preference for sensations and experiences that embody variation, novelty, and complexity, together with a willingness to incur physical and social risks in order to gain such experience. Reinforcement sensitivity reflects individual differences in susceptibility to reinforcing and aversive stimuli. Reinforcement sensitivity theory (Corr, 2008; Smillie, 2008; Box 5.2) relates propensity to behavior not only to the stimuli that have been consequential upon such behavior in the past but also to the mediating neurophysiological events that are the immediate precursors of responding.

Box 5.2 Reinforcement sensitivity theory

Reinforcement sensitivity theory (RST; Gray, 1982; Corr, 2008a; Smillie, 2008) reflects the excitatory (impulsivity) and inhibitory (executive) components of the CNBDS model but also permits us to make extensions relating to the expected behavior patterns that follow from each and the way in which individual differences may be summed up in terms of an ascription of personality types. There are several versions of RST. Here we focus on the fundamental elements of the version of the theory developed by Gray and McNaughton (2000), McNaughton and Corr (2004) and Corr (2008b). RST proposes that the basic behavioral processes of approach and avoidance are differentially associated with reinforcement and punishment, and that individuals show variations in their sensitivity to these stimuli. (Note that RST uses the term "reinforcement" to include both rewarding and punishing stimuli. As argued in Box I.1, this usage can be confusing in view of the confinement of "reinforcement" to instances in which consequential stimuli strengthen (i.e., increase) the rate at which a response is emitted and "punishment" to instances in which consequential stimuli reduce that rate, a usage common in behavior analysis in terms of which the CNBDS hypothesis is generally formulated. I have therefore tried to use the terms "reinforcement" and "punishment" consistently in their behavior analytical definitions. However, it is not always possible to do justice to RST by adhering to this rule and on occasion I have used "reward" rather than "reinforcement" where this is clearer.)

Approach is behavior under the control of positively reinforcing or appetitive stimuli and is mediated by neurophysiological reward circuitry that the theory categorizes as a Behavioral Approach System (BAS). The BAS consists in the basal ganglia, especially in the mesolimbic dopaminergic system that projects from the ventral tegmental area (VTA) to the ventral striatum (notably the nucleus accumbens) and mesocortical DA PFC (Smillie, 2008; cf. Pickering and Smillie, 2008). For recent discussion of the role of the striatum in decision-making and the processing of rewards, see Delgado and Tricomi (2011). Recent research demonstrating the role of this dopaminergic system in formulating reward prediction errors (RPEs; Box 4.2) is consonant with this understanding. In essence, unpredicted reward is followed by an increase in phasic dopaminergic activity whereas unpredicted non-reward is followed by a decrease and is unchanged when reward is entirely predicted (Schultz, 2000, 2002; Schultz and Dickinson, 2000; Schultz *et al.*, 2008). Unpredicted reward instantiates the activity of the BAS, therefore, and predicted reward maintains its operation. Moreover, BAS activity increases positive reward (pleasure) and motivates approach to reinforcing stimuli and stimuli that predict reinforcement. Such approach is characteristic of the extraverted personality; Corr (2008b, p. 10) sums up the personality type as "optimism, reward-orientation and impulsivity," and notes that it maps clinically on to addictive behaviors.

These emotional and motivational outcomes represent one pole of a continuum of individual differences that manifest differential BAS and Behavioral Inhibition System (BIS) reactions to stimuli. There is a corresponding though antithetical explanation of avoidance in RST. Avoidance is shaped by sensitivity to stimuli of punishment and threat and mediated by two bio-behaviorally based systems of emotion and motivation. The first of these, the Fight-Flight-Freeze system (FFFS), is triggered by aversive stimuli and the resulting feeling of fear, what Corr (2008b, p. 10) refers to as the "get me out of here emotion"; the FFFS's motivational output is a behavior pattern characterized as "defensive avoidance." However, if the consequential stimuli involved are mixed in terms of their emotional valence, then the BIS, which is generally involved in the resolution of goal conflict, is activated; in this case the emotional output is anxiety, the "watch out for danger" emotion Corr (2008b, p. 11) and the behavioral outputs are risk evaluation and cautiousness which are described as manifesting defensive approach. Hence, in summary, reward sensitivity leads to positive emotion and approach and a response pattern that is characterized as "extraversion" via behavioral observation or psychometric testing; by contrast, punishment sensitivity leads to negative emotion and avoidance and a personality characterized in terms of neuroticism (Smillie, 2008).

RST also relates the FFFS and BIS to specific neurophysiological systems (Figure 5.6). In the case of the FFFS this is the periaqueductal gray, which is implicated in acute or proximal threat, and the medial hypothalamus, amygdala, and interia cingulate cortex, implicated in distal threats. The BIS comprises the septo-hippocampal system and the amygdala. The emotional output of the FFFS is fearfulness while that of the BIS is anxiety. In either case, the emotional outputs are negative and most forms of RST relate this to neuroticism. The value of employing explanatory constructs referring to personality types such as extraversion and neuroticism is that they summarize individual differences in reinforcement sensitivity, adding both to the interpretation of behavior and its prediction in novel environments.

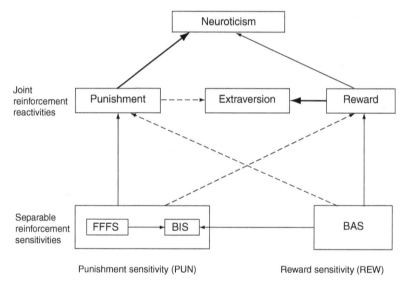

Figure 5.6 Summary of reinforcement sensitivity theory.

Source: Corr (2008a, pp. 1–43; 2008b)

Left to itself, Automatic Mind will act via the state impulsivities, in the absence of any influence of the behavioral inhibition, planning, and attention-maintaining tendencies of Algorithmic Mind: the result will be a failure to reflect upon the longer range outcomes of immediate behavior, so that the resulting behavior reflects a preference for SSR over LLR. Pursuit of this short-range interest can be overcome only by an intervention of Reflective Mind which initiates override of Automatic Mind via Algorithmic Mind.

Acting in response to Reflective Mind's initiation of override, Algorithmic Mind activates its executive functions that counter impulsivity (paying attention, drawing upon behavioral flexibility and disinhibition, planning and valuing future events) and which enable longer term interests to be explored and pursued. Override, which thus consists in the countering of the immediate short range of Automatic Mind by exercise of the executive functions, does not of itself result in the formulation of a plan for longer term behavior, however. Planning with foresight entails that Reflective Mind also initiates the decoupling of the representations for which Automatic Mind and Algorithmic Mind are responsible so that the simulation of alternative courses of action may take place. Simulation makes possible the hypothetical thinking that permits these alternatives to be generated and tested: an apparently satisfactory plan (one that is strategically consistent with long-term goals and capabilities) engenders a response from Reflective Mind such as the pursuit of a longer term objective in place of the impulsive action for which unencumbered Automatic Mind would have produced.

The trait impulsivities can promote or impede the operations of either Automatic Mind or Reflective Mind, working toward generation of either the short- or long-range interest. Trait impulsivities, sensation-seeking, and reward sensitivity are based on individual differences which are susceptible to learning history as well as the neurophysiological basis of behavior. How the trait impulsivity system works is debatable but it may be responsible for the *style* of thinking characteristic of or preferred by an individual, and his or her tendency toward an analytical or intuitive approach to problem-solving (Sadler-Smith, 2009). This would set limits to an individual's range of actual behaviors. Imagine a hypothetical range of behaviors from the most impulsive to the most executively controlled which contains all the actual ranges of behavior of which individuals in the population are capable. The actual range of any individual will be a subset of this. The extent of the actual subset that is the behavioral range of any individual will reflect his or her cognitive style, especially as it is determined by sensation-seeking and reinforcement sensitivity, the propensity of his or her behavior to be reinforced by highly arousing stimuli and immediate reward.

The tri-process configuration captures well the requirements of the CNDS model, especially in portraying those of its elements that have been shown to be antipodal, those that remain after the establishment of antipodality has been exhausted, and the relationships among them. The tri-process model comprises an Automatic Mind which responds rapidly to environmental circumstances (which captures well the imperatives of the impulsive system posited by the CNDS model). This Automatic Mind can, however, be checked by Algorithmic Mind (which includes the executive system that has precisely the antithetical imperatives required to counter the impulsive tendencies of Automatic Mind). Algorithmic Mind's countering the tendencies of Automatic Mind relies in turn upon its being directed by Reflective Mind to override Automatic Mind in order to inaugurated the decoupling of representations based on reality so that the procedure of simulation via hypothetical thought may occur. In simulation, alternative behaviors that may be enacted can be examined in terms of their outcomes in the short and long term. The information so gained is fed back to Reflective Mind which inaugurates action. Reflective Mind has additional functions which include monitoring environmental circumstances and being aware of the likely response of Automatic Mind to them in order to initiate decoupling and simulation. These are not the functions of Algorithmic Mind of the tri-process theory or the executive system of the CNDS model.

Metacognition and rationality

Styles of rationality

Both Algorithmic Mind and Reflective Mind play central roles in the exercise of reason, principally by bringing about the conditions required for *hypothetical thinking*. The capacity of type 2 systems to override Automatic Mind is essential to the decoupling that permits the inauguration of hypothetical thinking in which futures can be simulated in imagination; this is a prerequisite of the ability to substitute more appropriate responses for those dictated by the automaticity and immediacy on the basis of which TASS function. However, this involvement of type 2 systems is not inevitable. People may avoid this decoupling and the hypothetical thinking which it makes possible by dint of what Stanovich (2009b) terms *dysrationalia* which consists in "intelligent people taking injudicious actions or holding unjustified beliefs" (p. 12).

One source of dysrationalia – a problem of process – is that people are *cognitive misers*, choosing the less computationally demanding of two kinds of mental process (i.e., surrendering to Automatic Mind rather than engaging Algorithmic Mind to process information and solve problems). As a result, people do not practice fully disjunctive reasoning (i.e., they do not consider all the possibilities before reaching a conclusion). We also approach problems from our personal perspective, and since "every way of seeing is a way of not seeing," we exhibit a *my-side bias*, an incomplete view of how things stand.

Another source of dysrationalia – this time a problem of content – is that people exhibit *mindware gaps*: they do not possess the specific knowledge, rules, and strategies required to think rationally. Mindware refers to things that need to be retrieved from memory to solve problems: the ability to understand logic, risk, scientific inference, and so on.

Where it is engaged, however, the function of Reflective Mind is encapsulated in its emitting an appeal for the initiation of cognitive simulation or hypothetical reasoning that provides alternative behavioral options to those which would result from autonomous thinking and unreflective reaction, options that are based on consideration of long-range outcomes of behavior. These operations ensure the cognitive decoupling that permits inhibition of any confusion between representations of imagined states with representations of real world occurrences. In short, decoupling prevents the contamination of the hypothetically constructed future scenarios, including the goals they specifically assume, that may occur through intermingling with current events and the goals they entail. In the context of the examples of akrasia and addiction with which we are here concerned, it is essential for the rational decision-maker to be able to separate short-range goals and their probable consequences from the longer range goals that could be pursued as alternatives, and *their* likely outcomes. It is necessary to represent these competing goals in a way that keeps them clearly separated, especially as the time approaches when the first goal may be achieved. If this separation were not possible, it is conceivable that the decision-maker would confuse the consequences of a goal that is about to become realizable with the recently simulated outcomes of a longer range objective.

The necessity in the case of intertemporal valuation is to keep the two simulated hypothetical futures distinct from one another *and* from the decision-maker's representations of his or her current behavior (primary representations) *and* from representations in memory of previous activities and their after-effects. This entails high-level cognitive control: indeed, high-level metacognitive control. Stanovich (2011) notes that this "quarantining of representations" (Nichols and Stich, 2003) requires the representation of not only a series of states of affairs but also of *attitudes* toward each state of affairs. An important element in the attitude one projects toward each such set of circumstances in a simulated future (or series of simulated futures, depending on the complexity of the decision) is the evaluation of each of these imagined situations in terms of its contribution to an overall goal or set of goals. Intertemporal valuation also makes demands on the decision-maker to avoid cognitive miserliness and to draw upon the appropriate mindware. Costly cognitive effort can be economized by not bothering to make the comparison between alternative courses of action, not creating competing outcomes in imagination, not having to evaluate them, not getting involved in computations of behavioral effects and their meanings – in short, not deciding but reacting. Techniques of scenario creation, evaluation, and choosing mean drawing upon the appropriate knowledge, arithmetical techniques, understanding of risk, and past experience and its significance. These components of the necessary mindware may simply not be available or the individual may not expend the necessary mental effort in their recall and application. To make appropriate intertemporal evaluations is cognitively expensive. The underlying requirement is for a mental apparatus that engenders a timely call for, and accomplishment of, decoupling which in turn permits the hypothetical thinking upon which the contemplation and selection of alternative futures are contingent.

Decoupling is essential to working with the primary representation without compromising it with representations that feature cognitive simulations of future events. The mental operations that inhere in picoeconomic strategies for overcoming temptation similarly demand this capacity to disconnect depictions of future states of affairs, namely that which will obtain if the present course of behavior is continued and that which will result if some forestalling stratagem is enacted. Perhaps the most cognitively demanding of all, bundling requires two entire sequences of behaviors and their reinforcers and punishers to be conceived, the separate values of these outcomes to be assessed, their separate gross significance to be ascertained, and a comparison of the separate aggregations of worth to be compared with one another and with a superordinate goal. But the manipulations of intentionality entailed by the other picoeconomic strategies are also highly demanding. Precommitment, control of attention, and preparation of emotion all require similar faculties of looking ahead imaginatively to a future that may not resemble any previously encountered situation, foreseeing behavior patterns and their entailments, comparative appraisal, and decision-making. Now, engaging in all of these relies upon a willingness to avoid cognitive miserliness by actively imagining and computing. Each calls upon mindware in terms of mental techniques and appreciation of the import of hypothetical outcomes.

The transformation of a signal that one has lost a bet into an understanding that one is growing in skill or has even already accomplished a minor goal which foretells winning a jackpot makes demands on such imagination but it is not a behavior pattern that reflects rationality so much as cognitive miserliness and lack of the appropriate mindware. The tendency to continue playing, even doing so more intensively by gambling higher stakes, playing harder and longer, suggests an unwillingness or an inability to decouple, to hypothesize a different future, to give rein to the capabilities of Algorithmic Mind and Reflective Mind to suggest different goals and different ways of achieving them. It may equally reflect an inability to compute the odds, to appreciate the impact of current practices and their imaginable alternatives.

These considerations are germane to akrasia and addiction in general because a key component of both is a tendency toward hyperbolic discounting which exaggerates immediate values at the expense of those which call for patience. The unwillingness or inability to decouple and consider analytically means that intertemporal evaluation will act to encourage the pursuit of immediacy, with the consequence of incurring longer range deleterious effects that may have been avoided. The strategies that build on a successful re-evaluation of future results are available and can change lives. The acceptance of distorted perspectives on one's behavior and its effects may be overcome by the pursuit of such strategies.

What is evident following these cognitive interpretations is that we cannot conceive of the individual's activity as a result of metacognitive deliberation as of the same kind as the *behavior* that can be traced entirely to reinforcement contingencies or the responses that occur automatically in the presence of appropriate stimuli. Cognitive explanation enables us to conceive of metacognitively inspired behavior as *action*. This does not alter the ontological status of the activity; rather, it alters the methodological perspective assumed for its explanation.

Cognitive level and cognitive style

Stanovich (2011) differentiates Algorithmic Mind and Reflective Mind in terms of individual differences in cognitive ability and thinking dispositions. Cognitive abilities index the efficiency of Algorithmic Mind while thinking dispositions or cognitive styles refer to the way in which Reflective Mind functions. Thinking dispositions are concerned with "beliefs, belief structure, and, importantly, attitudes toward forming and changing beliefs" (Stanovich, 2011, p. 35). They also encapsulate an individual's set of goals including their hierarchical organization. Thinking dispositions embody individual differences in intellectual style which are often expressed prior to making a decision or reaching a conclusion. These may include the scope of information search, the examination of alternative perspectives, thinking deeply, establishing options on the basis of available evidence, evaluating the consequences of an action before taking it, and examining fine shades of meaning and their implications as opposed to dogmatism in resolving problems. After enumerating such sources of individual difference in cognitive style, Stanovich (2011, p. 36) sums up: "In short, individual differences in thinking dispositions are assessing variation in people's goal management, epistemic values, and epistemic self-regulation – differences in the operation of the reflective mind."

The kind of rationality required for the consideration of alternative futures in a manner that avoids cognitive miserliness and which can draw upon relevant mindware to advantage is exemplified by a number of tests of reasoning skill, exemplified by the so-called "Linda problem." This has been widely discussed in the literature and I will give only a synopsis of the main consideration. A short account is presented of a woman who is described as young, intelligent, willing to speak her mind, and single. She is a philosophy graduate and as a student was politically active. The respondent is then asked to assign probabilities to two statements about her: for example, (1) that she is a librarian, and (2) that she is a librarian and a committed feminist. There is a tendency for respondents, even those who are highly intelligent and educated, to assign a higher probability to (2) than to (1). However, it is statistically more likely that a woman is a librarian than that she is both a librarian and an active feminist. Not all librarians are active feminists. The capacity to assign probabilities accurately is not as widespread as might be imagined: most of us find it easier to draw unsubstantiated conclusions from the meager information provided than to reason logically.

The tendency to default to Automatic Mind rather than seek to overcome cognitive miserliness by engaging in type 2 processing is exemplified by the following problem (Levesque, 1986, 1989): "John is looking at Susan but Susan is looking at Fred. John is married but Fred is single. Is a married person looking at an unmarried person?" The proffered responses are "Yes," "No," and "It is impossible to say from the information given." Most respondents select the third, regardless of their intelligence. This common response, presumably the result of drawing the automatic inference that it is impossible to give an answer without further data, is an example of cognitive miserliness and unwillingness to draw upon mindware resources. If type 2 processing is engaged, however, the solution is not difficult. View the situation from Susan's point of view. Either she is married or she is not. If she is not, then a married person, John, is looking at an unmarried person. If she is, then she as a married person is looking at an unmarried person. The problem is resolvable by the application of resources that are generally available; yet most of us, upon initial contact with the problem, immediately default to the position that avoids further thought.

These aspects of reasoning ability are not the matters that IQ tests assess. The intelligence thus measured is important of course, and essential in ensuring that the operations of Algorithmic Mind can occur, particularly the decoupling necessary to ensure the opportunity for cognitive rehearsal. A certain minimal level of intellectual capacity and ability is required for both the initiation and the sustenance of these operations, but this is not the sole component of the rationality required for appropriate responding to particular situations. Intelligence as measured by the standard tests indexes cognitive level or ability, whereas the elements of qualitative intellectual differences in creativity, problem-solving, and decision-making to which Stanovich is referring as thinking dispositions are cognitive *styles*. Some consideration of cognitive style can elucidate the distinction between the kinds of rationality that Stanovich discusses as differences in the functioning of Reflective Mind and those captured by intelligence tests.

Among the numerous conceptions and measures of cognitive style, Kirton's (2003) adaption–innovation theory is of especial relevance to the individual differences reflected in sensation-seeking and reinforcement sensitivity, which figure in the tripartite cognitive theory. Moreover, it has been extensively used in the contexts of management and consumer behavior (Foxall, 1994, 1995; Foxall and James, 2009). *Cognitive style* refers to a person's persistent preferred *manner* of making decisions, the characteristic *way* in which he or she approaches problems, information gathering and processing, and the kinds of solution they are likely to work toward and attempt to implement. As such, it is orthogonal to cognitive level as manifested by measures of intelligence or cognitive capacity. Kirton (2003) proposes that individuals' cognitive styles can be arrayed on a continuum the polar extremes of which denote a predisposition toward "doing better" (which characterizes the extreme adapter) to that toward "doing differently" (the extreme innovator). Adaption–innovation is measured by the Kirton Adaption–Innovation Inventory (KAI), which evinces high levels of reliability and validity; KAI scores correlate with a number of personality variables including extraversion, sensation-seeking, and impulsivity. General population samples indicate that trait adaption–innovation is approximately normally distributed and general population scores, including of course those of managers, are arrayed over a limited continuum which falls within the theoretical spectrum of scores posited by adaption–innovation theory. As is suggested by the normal distribution of the trait, most consumers exhibit a mixture of adaptive and innovative tend-encies; they are not, for the most part, extreme in their behaviors, though some have scores toward the extremes of the bipolar construct of adaption–innovation. In the present context, however, it is the extreme cognitive styles and extreme modes of consumer choice that are of specific interest. Box 5.3 suggests the neurophysiological basis of adaption–innovation.

Box 5.3 Neurophysiological basis of adaption–innovation

The neurophysiological basis of adaption–innovation is of interest in placing this theory of cognitive style within the context of the temporal discounting/preference reversal framework which has been a guiding feature of this investi-gation. Evolutionary logic suggests that social animals are motivated by two counterposed tendencies: first, to compete with conspecifics for limited resources such as food, sexual partners, and territory upon which individual survival and biological fitness rely; second, to find satisfaction in the company of conspecifics which requires a degree of cooperation and conformity (van der Molen, 1994). These tendencies suggest biological bases for utilitarian and informational reinforcement, respectively. Individual differences in their influ-ence may also reflect predispositions to seek higher or lower levels of each kind of reinforcement and an overall pattern of reinforcement that is optimal for the sensation-seeking and reinforcement sensitivities of the individual. The person-ality characteristics which reflect these motivational forces are, in turn, the highly intercorrelated traits of:

> self-will, thing-orientation, individualism and innovative creativity on the one pole and compliance, person-orientation, sociability, conformity and creative adaptiveness on the other. Individuals differ from one another as far as the balance between these polarities [is] concerned. This variation between individuals must have genetic components.
>
> (Van der Molen, 1994, p. 140)

Drawing upon the work of Cloninger (1986, 1987), van der Molen (1994, pp. 150–152; Skinner and Fox-Francoeur, 2013) makes a strong case for the evolutionary and genetic components of adaption–innovation. Cloninger's "novelty-seeking" and "reward dependence" dimensions of personality are especially pertinent. The former is driven predominantly by the neurotransmit-ter dopamine which manifests in behavior that seeks to alleviate boredom and monotony, to deliver the sense of exhilaration and excitement that is generally termed "sensation-seeking" (Zuckerman, 1994); these individuals demonstrate a tendency to be "impulsive, quick-tempered and disorderly ... quickly dis-tracted or bored ... easily provoked to prepare for flight or fight" (van der Molen, 1994, p. 151). "Reward-dependent" individuals are, in contrast, highly dependent on "social reward and approval, sentiment and succor"; they are "eager to help and please others, persistent, industrious, warmly sympathetic, sentimental, and sensitive to social cues, praise and personal succour, but also able to delay gratification with the expectation of eventually being socially rewarded" (ibid.). These individuals' behavior is strongly controlled by the monoamine neuromodulator norepinephrine.

Which of these bundles of attributes manifests in behavior that marks out some individuals as leaders depends entirely on the demands of the managerial situation: retail banking, relying for the most part upon the implementation of standard operating procedures, may have a natural tendency to encourage and reward those behaviors that reflect an adaptive cognitive style; pharmaceutical companies, whose technological, demand, and competitive environments reflect a greater dynamism than is ordinarily the norm for retail banking, requires for a much larger part of its activities the presence of individuals whose cognitive and creative styles are predominantly innovative. Investment banking which is expected to reflect a large adaptively creative style of operation but which attracts innovators is in danger of becoming the kind of "casino banking" that has been so deleterious to both corporate and general social welfare in the past decade. But the inability of an organization to achieve the right cognitive and creative accommodation to its environment will predictably culminate in catastrophe. For the retail bank whose leaders fail to perceive and respond appropriately to the changing international competition in high street banking, the pharmaceutical firm that becomes overinvolved in the development and marketing of drugs that are novel in the extreme, and for the investment bank that overemphasizes innovative creativity to the point where reckless decisions are made, catastrophe is equally probable. Predominant organizational climate, adaptive or innovative, can be disastrous if either of these cognitive styles comes to predominate.

These behavioral styles are remarkably consonant with the cognitive styles described by Kirton (2003). Their prevalence and likely genetic basis is borne out by their consistency with the reinforcement sensitivity theory described above (Corr, 2008a; see also Eysenck, 2006), though the terminology may vary.

The behavior of the extreme adapter is generally characterized by a tendency toward caution in decision-making and problem-solving, use of tried-and-tested methods, efficiency, rule-conformity, and limited quantitative creativity manifesting in the generation of relatively few, workable solutions. The extreme innovator is, in contrast, more outlandish in selecting decisions, more likely to propose novel solutions to problems (many of which are impracticable), less efficient, and more likely to modify or even break the rules.

In contradistinction to innovators, adapters are typically prudent, using tried-and-tested methods, cautious, apparently impervious to boredom, and unwilling to bend, let alone break, the rules. They seek the kind of efficiency that manifests in accomplishing known tasks more effectively. An extremely adaptive cognitive style suggests hyperactivity of the executive system coupled with hypoactivity of the impulsive system. Those aspects of the executive system that involve ToM, the observation of social conventions, metacognition, and some facets of behavioral flexibility would be adapter characteristics that would confirm this categorization. The tentative conclusion is that adapters would cope well and perform advantageously when involved in the intellectual, long-term, detailed thinking that strategic planning requires. The downside to their overinvolvement in this kind of decision-making derives from the demands that strategic planning and commitment sometimes exert upon the ability to undertake "outside-the-paradigm" thinking. Such demands are likely to arise only occasionally but they are equally likely to arise at times of crisis and to benefit most from the kind of thinking which characterizes a more innovative cognitive style.

In contradistinction to adapters, innovators typically proliferate ideas that require the relatively radical change that can modify strategic direction, the modification of goals and goal hierarchies, the range of behaviors in which they desire to engage. At its extreme however, this cognitive style suggests hypoactivity of the executive system, with concomitant hyperactivity of the impulsive system. The impulsive system is geared to the rapid identification and evaluation of opportunities and threats, the capacity to envisage far-reaching, possibly disruptive, change which, in refocusing the entire strategic scope of the individual's behavior pattern can lead to upheaval in behavioral direction. To the extent that these are innovator traits, it is clear that decision-making needs to be balanced by an emphasis on adaptive traits which supply the capacity for sounder decision-making and for the acquisition of coping skills. Both of these tactics require that extreme innovators learn to appreciate the rationale behind the adaptive mode of problem-solving, which they will otherwise typically perceive as too slow-moving to be appropriate to a situation perceived as requiring a rapid response. More extreme adapters would correspondingly see the behavior of innovators as too outlandish to be consonant with their values. Innovators supply strengths to decision-making tasks: they are more likely to think outside the paradigm within which a problem has arisen, to be unconfined by the tried-and-tested methods currently in place, and to take risks. These can be relevant behaviors when the individual genuinely faces uncertainties that require radical strategic rethinking, but innovators may be unsuited to more short-term decision-making which requires the skills of prudence and caution which are the hallmark of the adapter.

There is no absolute right and wrong when it comes to the exercise of cognitive style; either may be appropriate or inappropriate to a specific situation. A situation that calls for strategic thinking and planning requires the adventurous outlook of the innovator, tempered by the prudence of the adapter. Unreconstructed adapters are likely to display a dysfunctional emphasis on caution in such situations at the expense of strategic decision-making. Insofar as situations demanding strategic decisions are unprogrammed, they require the inputs of innovative traits; a predominance of adaptive traits in such situations will engender imbalance. More routine decision-making calls for the efficient involvement of the adaptive cognitive style, tempered by the more outward-looking tendency of innovative traits. The presence of extremely innovative traits, leading to the assumption of risks in the pursuit of short-term benefits, is likely to interfere with the setting of long-term goals and the strategic planning and decision-making they require.

However, the adaption–innovation theory subtly captures aspects of behavior that are not apparent from more simplistic attempts to predict behavior psychometrically. An example is studies of consumer initiation of new behavior patterns, for instance, such as the purchase of new brands or products, in which consumers scoring innovatively on KAI were expected to exhibit higher levels of initiation. In practice, it was found that the consumers who displayed the lowest volumes of novel adoption were uninvolved adapters; those exhibiting significantly higher but moderate levels of initiation were innovators, regardless of level of involvement; the surprising result was that those responsible for the highest levels of initiation were involved adapters (Foxall, 1988, 1994).

The implication is that adapters and innovators will bring different thinking dispositions to the problems we have considered. In all three cases, individuals whose cognitive style is distinctly adaptive are more likely to act with caution, considering carefully the full range of options available to them in terms of the costs that will be imposed by their adoption and the benefits likely to accrue as a result. They are likely, when valuing intertemporally available rewards, to disengage from current concerns, and to calculate as far as possible the outcomes of the scenarios for further action that present themselves. Similar skills are required for the contemplation of the alternative future behaviors and their consequences that arise in the entertainment and prosecution of picoeconomic strategies for change. Finally, adapters may be more likely than innovators to recognize the appearance of two identical symbols as indicative of a loss and of the cognitive simulation necessary to consider alternative behavior patterns such as not continuing to play. Innovators may be more likely to exhibit cognitive miserliness, jumping to the conclusion that they are on their way to a major win, not because they lack the intelligence to know otherwise, but because they are more creatures of the moment. Similarly, they may fail to employ mindware resources, not because they are lacking but because, for them, drawing upon their skill and knowledge bases may be costly and interruptive of other behaviors.

There are three important considerations in judging these remarks. First, the likely reactions of adapters and innovators to these situations are speculative, drawing upon generalizations based, admittedly, on extensive investigations, but not specifically related to akrasia and addiction. They therefore invite the appropriate empirical research. As has been pointed out, most individuals do not exhibit an extreme cognitive style: their responses to situational demands are tempered by tendencies contrary to their predominant style; but we are interested here in extreme behavior and these interpretations are permissible so long as they are treated as hypotheses. Second, the main point is that thinking dispositions will influence the capacity for exercising the kind of reasoning that can bring executive functioning to the fore and forestall the deleterious effects of behaving on impulse. Cognitive styles will, in some manner or other, influence individuals' manner of processing information to arrive at decisions and this is germane to our understanding of the cognitive architecture within which future behavior is imagined, implemented, and maintained. Finally, behaving either adaptively or innovatively because of one's inherent cognitive style is of less import in assessing their behavior than considerations that arise in connection with coping. Even distinctly adaptive and distinctly innovative individuals can learn to cope with the situations in which they find themselves, by coming to understand the virtues of the opposite cognitive style in achieving their goals. If the time and circumstances are not opportune for acting in accord with their preferred style, they are able to behave in ways appropriate to the situation, while pursuing a longer term strategy that will enable them to alter their behavior pattern when the situation changes (Kirton, 2003). Hence, we are not slaves of our thinking dispositions but, depending upon our abilities to exhibit coping behaviors, can to some degree tailor our tendencies to circumstance.

Metacognition in intertemporal valuation

Behavioral continuity and discontinuity

Intertemporal valuation requires heuristic rationality when either of the instances of behavioral discontinuity considered in Chapter 4 arises: namely, (1) *addiction–abstinence discontinuity* which entails a move from substance abuse or other addictive behavior to abstinence, and (2) *addiction–aversion continuity* in which the individual persists in a pattern of behavior the consequences of which are increasingly hurtful. Intertemporal valuation actually involves the *re*-evaluation of alternative and competing behaviors and, especially, of their effects. The deliberative action entailed is metacognitive because it is the contemplation of the cognitions that have controlled behavior in the past and of those that will in future exert a governing role in decision-making. It is also a contemplation of how the individual will *feel* (1) if the course of behavior is not altered (perhaps shame), and (2) if the change is successfully made (perhaps pride or self-esteem). These felt emotions are, respectively, the ultimate informational rewards and punishers that will become somatic markers for the guidance of further decision-making, and thus influence the probability of similar behaviors being enacted in the future. But we are concerned at the present stage with the contemplation of these alternatives leading to a decision to change or maintain a pattern of behavior.

(1) involves switching from a pattern of behavior that has to date been under TASS control, perhaps habitually, in favor of the adoption of a course of action that is under the metacognitive control of Algorithmic Mind and Reflective Mind. More accurately than the word *adoption* here would be *trial*, since the individual can do no more at this stage than plan the inauguration of *what may become* a new behavior pattern. Such a change cannot be explained in the absence of clear modification of the contingencies of reinforcement and/or a

profound and unusual neurophysiological change in the individual. The objective contingencies have not altered, however, and even if the individual has received or self-generated rules of behavior, these can only be understood in terms of intentionality, since their very form entails aboutness. For the switch from the SSR to the LLR is effected even though there is no learning history for selecting LLR, no experience, or knowledge to call upon. Any change in the individual's behavior from repeated choice of the immediate reward to that of abstinence requires cognition, the positing of a deliberative process that leads to a change in behavior. The person's behavior must be interpreted as his or her having "decided" to change his or her behavior and inaugurate a new behavior pattern not previously enacted on the basis that he or she believes this will lead to superior outcomes. This intentional interpretation requires *something like* the disengagement of his or her behavior from the immediate sway of available reinforcers via the decoupling of TASS control, permitting a series of cognitive rehearsals in which hypotheticality can be given rein, new scenarios for future action worked out, and one selected and implemented. These are the logical steps required for the new behavior to come into being, regardless of whether one accepts the tripartite model as the sole depiction of them.

In (2), there is acquiescence in a pattern of behavior that once was gratifying, positively rewarded by pleasure, arousal, and dominance but which now has the effect of generating the antithetical emotional feelings and yet is not discontinued. We can describe this well in intentional language as the progression from the *binge/intoxication* stage that is positively reinforced, to the *withdrawal/negative affect* and eventually the *preoccupation/anticipation* stages (Koob *et al.*, 2014) with their negative emotional tone; we can also adduce reasons for this in terms of incentive salience which has replaced *liking* the drug with *wanting* or *craving* it (Berridge and Robinson, 1993). It is easy to imagine that there is no room here for cognition in the narrow sense of intellectualization – any "decision" to continue is surely unprogrammed to the point where it is unworthy to call it a decision at all – but that is to ignore the instances where change is certainly contemplated and worked toward, even it is not always efficacious (e.g., Vohs and Baumeister, 2011).

The personal level of exposition

At the level of intentional interpretation, we have ascribed desires and beliefs (including perceptions) to the individual to account for his or her behavior. The justification for this interpretation lies in the specification of the mental operations that would have to be going on here. The deliberation entailed in valuation of the SSR versus the LLR requires suspension of cognitive miserliness and the drawing upon mindware in the form of a series of beliefs that have been acquired through experience and prior deliberation. Thus the initial intentional interpretation of *intertemporal evaluation* which was arrived at in the argument that it was a cognitive operation is now cashed out in terms of the theory of mental processing that makes it feasible.

Delimitation of behavioral interpretation

This seems to be an area that behaviorists avoid by observing and describing only the observed behaviors – "Ego selects SSR," "Ego selects LLR," "Ego is valuing this or that." But a change in behavior can be explained only if the individual is conceived of as engaging in the mental representation of their past behavior and its consequences, and projecting mentally into their future behavior and its consequences. The only kind of valuation going on is mental. Behavioral interpretation is unjustified because it cannot point to the stimulus conditions required to stand up to its depiction. The intentional interpretation is a default position reached in view of this poverty of the stimulus (Chomsky, 1959); it is not amenable to direct empirical test owing to the unobservable nature of its variables. Rather, it must be cashed out in terms of a cognitive interpretation.

Stanovich (2011) contrasts intelligence with rationality, the former encapsulated in the idea of being smart and consisting in what IQ tests measure, the latter to "tendencies to take or not take judicious actions, make sensible decisions, or behave appropriately to the situation" (p. 15). Fully disjunctive thinking requires one to override being a cognitive miser, to avoid the superficial decision-making that results from shallow information processing. The cognitive miser relies on salient cues because they are easily processed, a tendency that has obvious parallels with the phenomenon of incentive salience, since elements in the immediate consumer behavior setting will be primed to initiate strong craving. The cognitive miser who is faced with having to value an SSR and a corresponding LLR will look for clues in the immediate environment rather than in longer term considerations. The latter are, by definition, not to hand; taking them into consideration demands applying oneself mentally to them, making an intellectual investment in summoning them to mind, appraising them, comparing them with the SSR, and making a choice. It is so much easier to confine consideration to the known outcomes of selecting this familiar choice and plumping for it again. In fact, behavior that is determined by the TASS operations need be preceded by no conscious deliberation at all. It is the *decision to engage in deliberation* that is the costly first stage of an effortful consideration of alternatives. Mindware gaps are, moreover, inevitable in the individual who has always chosen SSR over LLR: having no experience of being patient and reaping the larger reward, they have not formulated rules for acquiring the habit of persistence and for coping with the reception of larger payoffs. They do not have ready-to-hand heuristics for these skills. This is not a matter of intelligence; lack of the specific mindware that is prerequisite to solving particular problems can handicap even the brightest. Many highly intelligent people read their horoscopes and some believe them.

Metacognition in picoeconomic strategizing

Ordinarily, we assume that if the S1 system/Impulsive system is operating without conscious control, it will immediately motivate precipitate behavior in response to environmental stimuli. Only if the S2/executive system operates to forestall it will more considered behavior arise. At its most basic, the interaction between the two decision systems will require the specification of the options available in the form of mental representation (Figure 5.7).

Whether there ever actually exists at level (A) a single short-range interest (SRI) and a corresponding long-range interest (LRI) that can be specified as objectively in life as in the laboratory is questionable. The behavior of laboratory animals who have known no life other than service to operant psychology may be attributed to the contingencies of reinforcement that have faced them since their introduction to the experimental situation. Their learning histories may be known fully and their behavior in similar contexts may, therefore, be accurately predicted. Even human beings in laboratory settings are not so amenable to the goals of science, since their earlier learning history cannot be ascertained, let alone controlled by the investigator, and their current behavior may well be influenced by their earlier experience. The individual who is acting in the course of a busy lifestyle is even further from enacting a behavior pattern that can be unambiguously attributed to operant schedules. As discussed in Chapter 4, an interpretation of this behavior in terms of cognitive functioning is inevitable. It follows that such an individual must form a representation of what he or she thinks will be the situation facing him or her in the future, the behavior it will encourage or inhibit, and the likely consequences of that behavior, at level (B). The formation of these representations requires perceptual awareness, memory, and imagination. The representations so formed provide the basic cognition; what the individual does with it mentally, the metacognition, at level (C). In order to act consciously, he or she must perceive the nature of the options likely to be available, weigh them in terms of their consequences, weight them comparatively in relationship to his or her goal structure, and then act. This is decision-making. The initial act may simply be a matter of taking steps toward more concrete behavior, namely preparation.

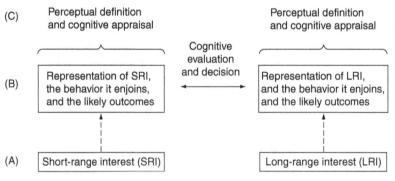

Figure 5.7 Metacognitive analysis of SRI and LRI.

It is difficult to envision an entirely bottom-up approach to the explanation of akrasia on the basis of the interaction of the SRI and LRI conceived of objectively as in level (A). Each interest is the result of a particular reinforcement history and its strength is determined by the pattern of reinforcement and punishment that has accompanied it in the past. However, since this pattern cannot be known empirically by the would-be explicator of an individual's behavior, this is not a matter settled by extensional behavioral science; rather, it is an informed speculation, feasible and plausible but no more than an interpretation in terms of observed behavior in a highly circumscribed context, that of the operant chamber. If this is designated a bottom-up approach to the explanation of behavior, we must recognize it as an abstraction rather than as a concrete fact based on observations of the three-term contingency in operation.

To describe the interests as sub-personal is against the spirit of Intentional Behaviorism. If there is an agent or self, there is only one: the person as a whole, or at an analytical level the attributes that must be ascribed at the personal level. The interests are not sub-personal; they are a matter of the whole person considering first this option, then that, then weighing the two together. This is all done by a single individual, self, or agent. The interests may have unique utility functions but only one interest can be *followed* (i.e., behaviorally) at one time and the utility function is that of the person; therefore he or she is the agent. There is only one person, one decision-maker, one agent.

Metacognitive rehearsal in picoeconomic strategizing

The picoeconomic strategies proposed by Ainslie all involve metacognitive operations. *Precommitment* requires the capacity to envision the state of affairs that would obtain if no attempt was made to restrain one's behavior, to predict the effect of so doing, to weigh the difference in outcome that would probably be the result of placing oneself under the obligation to behave differently, and so on. There is a precommitment to forgo immediate pleasure, which is almost certain, in favor of a potential larger gain that is more precarious simply because of its being delayed. This entails considerable imagination on the part of the decider. *Precommitment* which involves the manipulation of the pattern of reinforcement that each of two separate outcomes will engender also demands an ability to perceive future scenarios, to recognize the changes that one will need to make in one's physical and social surroundings and the avoidances these will facilitate. Both the abstracting and the devising require disengagement from TASS, cognitive rehearsal, hypothetical thinking. The individual's desires and beliefs are necessary to inaugurate this process and provide the raw materials for it.

Control of attention similarly requires a capacity to project oneself into a different scenario from that which would otherwise obtain, to envision the consequences of being in that situation, not in isolation but in direct evaluative comparison with the circumstances that would be the case. It requires an emotional capacity, that of feeling the difference in affective texture between the situations, perhaps as a result of somatic markers activated by thoughts of each, the possibility of empathizing with one's future self in each case, and of making a judgment not just between the outcomes of each but between the shame of the easier option, compared with the immediate pleasure it will bring, compared with the pride of the more strenuous option, compared with the pain of waiting. The comparison involves imagining what each will feel like and judging not only between *pride and shame* (the continuum shown in Figure 3.7), but between *shame + gratification and enjoyment* versus *pride + patience*. These are considerable tasks, and cognitively demanding. It is difficult to conceive of how the behaviorist would describe this state of affairs: there is no closely observed learning history to appeal to, only the dogma of a contingency-shaped and rule-governed past that is not empirically available or a vain reliance upon some sort of action at a distance to account for a stimulus field that cannot be sensuously apprehended and which almost certainly does not exist. The sole alternative is to employ intentional language and hence intentional interpretation.

Preparation of emotion is all the more demanding of metacognitive skills, since it is that part of preparing for the future which relies on representations of one's future feelings; moreover, it depends on an ability to forestall the pleasant emotions that accrue from the acceptance of a more immediate gratification in favor of a longer term and less dependable pleasure if one waits. It entails also enacting in imagination the feelings that would accompany the optimization of a pattern of utilitarian and informational reinforcement if the SSR were chosen, including the immediate self-esteem of having one's own way, seemingly being able to judge one's own best interests, or in any case to act as one "chooses." This has to be actively compared in consciousness with the imagined outcomes of sobriety, both functional and symbolic. The problem is that an akrasic, let alone an addict, may have little in the way of a learning history of selecting the delayed option to influence this projective process. We must not be pessimistic: people do change their thinking and are therefore capable of metacognitive control of their actions.

Bundling is metacognitive control *par excellence*: bringing forward in time two streams of reward so that they can be contrasted and making a choice between them. This means temporally advancing two streams of reward that exist only in consciousness, cumulating each stream, and making an informed comparison. This is Ainslie's view of willpower. If I eat salad rather than fruitcake, not once but always over an extended period of months or possibly years, I will realize my dream of weighing less, being fitter, living longer. I will accomplish not only the utilitarian benefits that inhere in feeling better and being more active but also the informational benefits of my family's approval and my own self-esteem. Is this sufficient to engender the *resolve* to change my behavior in this way? Is the resolve sufficient to ensure that I *can* change my behavior in this way? All of these considerations entail the cognitive ability to represent alternative courses of action, alternative utilitarian and informational patterns of reinforcement, and the emotional rewards they bring in their wake. I am not concerned with whether these strategies work, only in the cognitive operations necessary to make them feasible.

The picoeconomic strategies proposed by Ainslie as means of surmounting akrasia suggest an ability to overcome cognitive miserliness and to draw upon the necessary mindware. We have established that there is no learning history to account for this behavior; we have therefore to propose intentional precursors of the choices made, in thought and/or in action; and we have to undergird this intentional interpretation with a structured cognitive method of functioning which will enable these intellectual and/or behavioral events to take place. Ainslie's description of the processes involved provides the intentional interpretation. The enabling cognitive structure is proposed by the tripartite model. In order to consider adopting one of these picoeconomic strategies, the individual must be capable of taking TASS offline and engaging in considerable bouts of cognitive rehearsal so that they can imagine and appraise the outcomes of continuing in the current behavior pattern, project themselves into performing an alternative, and imagine and appraise the possible consequences in which that alternative behavior might eventuate. There is also a need to assess the probabilities of the consequences of both kinds of behavior and to weigh these in comparative evaluation. We noted in Chapter 3 that some people are apparently unable to undertake the mental deliberations inherent in bundling (Ross *et al.*, 2008); we now propose that this is presumably because either Reflective Mind's function of initiating a call to decouple is absent from their repertoire, or because Algorithmic Mind's capacity to undertake and, especially, to sustain decoupling prevents the hypothetical thinking upon which bundling relies.

Precommitment, control of attention, and *preparation of emotion* all depend on a repudiation of cognitive miserliness, the engagement of Algorithmic Mind and the action of Reflective Mind to override TASS. The latter is not a conscious matter.

Bundling is especially demanding in all of these respects, since it requires the ability to cumulate two streams of potential benefit, the larger but later of which may never have been encountered as actual behavioral consequences and of which the individual thus has no learning history. Imagining what these consequences would be like if they were received is a matter not simply of intellectual accumulation of imagined events; it is a matter of assessing them by emotional means. Rolls's theory of emotion, the SMH, the BPM shame–pride continuum, are all relevant here. The emphasis the SMH places on the evocation of feelings by thoughts of possible future actions is central but, as has been pointed out, the individual will have very limited learning history upon which this operation may draw. The feelings experienced will therefore be based on generalized previous behavior and its outcomes, requiring an extension capacity for imagining the affective responses that would be contingent upon a particular course of action.

The near-miss

It is more problematic to configure the cognition involved in the near-miss phenomenon in terms of the tripartite model because the behavior results from the omission of the call for an execution of sustained decoupling and the cognitive rehearsal that the model deals in. The underlying cognitive systems that would support the intentional interpretations in terms of cognitive distortions and players' fallacious reasoning are the absence of measures to counter the stimulus–response reactions that maintain this behavior pattern. Is the arousal that is the outcome of hearing and seeing the stimuli produced by the slot-machine, which signal only ill-luck, instrumental in establishing somatic markers that make playing on in the face of an outcome marked by two identical icons more probable? Must we conclude that the gambler whose behavior is sustained by this outcome, symbolic of not winning yet somehow construed into a reinforcing state of affairs, is simply cognitively deficient, unable to disengage by overriding the TASS-engendered tendency toward automaticity of response? Most of us are aware of a tendency to react at a choice point by feeding a short-range interest. Deciding in an instant that, in spite of having had enough to drink or to eat, you will on this occasion finish the bottle or the packet in the privacy of your home may not have implications for others. And if it is genuinely an occasional occurrence it may not be detrimental to health. But to maintain such behavior over time is to show signs that a neurophysiological system concerned with the learning of skills has been harnessed in a context where skill learning is actually irrelevant (Clark, 2010).

To understand two identical symbols as a near-miss is to display cognitive miserliness. Rather than comprehending the actual probabilities involved and reminding themselves that they are no closer to winning a jackpot as a result of this two-symbol arrangement, because the chances of their winning do not depend on building up skill (tasks which would involve drawing on Algorithmic Mind), slot-machine gamblers allow TASS to motivate further play. It is easier to adopt the belief that things are going their way. These players may simply lack the mindware required to reflect upon the probabilities involved in their playing and thus to recognize the erroneous reasoning underlying the gambler's fallacy, whether it relies upon straightforward superstition or masquerades in terms of entrapment or the illusion of skill acquisition. These conclusions are not startling and would not in themselves require the tri-process theory. However, some explanation is required and the mechanisms behind the gambler's behavior suggest a failure to decouple from the behavioral imperatives which the TASS promotes with automaticity, and to engage in cognitive rehearsal to work out a clearer understanding of the nature of the probability of winning. Cognitive distortion is not simply a mentalistic attribution: it is analyzable.

Those slot-machine gamblers whose behavior is increased in response to so-called near-misses also display a my-side bias, tending to see things from their point of view rather than from that of the probabilities of winning and their determination or from the point of view of the owners of the gambling premises or manufacturers of the machines. Their own point of view is seriously biased in favor of the logical misrepresentation that (1) they are able to improve their performance by gaining a skill, or (2) a run of losses must be followed by a run of successes (the gambler's fallacy), or (3) entrapment: namely that having invested so much in gambling without success their sunk costs will ensure a large win. This myopia may be combined with a mindware gap: many people seem unable to grasp easily the logic of probability and risk; many believe they will be lucky next time. Moreover, most people interpret the occasional win as confirming whatever logic they have entertained about the course of the game.

The key function of Reflective Mind is the inauguration of the call to begin cognitive simulation or hypothetical reasoning. The key operation of Algorithmic Mind in this is the decoupling it carries out. Decoupling is cognitively demanding, assisted by language which provides "the discrete representational medium that greatly enables hypotheticality to flourish as a culturally acquired mode of thought" (Stanovich, 2009a, p. 63). Hypothetical thought requires the representation of assumptions, for instance, and linguistic forms like conditionals readily allow this. Decoupling abilities differ in their recursiveness and complexity. Decoupling makes it possible to distance oneself from the representations so that they can be reflected upon and improved. Decoupling is therefore the key function of Algorithmic Mind. It is clearly a system 2 operation in that its operation occurs serially and incurs high computational expense. The literature on executive function and working memory, Stanovich argues, supports the view that the main function of Algorithmic Mind is to achieve decoupling among representations while conducting cognitive simulation.

Conclusion

This study has spoken of addiction as a mode of consumption marked by steep temporal discounting and preference reversal, involving the pursuit of a substance or behavior pattern to the point of economic irrationality, where it fundamentally disrupts the individual's lifestyle, and is sustained by neurophysiological excess, "midbrain mutiny," as Ross et al. (2008) characterize it. It has, in particular, explored the role of cognition in the explanation of addictive behavior via the methodology of Intentional Behaviorism.

The investigation belongs to a larger research program concerned to examine critically whether there is a case for cognitive explanation at all, to generate, as it may be required, an appropriate intentional interpretation, treating the consumer as an idealized (utility-maximizing) system, and deducing the intentionality necessary for its being in its current state, and, then, undergirding this interpretation by a facilitative cognitive interpretation (Foxall, 2007a, 2016a). The assumptions on which the psychological explanation is founded are based on empirical investigations of consumer choice through the rigorous and critical testing of a parsimonious behaviorist model. For example, the attribution of optimality to consumer behavior is not simply a carry-over from economic theory but a feature of consumer choice that has proved demonstrable in the specific context of economic behavior. Rather than try to summarize the entire research program and its context, I will endeavor to point out how its essence has been served by the investigation of addiction by describing a case, rule governance, which epitomizes the Intentional Behaviorist method.

An important development with respect to the extensional model (Chapter 3) is the enhanced understanding of rule governance in the explanation of consumer choice. This is especially pertinent to the formulation of self-rules in the context of overcoming the temptation to act impulsively through such picoeconomic strategies as bundling. The sole avenue toward incorporating rule-governed behavior into an extensional model is to treat the elements of a spoken, written, or thought rule as a matrix of auditory and visual stimuli that act as learned discriminative stimuli and motivating operations in an n-term contingency that behaves exactly as do the contingent environment–behavior relationships that serve to account for contingency-shaped behavior. There need be no intentional inference here: the stimuli involved are not *about* anything; they are simply elements of the physical environment that have acquired control of behavior in the course of operant learning. However, when the stimuli concerned cannot be readily identified in the course of an operant analysis of complex behavior (that which is not amenable to a direct experimental analysis), then explanatory rules may be generated by the investigator. Such rules embody the intentionality in accordance with which an idealized consumer, maximizing a pattern of utilitarian and informational reinforcement, would behave.

In adopting this mode of interpretation, we have left behind the realm of extensional explanation. Rather than construct a quasi-behavioral interpretation that employs extensional terminology but which is incapable of realization because its posited stimuli cannot be shown by experimental or correlational method to be systematically related to behavior, we must adopt the apparently more authentic methodology of explicit intentional interpretation. Rules in this context constitute propositional attitudes. That is, rules delivered orally or in writing may be viewed as instructions to accept a propositional attitude ("I believe that Macy's is located at the next intersection"), which, combined with a desire to get to Macy's, motivates the appropriate pattern of movement. This is the logic underlying the understanding of intertemporal valuation as necessarily intentional (summarized in Box 4.1). Just as the values of SSR and LLR can have only mental reality at the point at which the consumer's initial preference is expressed (t_0), so do the elements in an other-rule and certainly those of a self-rule. I believe that even radical behaviorists often employ the notion of rule-governed behavior in this spirit, albeit with the explanatory ideology that seeks to preclude a non-extensional comprehension of what is happening.

Another consideration to emerge from this investigation is that contingency-shaped behavior, which is the result of the stimulus control of the rate of behaving, falls within the domain of the S1 level of processing, which is of great importance, therefore, integrating cognitive processing with environmental influence on choice. Rule governance is also an environmentally sensitive influence on behavior, but one that requires metacognitive concepts in order to explicate its origins and effects on behavior. In short, rule-governed behavior is an output of cognitive rehearsal which draws on the S2 level of cognitive processing.

The generation of intentional interpretations in Chapter 4 and their underpinning by means of theories of neurobehavioral decision-making and cognitive processing in Chapter 5 have been described and evaluated in some detail there. I shall concentrate here, therefore, on the current and future development of the Intentional Behaviorist strategy. This approach, with its sequence of theoretical minimalism, followed by intentional interpretation and cognitive interpretation, offers a means of exposing the bounds of behaviorism and providing an account of behavior in the face of "misrepresentation," notably that which arises through the absence of an appropriate stimulus field to provide an operant explanation. However, perhaps as a consequence of the concentration in this investigation on addiction, which has significant and extensive connections with neurophysiology, the emphasis has been on cashing out the intentional interpretation of addictive behavior in terms of a cognitive psychology that is oriented toward the sub-personal dimension of brains and neuronal operations. We might allude to this as *microcognitive psychology* in order to distinguish it from the possibility of a *macrocognitive psychology* which is required to link intentional interpretation more firmly with the super-personal dimension of explanation, namely the realm of operancy. The promise of this phase of the research program is the provision of a cognitive theory of consumer choice that embraces both micro and macro dimensions.

The cognitive interpretation presented here is as much a competence theory as the intentional interpretation; both are, moreover, conceived of as personal-level accounts. The performance theories relevant to the empirical testing of propositions derived from these interpretations belong to extensional neuroscience and behavioral science. This will doubtless be the case also for the macrocognitive psychology of consumer choice.

So, how has this investigation enhanced our understanding of the choice or decision point illustrated in the frontispiece, not as part of a single second of dalliance but, potentially, as the initiation of a *sequence* of behavior that engenders a *sequence* of positive and negative consequence? The situation depicted by Bronzino reflects the problem of intertemporal valuation, which we have noted as the central index employed by the CNDS model of balance between the impulsive and executive systems. Intertemporal valuation depends crucially on interaction between Reflective Mind and Algorithmic Mind in their determination of the overriding of S1-inspired tendencies to act with alacrity in generating a pattern of utilitarian and informational reinforcement and the consequent pattern of emotional reward. Individual differences in reinforcement sensitivity and sensation-seeking may disturb this override procedure. Depending on the relative strengths of these behavioral dispositions compared with that of the fluid intelligence necessary for the initiation and maintenance of decoupling, their influence on the Algorithmic Mind–Automatic Mind axis (Figure 5.6) will determine the steepness of the temporal discounting reflected in decision-making and response. The recognition at the Algorithmic Mind level of a call for decoupling depends on the capacity to register the need for such an inauguration of cognitive rehearsal and this depends on not being overwhelmed by reinforcement sensitivity and sensation-seeking to the extent that the environmental demands for immediacy are exaggerated. If this is the case, the automaticity of TASS-derived responses will be unchecked. The urgency and strength of the call to disengage or decouple emitted by Reflective Mind depends on the capacity of the latter to recognize the urgency of environmental demands and the deleterious consequences of an impulsive response. This in turn depends on the thinking disposition, possibly conceived of in terms of adaptive–innovative cognitive style, which reflects both extraversion and sensation-seeking and is closely related also to reinforcement sensitivity. The importance of the competence of an appropriate cognitive style to temper reinforcement sensitivity and sensation-seeking is evident, as is the contribution of fluid intelligence to the ability to cope with one's predominant cognitive style in the face of unfavorable environmental conditions.

The influence of the trait-impulsive system may depend on the capacity of reinforcement sensitivity and sensation-seeking to modify the incentive salience of the utilitarian and informational reinforcers either available in the current consumer behavior setting or for which the elements of the consumer situation set the occasion, conditional upon the enactment of the requisite behavior. The pattern of reinforcement, however represented by the consumer situation, would thus exert a motivating effect based on the release or retention of dopamine in the mesocoritolimbic system. This observation, if it is borne out, may extend the explanation how incentive salience operates generally.

Bibliography

Ainslie, G. (1986). Beyond microeconomics: Conflict among interests in a multiple self as a determinant of value. In Elster, J. (Ed.) *The Multiple Self* (pp. 133–175). Cambridge: Cambridge University Press.

Ainslie, G. (1989). Freud and picoeconomics. *Behaviorism*, 17, 11–19.

Ainslie, G. (1992). *Picoeconomics: The Strategic Interaction of Successive Motivational States within the Person*. Cambridge: Cambridge University Press.

Ainslie, G. (2001). *Breakdown of Will*. Cambridge: Cambridge University Press.

Ainslie, G. (2007). Emotion: The gaping hole in economic theory. In Montero, B. and White, M.D. (Eds) *Economics and the Mind* (pp. 11–28). London and New York: Routledge.

Ainslie, G. (2010). Procrastination: The basic impulsive. In Andreou, C. and White, M. (Eds) *The Thief of Time* (pp. 11–27). Oxford: Oxford University Press.

Ainslie, G. (2011). Free will as recursive self-prediction: Does a deterministic mechanism reduce responsibility? In Poland, J. and Graham, G. (Eds) *Addiction and Responsibility* (pp. 55–87). Cambridge, MA: MIT Press.

Ainslie, G. (2013). Money as MacGuffin: A factor in gambling and other process addictions. In Levy, N. (Ed.) *Addiction and Self-control: Perspectives from Philosophy, Psychology, and Neuroscience* (pp. 16–37). Oxford: Oxford University Press.

Ainslie, G. (2015). The cardinal anomalies that led to behavioral economics: Cognitive or motivational? *Managerial and Decision Economics*.

Ainslie, G. and Monterosso, J. (2003). Hyperbolic discounting as a factor in addiction: A critical analysis. In Vuchinich, R.E. and Heather, N. (Eds) *Choice, Behavioral Economics and Addiction* (pp. 35–70) Oxford: Pergamon.

Alcaro, A., Huber, R., and Panksepp, J. (2007). Behavioral functions of the mesolimbic dopaminergic system: An affective neuroethological perspective, *Brain Research Review*, 56, 283–321.

Alessi, S.M. and Petry, M.N. (2003). Pathological gambling severity is associated with impulsivity in a delay discounting procedure. *Behavioural Processes*, 64, 345–354.

Altman, J., Everitt, B.J., Glautier, S., Markou, A., Butt, D., Oretti, R., Phillips, G.D., and Robbins, T.W. (1996). The biological, social and clinical bases of drug addiction: Commentary and debate. *Psychopharmacology*, 125, 285–345.

American Psychiatric Association (2013). *Diagnostic and Statistical Manual of Mental Disorders*, 5th edn. Arlington, VA: American Psychiatric Association.

Ardila, A. (2008). On the evolutionary origins of executive functions. *Brain and Cognition*, 68, 92–99.

Ariyabuddhiphongs, V. and Phengphol, V. (2008). Near miss, gambler's fallacy and entrapment: Their influence on lottery gamblers in Thailand. *Journal of Gambling Studies*, 24, 295–305.

Audrain-McGovern, J., Rodruigez, D., Epstein, L.H., Cuevas, J., Rodgers, K., and Wilyeto, E.P. (2009a). Does delay discounting play an etiological role in smoking or is it a consequence of smoking? *Drug and Alcohol Dependence*, 103, 99–106.

Audrain-McGovern, J., Rodruigez, D., Epstein, L.H., Rodgers, K., Cuevas, J., and Wilyeto, E.P. (2009b). Young adult smoking: What factors differentiate ex-smokers, smoking cessation treatment seekers and nontreatment seekers? *Addictive Behaviors*, 34, 1036–1042.

Baboushkin, H.R., Hardoon, K.R., Derevensky, J.L., and Gupta, R. (2001). Underlying cognitions in gambling behaviour among university students. *Journal of Applied Social Psychology*, 31, 1409–1430.

Baker, F., Johnson, M.W., and Bickel, W.K. (2003). Delay discounting differs between current and never-smokers across commodities, sign, and magnitudes. *Journal of Abnormal Psychology*, 112, 382–392.

Bandura, A. (1986). *Social Foundations of Thought and Action: A Social Cognitive Theory*. Englewood Cliffs, NJ: Prentice Hall.

Bandura, A. (1997). *Self-Efficacy: The Exercise of Control*. New York: Freeman.

Banich, M.T. (2009). Executive function: The search for an integrated account. *Current Directions in Psychological Science*, 10, 89–94.

Barkley, R.A. (1997a). Behavioral inhibition, sustained attention, and executive functions: Constructing a unified theory of ADHD. *Psychological Bulletin*, 121, 65–94.

Barkley, R.A. (1997b). *ADHD and the Nature of Self-control*. New York: Guilford Press.

Barkley, R.A. (2001). The executive functions and self-regulation: An evolutionary neuropsychological perspective. *Neuropsychology Review*, 11, 1–29.

Barkley, R.A. (2012). *Executive Functions: What They Are, How They Work, and Why They Evolved*. New York: Guilford Press.

Barkley, R.A. (2013). Attention-deficit-hyperactivity disorder, self-regulation, and executive functioning. In Vohs, K.D. and Baumeister, R.F. (Eds) *Handbook of Self-regulation: Research, Theory, and Applications*, 2nd edn (pp. 551–563). New York: The Guilford Press.

Barkow, J., Cosmides, L., and Tooby, J. (Eds) (1990). *The Adapted Mind: Evolutionary Psychology and the Generation of Culture*. New York: Oxford University Press.

Barrett, L.F. (2005). Feeling is perceiving: Core affect and conceptualization in the experience of emotion. In Barrett, L.F., Niedenthal, P.M., and Winkielman, P. (Eds) *Emotion and Consciousness* (pp. 255–285). New York: Guilford Press.

Barrett, L.F., Mesquita, B., Ochsner, K.N., and Gross, J.J. (2007). The experience of emotion. *Annual Review of Psychology*, 38, 173–401.

Bauer, I.M. and Baumeister, R.F. (2013). Self-regulatory strength. In Vohs, K.D. and Baumeister, R.F. (Eds) *Handbook of Self-regulation: Research, Theory, and Applications*, 2nd edn (pp. 64–82). New York: Guilford Press.

Baum, W.M. (1973). The correlation-based law of effect. *Journal of the Experimental Analysis of Behavior*, 20, 137–153.

Baum, W.M. (1974). On two types of deviation from the matching law: Bias and undermatching. *Journal of the Experimental Analysis of Behavior*, 231–242.

Baum, W.M. (1979). Matching, undermatching, and overmatching in studies of choice. *Journal of the Experimental Analysis of Behavior*, 23, 45–53.

Baum, W.M. (2002). Molar versus molecular as a paradigm clash. *Journal of the Experimental Analysis of Behavior*, 75, 338–341.

Baum, W.M. (2004). Molar and molecular views of choice. *Behavioral Processes*, 66, 349–359.

Baum, W.M. (2006). *Understanding Behaviorism: Behavior, Culture, and Evolution*, 2nd edn. Malden, MA: Blackwell.

Baum, W.M. (2015). Driven by consequences: The multiscale view of choice. *Managerial and Decision Economics*.

Baumeister, R.F. and Tierney, J. (2012). *Willpower: Rediscovering our Greatest Strength*. New York: Penguin.

Bechara, A. (2005). Decision-making, impulse control and loss of willpower to resist drugs: A neurocognitive perspective. *Nature Neuroscience* 8(11), 1458–1463.

Bechara, A. (2011). Human emotions in decision making: Are they useful or disruptive? In Vartanian, O. and Mandel, D.R. (Eds) *Neuroscience of Decision Making* (pp. 73–95). New York and Hove: Psychology Press.

Bechara, A. and Damasio, D.R. (2005). The somatic marker hypothesis: A neural theory of economic decision. *Games and Economic Behavior*, 52, 336–372.

Bechara, A., Damasio, H., and Damasio A.R. (2000). Emotion, decision making and the orbitofrontal cortex. *Cerebral Cortex*, 10, 295–307.

Becker, G.S. and Murphy, K.M. (1988). A theory of rational addiction. *Journal of Political Economy*, 96, 675–700.

Bennett, M.R. (2007). Neuroscience and philosophy. In Bennett, M., Dennett, D., Hacker, P., and Searle, J. *Neuroscience and Philosophy: Brain, Mind, and Language* (pp. 49–69). New York: Columbia University Press.

Bennett, M.R. and Hacker, P.M.S. (2003). *Philosophical Foundations of Neuroscience*. Oxford: Blackwell.

Bennett, M.R. and Hacker, P.M.S. (2007). The conceptual presuppositions of cognitive neuroscience: A reply to critics. In Bennett, M., Dennett, D., Hacker, P., and Searle, J. *Neuroscience and Philosophy: Brain, Mind, and Language* (pp. 127–170). New York: Columbia University Press.

Bermúdez, J.L. (2003). *Thinking Without Words*. Oxford: Oxford University Press.

Bermúdez, J.L. (2005). *Philosophy of Psychology: A Contemporary Introduction*. New York and London: Routledge.

Bermúdez, J.L. (2009). *Decision Theory and Rationality*. Oxford: Oxford University Press.

Berns, G. (2005). *Satisfaction: The Science of Finding True Fulfillment*. New York: Henry Holt.

Berridge, K.C. (2007). The debate over dopamine's role in reward: The case for incentive salience. *Psychopharmacology*, 191, 391–431.

Berridge, K.C. and Kringelbach, M.L. (2015). Pleasure systems in the brain. *Neuron*, 86, 646–664.

Berridge, K.C. and Robinson, T.E. (1993). The neural basis of drug craving: An incentive-sensitization theory of addiction. *Brain Research Reviews*, 18, 247–291.

Berridge, K.C. and Robinson, T.E. (1995). The mind of an addicted brain: Neural sensitization and wanting versus liking. *Current Directions in Psychological Science*, 4, 71–76.

Berridge, K.C. and Robinson, T.E. (1998) What is the role of dopamine in reward: Hedonic impact, reward learning, or incentive salience? *Brain Research Reviews*, 28, 309–369.

Berridge, K.C. and Robinson, T.E. (2003). Parsing reward. *Trends in Neurosciences*, 26, 507–513.

Berridge, K.C. and Robinson, T.E. (2012). Drug addiction as incentive sensitization. In Poland, J. and Graham, G. (Eds) *Addiction and Responsibility* (pp. 21–53). Cambridge, MA: MIT Press.

Berridge, K.C., Venier, I.L., and Robinson, T.E. (1989). Taste reactivity analysis of 6-hydroxydopamine-induced aphagia: Implications for arousal and anhedonia hypotheses of dopamine function. *Behavioral Neuroscience*, 103, 36–45.

Bickel, W.K. and Johnson, M.W. (2003). Delay discounting: A fundamental behavioral process in drug dependence. In Lowenstein, G., Read, D., and Baumeister, R. (Eds) *Time and Decision: Economic and Psychological Perspectives on Intertemporal Choice* (pp. 419–440). New York: Russell Sage Foundation.

Bickel, W.K. and Marsch, L.A. (2000). The tyranny of small decisions: Origins, outcomes, and proposed solutions. In Bickel, W.R. and Vuchinich, R.E. (Eds) *Reframing Health Behavioral Change with Behavioral Economics* (pp. 341–391). Mahwah, NJ: Erlbaum.

Bickel, W.K. and Marsch, L.A. (2001). Toward a behavioral economic understanding of drug dependence: Delay discounting processes. *Addiction*, 96, 73–86.

Bickel, W.K. and Vuchinich, R.E. (Eds) (2000). *Reframing Health Behavior Change with Behavioral Economics*. Mahwah, NJ: Erlbaum.

Bickel, W.K. and Yi, R. (2008). Temporal discounting as a measure of executive function: Insights from the competing neuro-behavioral decisions systems hypothesis of addiction. *Advances in Health Economics and Health Services Research*, 20, 289–309.

Bickel, W.K. and Yi, R. (2010). Neuroeconomics of addiction: The contribution of executive dysfunction. In Ross, D., Kincaid, H., Spurrett, D., and Collins, P. (Eds) *What is Addiction?* (pp. 1–25). Cambridge, MA: MIT Press.

Bickel, W.K., Odum, A.L., and Madden, G.J. (1999). Impulsivity and cigarette smoking: Delay discounting in current, never, and ex-smokers. *Psychopharmacology*, 146, 447–454.

Bickel, W.K., Kowal, B.P., and Gatchalian, K.M. (2006). Understanding addiction as a pathology of temporal horizon. *The Behavior Analyst Today*, 7, 32–47.

Bickel, W.K., Miller, M.L., Yi, R., Kowal, B.P., Lindquist, D.M., and Pitcock, J.A. (2007a). Behavioral and neuroeconomics of drug addiction: Competing neural systems and temporal discounting processes. *Drug and Alcohol Dependence*, 90S, S85–S91.

Bickel, W.K., Miller, M.L., Yi, R., Kowal, B.P., Lindquist, D.M., and Pitcock, J.A. (2007b). Behavioral and neuroeconomics of drug addiction: Competing neural systems and temporal discounting processes. *Drug and Alcohol Dependence*, 90S, S85–S91.

Bickel, W.K., Jones, B.A., Landes, R.D., Christensen, D.R., Jackson, L., and Mancino, M. (2010). Delay discounting predicts voucher redemptions during contingency-management procedures. *Experimental and Clinical Psychopharmacology*, 18, 546–552.

Bickel, W.K., Jarmolowicz, D.P., Mueller, E.T., and Gatchalian, K.M. (2011a). The behavioral economics and neuroeconomics of reinforcer pathologies: Implications for etiology and treatment of addiction. *Current Psychiatry Reports*, 13, 406–415.

Bickel, W.K., Landes, R.D., Christensen, D.R., Jackson, L., Jones, B.A., Kurth-Nelson, Z., and Redish, D. (2011b). Single- and cross-commodity discounting among cocaine addicts: The commodity and its temporal location determine discounting rate. *Psychopharmacology*, 217, 177–187.

Bickel, W.R., Jarmolowicz, D.P., Mueller, E.T., and Gatchalian, K.M. (2011c). The behavioral economics and neuroeconomics of reinforcer pathologies: Implications for etiology and treatment of addiction. *Current Psychiatry Reports*, 13, 406–415.

Bickel, W.K., Jarmolowicz, D.P., Mueller, E.T., Gatchalian, K.M., and McClure, S.M. (2012a). Are executive function and impulsivity antipodes? A conceptual reconstruction with special reference to addiction. *Psychopharmacology*, 221, 361–387.

Bickel, W.K., Jarmolowicz, D.P., MacKillop, J., Epstein, L.H., Carr, K., Mueller, E.T., and Waltz, T.J. (2012b). The behavioral economics of reinforcer pathologies: Novel approaches to addictive disorders. In Shaffer, H.J. (Ed.) *APA Addiction Syndrome Handbook* (pp. 333–363). Washington, DC: American Psychological Association.

Bickel, W.K., Jarmolowicz, D.P., MacKillop, J., and Epstein, L.H. (2013). What is addiction? In McCrady, B.S. and Epstein, E.E. (Eds) *Addictions: A Comprehensive Guidebook*, 2nd edn (pp. 3–16). New York: Oxford University Press.

Bjork, J.M., Knutson, B., Fong, G.W., Caggiano, D.M., Bennett, S.M., and Hommer, D.W. (2004). Incentive-elicited brain activation in adolescents: Similarities and differences from young adults. *Journal of Neuroscience*, 24, 1793–1802.

Blair, C. and Ursache, A. (2013). A bidirectional model of executive functions and self-regulation. In Vohs, K.D. and Baumeister, R.F. (Eds) *Handbook of Self-regulation: Research, Theory, and Applications*, 2nd edn (pp. 300–320). New York: Guilford Press.

Bolles, R.C. (1979). *Learning Theory*, 2nd edn. New York: Holt, Rinehart & Winston.

Brentano, F. (1874). *Psychology from an Empirical Standpoint*. Leipzig: Meiner.

Brook, A. and Ross, D. (Eds) (2002) *Daniel Dennett*. Cambridge: Cambridge University Press.

Brown, P.L. and Jenkins, H.M. (1968). Autoshaping the pigeon's keypeck. *Journal of the Experimental Analysis of Behavior*, 11, 1–8.

Brown, R.I.F. (1986). Arousal and sensation-seeking components in the general explanation of gambling and gambling addictions. *International Journal of the Addictions*, 21, 1001–1016.

Brown, R.I.F. (1987). Classical and operant paradigms in the management of compulsive gamblers. *Behavioural Psychotherapy*, 15, 111–122.

Bui Huynh, N. and Foxall, G.R. (2015). Consumer store choice: A matching analysis. In Foxall, G.R. (Ed.) *The Routledge Companion to Consumer Behavior Analysis* (pp. 96–120). London and New York: Routledge.

Businelle, M.S., McVay, M.A., Kendzor, D., and Copeland, A. (2010). A comparison of delay discounting among smokers, substance abusers, and non-dependent controls. *Drug and Alcohol Dependence*, 112, 247–250.

Cabanac, M. (2010). The dialectics of pleasure. In Kringelbach, M.L. and Berridge, K.C. (Eds) *Pleasures of the Brain* (pp. 113–124). Oxford: Oxford University Press.

Camerer, C., Loewenstein, G. and Prelec, D. (2005). Neuroeconomics: How neuroscience can inform economics. *Journal of Economic Literature*, 43, 9–64.

Carlson, N.R. (2010). *Physiology of Behavior*, 10th edn. Boston, MA: Pearson.

Carlton, P.L. and Manowitz, P. (1987). Physiological factors in determinants of pathological gambling. *Journal of Gambling Behavior*, 3, 274–285.

Carver, C.S. and Scheier, M.F. (2013). Self-regulation of action and affect. In Vohs, K.D. and Baumeister, R.F. (Eds) *Handbook of Self-regulation: Research, Theory, and Applications*, 2nd edn (pp. 2–21). New York: Guilford Press.

Chambers, R.A., Bickel, W.K., and Potenza, M.N. (2007). A scale-free systems theory of motivation and addiction. *Neuroscience and Biobehavioral Reviews*, 31(7), 1017.

Chase, H.W. and Clark, L. (2010). Gambling severity predicts midbrain response to near-miss outcomes. *Journal of Neuroscience*, 30, 6180–6187.

Childe, G. (1936). *Man Makes Himself*. London: Watts.

Childe, G. (1958). *The Prehistory of European Society*. Harmondsworth: Penguin.

Chisholm, R.M. (1957). *Perceiving: A Philosophical Study*. Ithaca, NY: Cornell University Press.

Chomsky, N. (1959). A review of Skinner's *Verbal Behavior*. *Language*, 35, 26–58.

Chomsky, N. (1980). *Rules and Representations*. New York: Columbia University Press.

Clark, L. (2010). Decision making during gambling: An integration of cognitive and psychobiological approaches. *Philosophical Transactions of the Royal Society B*, 365, 319–330.

Clark, L., Lawrence, A.J., Astley-Jones, F., and Gray, N. (2009). Gambling near-misses enhance motivation to gamble and recruit win-related brain circuitry. *Neuron*, 61, 481–490.

Clark, L., Crooks, B., Clarke, R., Aitken, M.R., and Dunn, B.D. (2012). Physiological responses to near-miss outcomes and personal control during simulated gambling. 28, 123–137.

Cloninger, C.R. (1986). A unified biosocial theory of personality and its role in the development of anxiety states. *Psychiatric Development*, 3, 167–226.

Cloninger, C.R. (1987). A systematic method for clinical description and classification of personality variants. *Archives of General Psychiatry*, 44, 573–588.

Coffey, S.F., Gudleski, G.D., Saladin, M.E., and Brady, K.T. (2003). Impulsivity and rapid discounting of delayed hypothetical rewards in cocaine-dependent individuals. *Experimental and Clinical Psychopharmacology*, 11, 18–25.

Coolidge, F.L. and Wynn, T. (2005). Working memory, its executive functions, and the emergence of modern thinking. *Cambridge Archaeological Journal*, 15, 5–26.

Coolidge, F.L. and Wynn, T. (2009). *The Rise of Homo Sapiens: The Evolution of Modern Thinking*. Chichester: Wiley-Blackwell.

Corr, P.J. (2008a). Reinforcement sensitivity theory (RST): Introduction. In Corr, P.J. (Ed.) *The Reinforcement Sensitivity Theory of Personality* (pp. 1–43). Cambridge: Cambridge University Press.

Corr, P.J. (Ed.) (2008b). *The Reinforcement Sensitivity Theory of Personality*. Cambridge: Cambridge University Press.

Côté, D., Caron, A., Aubert, J., Desrochers, V., and Ladouceur, R. (2003). New wins prolong gambling on a video lottery terminal. *Journal of Gambling Studies*, 18, 433–438.

Crane, T. (1998). Intentionality as the mark of the mental. *Royal Institute of Philosophy Supplement*, 43, 229–251.

Crane, T. (2002). *The Mechanical Mind: A Philosophical Introduction to Minds, Machines and Mental Representations*, 2nd edn. London and New York: Routledge.

Crane, T. (2009). Intentionalism. In McLaughlin, B.P., Beckerman, A., and Walter, S. (Eds) *The Oxford Handbook of Philosophy of Mind* (pp. 474–493). Oxford: Oxford University Press.

Curry, B., Foxall, G.R., and Sigurdsson, V. (2010). On the tautology of the matching law in Consumer Behavior Analysis. *Behavioral Processes*, 84, 390–399.

Damasio, A.R. (1994). *Descartes' Error: Emotion, Reason and the Human Brain*. New York: Putnam.

Damasio, A.R. (1999). *The Feeling of What Happens: Body, Emotion and the Making of Consciousness*. London: Vintage.

Damasio, A.R. (2009). Neuroscience and the emergence of neuroeconomics. In Glimcher, P.W., Camerer, C.F., Fehr, E., and Poldrack, R.A. (Eds) *Neuroeconomics: Decision Making and the Brain* (pp. 209–214). New York: Academic Press.

Daruna, J.H. and Barnes PA. (1993). A neurodevelopmental view of impulsivity. In McCown, W.G., Johnson, J.L., and Shure, M.B. (Eds) *The Impulsive Client: Theory, Research and Treatment* (pp. 23–37). Washington, DC: American Psychological Association.

Daugherty, D. and MacLin, O.H. (2007). Perceptions of luck: Near wins and near loss experiences. *Analysis of Gambling Behavior*, 1, 123–132.

Davison, M. and McCarthy, D. (1988). *The Matching Law: A Research Review*. Hillsdale, NJ: Erlbaum.

Daw, N.D. (2013). Advanced reinforcement learning. In Glimcher, P.W. and Fehr, E. (Eds) *Neuroeconomics: Decision-making and the Brain*, 2nd edn (pp. 299–320). London: Elsevier.

Daw, N.D. and Tobler, P.N. (2013). Value learning through reinforcement: The basics of dopamine and reinforcement learning. In Glimcher, P.W. and Fehr, E. (Eds) *Neuroeconomics: Decision-making and the Brain*, 2nd edn (pp. 283–298). London: Elsevier.

Dawkins, R. (1976). *The Selfish Gene*. Oxford: Oxford University Press.

Dawkins, R. (1982). *The Extended Phenotype*. Oxford: Oxford University Press.

Dayan, P. (2012). Models of value and choice. In Dolan, R.J. and Sharot, T. (Eds) *Neuroscience of Preference and Choice: Cognitive and Neural Mechanisms* (pp. 33–52). Amsterdam: Academic Press.

de Villiers, P.A. and Herrnstein, R.J. (1976). Toward a law of response strength. *Psychological Bulletin*, 83, 1131–1153.

de Waal, E. (2011). *The Pot Book*. London: Phaidon.

Delgado, M.R. and Tricomi, E. (2011). Reward processing and decision making in the human striatum. In Vartanian, O. and Mandel, D.R. (Eds) *Neuroscience of Decision Making* (pp. 145–172). New York and Hove: Psychology Press.

Denckla, M.B. (1996). A theory and model of executive function: A neuropsychological perspective. In Lyon, G.R. and Krasnegor, N.A. (Eds) *Attention, Memory, and Executive Function* (pp. 263–278). Baltimore, MD: Paul H. Brookes.

Dennett, D.C. (1969). *Content and Consciousness*. London: Routledge & Kegan Paul.

Dennett, D.C. (1978). *Brainstorms*. Montgomery, VT: Bradford.

Dennett, D.C. (1987). *The Intentional Stance*. Cambridge, MA: MIT Press.

Dennett, D.C. (1991a). *Consciousness Explained*. London: Penguin Books.

Dennett, D.C. (1991b). Real patterns. *Journal of Philosophy*, 88, 27–51.

Dennett, D.C. (1995). *Darwin's Dangerous Idea*. London: Allen Lane.

Dennett, D.C. (1996). *Kinds of Minds: Towards an Understanding of Consciousness*. London: Weidenfeld & Nicolson.

Dennett, D.C. (2006). *Sweet Dreams: Philosophical Obstacles to a Science of Consciousness*. Cambridge, MA: MIT Press.

Dennett, D.C. (2007). Philosophy as naïve anthropology. In Bennett, M., Dennett, D.C., Hacker, P., and Searle, J. *Neuroscience and Philosophy: Brain, Mind and Language* (pp. 73–95). New York: Columbia University Press.

Dennett, D.C. (2009). Intentional systems theory. In McLaughlin, B.P., Beckerman, A., and Walter, S. (Eds) *The Oxford Handbook of Philosophy of Mind* (pp. 339–350). Oxford: Oxford University Press.

DeYoung, C.G. (2013). Impulsivity as a personality trait. In Vohs, K.D. and Baumeister, R.F. (Eds) *Handbook of Self-regulation: Research, Theory, and Applications*, 2nd edn (pp. 485–502). New York: Guilford Press.

Di Chiara, G. (2002). Dopamine and reward. In Di Chiara, G. (Ed.) *Dopamine in the CNS II* (pp. 265–319). Berlin: Springer.

Dixon, M.J., Harrigan, K.A., Sandhu, R., Collins, K., and Fufelsang, J.A. (2010). Losses disguised as wins in modern multi-line video slot machines. *Addiction*, 105, 1819–1824.

Dixon, M.R. (2000). Manipulating the illusion of control: Variations in risk-taking as a function of perceived control over chance outcomes. *The Psychological Record*, 50, 705–720.

Dixon, M.R. and Belisle, J. (2015). Gambling behavior. In Foxall, G.R. (Ed.) *The Routledge Companion to Consumer Behavior Analysis* (pp. 231–241). London and New York: Routledge.

Dixon, M.R. and Delaney, J. (2006). The impact of verbal behavior on gambling behavior. In Ghezzi, P.M., Lyons, C.A., Dixon, M.R., and Wilson, G.R. (Eds) *Gambling: Behavior Theory, Research and Application* (pp. 171–189). Reno, NV: Context Press.

Dixon, M.R. and Schreiber, J.B. (2004). Near-miss effects on response latencies and win estimations of slot machine players. *The Psychological Record*, 54, 335–348.

Dixon, M.R., Marley, J., and Jacobs, E.A. (2003). Contextual control of delay discounting by pathological gamblers. *Journal of Applied Behavior Analysis*, 36, 449–458.

Dixon, M.R., Jackson, J.W., Delaney, J., Holton, B., and Crothers, M.C. (2007). Assessing and manipulating the illusion of control of video poker players. *Analysis of Gambling Behavior*, 1, 90–108.

Dixon, M.R., Nastally, B.L., Jackson, J.W., and Habib, R. (2009a). Altering the "near-miss" effect in slot machine gamblers. *Journal of Applied Behavior Analysis*, 42, 913–918.

Dixon, M.R., Nastally, B.L., Haha, A.D., Horner-King, M., and Jackson, J.W. (2009b). Blackjack players demonstrate the near miss effect. *Analysis of Gambling Behavior*, 3, 56–61.

Dixon, M.R., Nastally, B.L., and Waterman, A. (2010). The effect of gambling activities on happiness levels of nursing home residents. *Journal of Applied Behavior Analysis*, 43, 531–535.

Dretske, F. (1969). *Seeking and Knowing*. London: Routledge & Kegan Paul.

Dretske, F. (1988). *Explaining Behavior: Reasons in a World of Causes*. Cambridge, MA: MIT Press.

Duka, T., Sahakian, B., and Turner, D. (2007). Experimental psychology and research into brain science, addiction and drugs. In Nutt, D., Robbins, T.W., Stimson, G.V., Ince, M., and Jackson, A. (Eds) *Drugs and the Future: Brain Science, Addiction and Society* (pp. 133–168). Oxford: Elsevier.

Dunbar, R. (2014). *Human Evolution*. London: Penguin Books.

Ellis, B.J., Figueredo, A.J., Brumbach, B.H., and Schlomer, G.L. (2009). Fundamental dimensions of environmental risk: The impact of harsh versus unpredictable environments on the evolution and development of life history strategies. *Human Nature*, 20, 204–268.

Eisenberger, N.I. and Cole, S.W. (2012). Social neuroscience and health: Neurophysiological mechanisms linking social ties with physical health. *Nature Neuroscience*, 15, 669–674.

Elster, J. (ed.) (1987). *The Multiple Self*. Cambridge: Cambridge University Press.

Elster, J. (ed.) (1999a). *Getting Hooked: Rationality and Addiction*. Cambridge: Cambridge University Press.

Elster, J. (1999b). *Strong Feelings: Emotion, Addiction and Human Behavior*. Cambridge, MA: MIT Press.

Elster, J. (2015). *Explaining Social Behavior: More Nuts and Bolts for the Social Sciences*, revised edn. Cambridge: Cambridge University Press.

Elton, M. (2003). *Dennett: Reconciling Science and Our Self-conception*. Cambridge: Polity Press.

Euston, D.R., Gruber, A.J., and McNaughton, B.L. (2012). The role of medial prefrontal cortex in memory and decision-making. *Neuron*, 76, 1057–1070.

Evans, J.St.B.T. (2010). *Thinking Twice: Two Minds in One Brain*. Oxford: Oxford University Press.

Evans, J.St.B.T. and Stanovich, K.E. (2013). Dual-process theories of higher cognition: Advancing the debate. *Perspectives on Psychological Science*, 8, 223–241.

Eysenck, H.J. (2006). *The Biological Basis of Personality*, 2nd edn. New Brunswick: Transaction.

Faber, R.J. and Vohs, K.D. (2013). Self-regulation and spending: Evidence from impulsive and compulsive buying. In Vohs, K.D. and Baumeister, R.F. (Eds) *Handbook of Self-regulation: Research, Theory, and Applications*, 2nd edn (pp. 537–550). New York: Guilford Press.

Fagerstrøm, A. and Sigurdsson, V. (2015). Experimental analysis of consumer choice. In Foxall, G.R. (Ed.) *The Routledge Companion to Consumer Behavior Analysis* (pp. 25–39). London and New York: Routledge.

Fantino, E. and Logan, C.A. (1979). *The Experimental Analysis of Behavior: A Biological Perspective*. San Francisco, CA: W.H. Freeman.

Faucher, L. and Tappolet, C. (Eds) (2006a). *The Modularity of Emotions*. Calgary, Alberta: University of Calgary Press.

Faucher, L. and Tappolet, C. (2006b). Introduction: Modularity and the nature of emotions. In Foucher, L. and Tappolet, C. (Eds) *The Modularity of Emotions*. (pp. xii–xxxi). Calgary, Alberta: University of Calgary Press.

Fessler, D.M.T. (2001). Emotion and cost–benefit assessment: The role of shame and self-esteem in risk taking. In Gigerenza, G. and Selten, R. (Eds) *Bounded Rationality: The Adaptive Toolbox*. (pp. 191–214). Cambridge, MA: MIT Press.

Figner, B., Knoch, D., Johnson, E.J., Krosch, A.R., Lisanby, S.H., Fehr, E., and Weber, E.U. (2015). Lateral prefrontal cortex and self-control in intertemporal choice. *Nature Neuroscience*, 13, 538–539.

Finkel, E.J. and Fitzsimons, G.M. (2013). The effects of social relationships on self-regulation. In Vohs, K.D. and Baumeister, R.F. (Eds) *Handbook of Self-regulation: Research, Theory, and Applications*, 2nd edn (pp. 390–406). New York: Guilford Press.

Fishbach, A. and Converse, B.A. (2013). Identifying and battling temptation. In Vohs, K.D. and Baumeister, R.F. (Eds) *Handbook of Self-regulation: Research, Theory, and Applications*, 2nd edn (pp. 244–260). New York: Guilford Press.

Fishbein, M. and Ajzen, I. (2010). *Predicting and Changing Behavior*. New York: Psychology Press.

Fisher, W.W. and Mazur, J.E. (1997). Basic and applied research on choice responding. *Journal of Applied Behavior Analysis*, 30, 387–410.

Fitzsimons, G.M. and Finkel, E.J. (2013). The effects of self-regulation on social relationships. In Vohs, K.D. and Baumeister, R.F. (Eds) *Handbook of Self-regulation: Research, Theory, and Applications*, 2nd edn (pp. 407–421). New York: Guilford Press.

Fodor, J.A. (1968). *Psychological Explanation: An Introduction to the Philosophy of Psychology*. New York: Random House.

Fodor, J.A. (1975). *The Language of Thought*. New York: Crowell.

Fodor, J.A. (2008). *LOT2: The Language of Thought Revisited*. Oxford: Clarendon Press.

Foxall, G.R. (1988). Consumer innovativeness: Novelty-seeking, creativity and cognitive style. In Hirschman, E.C. and Sheth, J.N. (Eds) *Research on Consumer Behavior*, 3 (pp. 73–113). Greenwich, CT: JAI Press.

Foxall, G.R. (1990/2004). *Consumer Psychology in Behavioral Perspective*. London and New York: Routledge; reprinted 1994 by Beard Books, Frederick, MD.

Foxall, G.R. (1994). Consumer initiators: Adaptors and innovators, *British Journal of Management*, 5, S3–S12.

Foxall, G.R. (1995). Cognitive styles of consumer initiators. *Technovation*, 15, 269–288.

Foxall, G.R. (1997a). *Marketing Psychology: The Paradigm in the Wings*. London: Macmillan; New York: St. Martin's Press.

Foxall, G.R. (1997b). Affective responses to consumer situations. *International Review of Retail, Distribution and Consumer Research*, 7, 191–225.

Foxall, G.R. (1998). Radical behaviorist interpretation: Generating and evaluating an account of consumer behavior. *The Behavior Analyst*, 21, 321–354.

Foxall, G.R. (1999a). The contextual stance. *Philosophical Psychology*, 12, 25–46.

Foxall, G.R. (1999b). The substitutability of brands. *Managerial and Decision Economics*, 20, 241–257.

Foxall, G.R. (2001). Foundations of consumer behaviour analysis. *Marketing Theory*, 1, 165–199.

Foxall, G.R. (2002). *Consumer Behaviour Analysis: Critical Perspectives in Business and Management*. London and New York: Routledge.

Foxall, G.R. (2004). *Context and Cognition: Interpreting Complex Behavior*. Reno, NV: Context Press.

Foxall, G.R. (2005). *Understanding Consumer Choice*. London and New York: Palgrave Macmillan.

Foxall, G.R. (2007a). *Explaining Consumer Choice*. London and New York: Macmillan.

Foxall, G.R. (2007b). Explaining consumer choice: Coming to terms with intentionality. *Behavioral Processes*, 75, 129–145.

Foxall, G.R. (2007c). Intentional Behaviorism. *Behavior and Philosophy*, 35, 1–56.

Foxall, G.R. (2008a). Reward, emotion and consumer choice: From neuroeconomics to neurophilosophy. *Journal of Consumer Behaviour*, 7, 368–396.

Foxall, G.R. (2008b). Intentional Behaviorism revisited. *Behavior and Philosophy*, 37, 113–156.

Foxall, G.R. (2009). Ascribing intentionality. *Behavior and Philosophy*, 37, 217–222.

Foxall, G.R. (2010a). Accounting for consumer choice: Inter-temporal decision-making in behavioral perspective. *Marketing Theory*, 10, 315–345.

Foxall, G.R. (2010b). *Interpreting Consumer Choice: The Behavioral Perspective Model*. New York: Routledge.

Foxall, G.R. (2011). Brain, emotion and contingency in the explanation of consumer behavior. *International Review of Industrial and Organizational Psychology*, 26, 47–92.

Foxall, G.R. (2013). Intentionality, symbol, and situation in the interpretation of consumer choice. *Marketing Theory*, 13, 105–127.

Foxall, G.R. (2014a). Neurophilosophy of explanation in economic psychology: An exposition in terms of neuro-behavioral decision systems. In Moutinho, L. *et al.* (Eds) *Routledge Companion to the Future of Marketing* (pp. 134–150). London and New York: Routledge.

Foxall, G.R. (2014b). Cognitive requirements of competing neuro-behavioral decision systems: Some implications of temporal horizon for managerial behavior in organizations. *Frontiers in Human Neuroscience*, 8, 184.

Foxall, G.R. (2015a). Operant behavioral economics. *Managerial and Decision Economics* (published online May 2015).

Foxall, G.R. (Ed.) (2015b). *The Routledge Companion to Consumer Behavior Analysis*. London and New York: Routledge.

Foxall, G.R. (2015c). Consumer Behavior Analysis comes of age. In Foxall, G.R. (Ed.) *The Routledge Companion to Consumer Behavior Analysis* (pp. 3–21). London and New York: Routledge.

Foxall, G.R. (2015d). Consumer heterophenomenology. In Foxall, G.R. (Ed.) *The Routledge Companion to Consumer Behavior Analysis* (pp. 417–430). London and New York: Routledge.

Foxall, G.R. (2015e). Consumer Behavior Analysis and the marketing firm: Bilateral contingency in the context of environmental concern. *Journal of Organizational Behavior Management*, 35, 44–69.

Foxall, G.R. (2016a). *Explaining Consumer Choice: Intentionality, Behavior, and Neuroscience*. London and New York: Palgrave Macmillan.

Foxall, G.R. (2016b). *Context and Cognition in Consumer Psychology*. Hove: Psychology Press.

Foxall, G.R. and James, V.K. (2002). Behavior analysis of consumer brand choice: A preliminary analysis. *European Journal of Behavior Analysis*, 2, 209–220.

Foxall, G.R. and James, V.K. (2003). The behavioral ecology of brand choice: How and what do consumers maximize? *Psychology and Marketing*, 20, 811–836.

Foxall, G.R. and James, V.K. (2009). The style/involvement model of consumer innovativeness. In Rickards, T. and Moger, S. (Eds) *The Routledge Companion to Creativity* (pp. 71–87). London: Routledge.

Foxall, G.R. and Oliveira-Castro, J.M. (2009). Intentional consequences of self-instruction. *Behavior and Philosophy*, 37, 87–104.

Foxall, G.R. and Schrezenmaier, T.C. (2003). The behavioural economics of consumer brand choice: Establishing a methodology. *Journal of Economic Psychology*, 24, 675–695.

Foxall, G.R. and Sigurdsson, V. (2011). Drug use as consumer behavior. *Behavioral and Brain Sciences*, 34, 313–314.

Foxall, G.R. and Sigurdsson, V. (2012). When loss rewards: The near-miss effect in slot machine gambling. *Analysis of Gambling Behavior*, 6, 5–22.

Foxall, G.R. and Sigurdsson, V. (2013). Consumer Behavior Analysis: Behavioral economics meets the marketplace. *The Psychological Record*, 62, 231–237.

Foxall, G.R. and Yani-de-Soriano, M.M. (2005). Situational influences on consumers' attitudes and behavior. *Journal of Business Research*, 58, 518–525.

Foxall, G.R. and Yani-de-Soriano, M.M. (2011). Influence of reinforcement contingencies and cognitive styles on affective responses: An examination of Rolls' theory of emotion in the context of consumer choice. *Journal of Applied Social Psychology*, 41, 2508–2537.

Foxall, G.R., Oliveira-Castro, J.M., and Schrezenmaier, T.C. (2004). The behavioral economics of consumer brand choice: Patterns of reinforcement and utility maximization. *Behavioural Processes*, 65, 235–260.

Foxall, G.R., James, V.K., Oliveira-Castro, J.M., and Ribier, S. (2010a). Product substitutability and the matching law. *The Psychological Record*, 60, 185–216.

Foxall, G.R., James, V.K., Chang, J., and Oliveira-Castro, J.M. (2010b). Substituta-bility and complementarity: Matching analyses of brands and products. *Journal of Organizational Behavior Management.* 30(2), 145–160.

Foxall, G.R., Yani-de-Soriano, M., Yousafzai, S., and Javed, U. (2012). The role of neurophysiology, emotion and contingency in the explanation of consumer choice. In Wells, V.K. and Foxall, G.R. (Eds) *Handbook of Developments in Consumer Behaviour* (pp. 461–522). Cheltenham, Glos., and Northampton, MA: Edward Elgar.

Foxall, G.R., Yan, J., Oliveira-Castro, J.M., and Wells, V.K. (2013). Brand-related and situational influences on demand elasticity. *Journal of Business Research*, 66, 73–81.

Frankish, K. and Evans, J. St. B.T. (2009). The duality of mind: An historical per-spective. In Evans, J.St.B.T. and Frankish, K. (Eds) *In Two Minds: Dual Processes and Beyond* (pp. 1–29). Oxford: Oxford University Press.

Freeman, W.J. (2000). Emotion is essential to all intentional behaviors. In Lewis, M.D. and Granic, I. (Eds) *Emotion, Development, and Self Organization Dynamic Systems Approaches to Emotional Development* (pp. 209–235). Cambridge: Cambridge University Press.

Gaboury, A. and Ladouceur, R. (1989). Erroneous perceptions and gambling. *Journal of Social Behavior and Personality*, 4, 411–420.

Gergely, G. and Csibra, G. (2003). Teleological reasoning in infancy: The naïve theory of rational action. *Trends in Cognitive Sciences*, 7, 287–292.

Gergely, G., Nidasdy, Z., Csibra, G., and Bíró, S. (1995). Taking the intentional stance at 12 months of age. *Cognition*, 56, 165–193.

Ghezzi, P.M., Wilson, G.R., and Porter, J.C.K. (2006). The near-miss effect in simu-lated slot machine play. In Ghezzi, P.M., Lyons, C.A., Dixon, M.R., and Wilson, G.R. (Eds) *Gambling: Behavior Theory, Research and Application* (pp. 155–170). Reno, NV: Context Press.

Gigerenzer, G. (2002). *Reckoning with Risk: Learning to Live with Uncertainty.* London: Penguin.

Glimcher, P.W. (2004). *Decisions, Uncertainty, and the Brain: The Science of Neuroeco-nomics.* Cambridge, MA: MIT Press.

Glimcher, P.W. (2011). *Foundations of Neuroeconomic Analysis.* New York: Oxford University Press.

Glimcher, P.W., Camerer, C.F., Fehr, E., and Poldrack, R.A. (Eds) (2009). *Neuroeco-nomics: Decision Making and the Brain.* New York: Academic Press.

Goldberg, E. (2002). *The Executive Brain: Frontal Lobes and the Civilized Mind.* Oxford: Oxford University Press.

Gollwitzer, P.M. and Oettingen, G. (2013). Planning promotes goal striving. In Vohs, K.D. and Baumeister, R.F. (Eds) *Handbook of Self-regulation: Research, Theory, and Applications*, 2nd edn (pp. 162–185). New York: Guilford Press.

Gottfried, J.A., O'Doherty, J., and Dolan, R.J. (2003). Encoding predictive reward value in human amygdala and orbitofrontal cortex. *Science*, 301, 1104–1107.

Gould, T. J. (2010). Addiction and cognition, *Addiction Science and Clinical Practice*, 5(2), 4–14.

Gray, J.A. (1982). *The Neuropsychology of Anxiety: An Enquiry into the Functions of the Septo-hippocampal System.* Oxford: Oxford University Press.

Gray, J.A. and McNaughton, N. (2000). *The Neuropsychology of Anxiety.* Oxford; Oxford University Press.

Green, C.W. and Reid, D.H. (1996). Defining, validating, and increasing indices of happiness among people with profound multiple disabilities. *Journal of Applied Behavior Analysis*, 29, 67–78.

Griffiths, M. (1990a). The cognitive psychology of gambling. *Journal of Gambling Studies*, 6, 31–42.

Griffiths, M. (1990b). Addiction to fruit machines: A preliminary study among males. *Journal of Gambling Studies*, 6, 113–126.

Griffiths, M. (1990c).The acquisition, development and maintenance of fruit machine gambling in adolescents. *Journal of Gambling Studies*, 6, 193–204.

Griffiths, M. (1991). Pyschobiology of the near-miss in fruit machine gambling. *The Journal of Psychology*, 125, 347–357.

Griffiths, M. (1994). The role of cognitive bias and skill in fruit machine gambling. *British Journal of Psychology*, 85, 351–369.

Griffiths, M. (1995). *Adolescent Gambling*. London and New York: Routledge.

Gupta, A.K. (2004). Origin of agriculture and domestication of plants and animals linked to early Holocene climate and amelioration. *Current Science*, 87, 54–59.

Haber, S.N. (2009). Anatomy and connectivity of the reward circuit. In Dreher, J.-C. and Tremblay, L. (Eds) *Handbook of Reward and Decision Making* (pp. 1–27). Amsterdam: Academic Press.

Habib, R. and Dixon, M.R. (2010) Neurobehavioral evidence for the "Near-Miss" effect in pathological gamblers. *Journal of the Experimental Analysis of Behavior*, 93, 313–328.

Hanson, C. (2009). *Thinking about Addiction: Hyperbolic Discounting and Responsible Agency*. Amsterdam: Rodopi.

Haw, J. (2008). The relationship between reinforcement and gambling machine choice. *Journal of Gambling Studies*, 24, 55–61.

Haw, J. (2009). The multiplier potential of slot machines predict (*sic*) bet size. *Analysis of Gambling Behavior*, 3, 1–6.

Hayes, S.C., Wilson, K.W., Gifford, E.V., Follette, V.M., and Strosahl, K. (1996). Experiential avoidance and behavioral disorders: A functional dimensional approach to diagnosis and treatment. *Journal of Consulting and Clinical Psychology*, 64, 1152–1168.

Hebb, D.O. (1949). *The Organization of Behavior: A Neuropsychological Theory*. New York: Wiley.

Heil, J. (1998). *Philosophy of Mind*. London: Routledge.

Heil, J. (2013). Mental causation according to Davidson. In D'Oro, G. and Sandis, C. (Eds) *Reasons and Causes: Causalism and Anti-causalism in the Philosophy of Action* (pp. 75–96). Basingstoke: Palgrave Macmillan.

Heil, S.H., Johnson, M.W., Higgins, S.T., and Bickel, W.K. (2006). Delay discounting in currently using and currently abstinent cocaine-dependent outpatients and non-drug matched controls. *Addictive Behaviors*, 31, 1290–1294.

Heilbronner, S.R., Hayden, B.Y., and Platt, M.L. (2010). Neuroeconomics of risk-sensitive decision making. In Madden, G.J. and Bickel, W.K. (Eds) *Impulsivity: The Behavioral and Neurological Science of Discounting*. (pp. 159–188). Washington, DC: American Psychological Association.

Herrnstein, R.J. (1961). Relative and absolute strength of response as a function of frequency of reinforcement. *Journal of the Experimental Analysis of Behavior*, 4, 267–272.

Herrnstein, R.J. (1970). On the law of effect. *Journal of the Experimental Analysis of Behavior*, 13, 243–266.

Herrnstein, R.J. (1979). Derivatives of matching. *Psychological Review*, 86, 486–495.

Herrnstein, R.J. (1982). Melioration as behavioral dynamism. In Commons, M.I., Herrnstein, R.J., and Rachlin, H. (Eds) *Quantitative Analyses of Behavior: Vol. II. Matching and Maximizing Accounts* (pp. 433–458). Cambridge, MA: Ballinger.

Herrnstein, R.J. (1997). *The Matching Law: Papers in Psychology and Economics*, edited by Rachlin, H. and Laibson, D.I. Cambridge, MA: Harvard University Press; New York: Russell Sage Foundation.

Herrnstein, R.J. and Prelec, D. (1992). A theory of addiction. In Loewenstein, G. and Elster, J. (Eds) *Choice Over Time* (pp. 331–360). New York: Russell Sage Foundation.

Herrnstein, R.J. and Vaughan, W., Jr. (1980). Melioration and behavioral allocation. In Staddon, J.E.R. (Ed.) *Limits to Action: The Allocation of Individual Behavior*. New York: Academic Press.

Heyes, C. (2000). Evolutionary psychology in the round. In Heyes, C. and Huber, L. (Eds) *The Evolution of Cognition* (pp. 3–22). Cambridge, MA: MIT Press.

Heyes, C. and Huber, L. (Eds) (2000). *The Evolution of Cognition*. Cambridge, MA: MIT Press.

Heyman, G.M. (1996). Resolving the contradictions of addication. *Behavioral and Brain Sciences*, 19, 561–574.

Heyman, G.M. (2009). *Addiction: A Disorder of Choice*. Cambridge, MA: Harvard University Press.

Higley, J.D., Mehlman, P.T., Poland, R.E., Taub, D.M., Vickers, J., and Suomi, S.J. (1996). CSF testosterone and 5-H1AA correlate with different types of aggressive behaviors. *Biological Psychiatry*, 40, 1067–1082.

Hofmann, W., Friese, M., Schmeichel, B.J., and Baddeley, A.D. (2013). Working memory and self-reg. In Vohs, K.D. and Baumeister, R.F. (Eds) *Handbook of Self-regulation: Research, Theory, and Applications*, 2nd edn (pp. 204–225). New York: Guilford Press.

Hoffman, W.F., Moore, M., Templin, R., McFarland, B., Hitzemann, R.J., and Mitchel, S.H. (2006). Neuropsychological function and delay discounting in methamphetamine-dependent individuals. *Psychopharmacology*, 188, 162–170.

Hoon, A., Dymond, S., Jackson, J.W., and Dixon, M.R. (2008). Contextual control of slot-machine gambling: Replication and extension. *Journal of Applied Behavior Analysis*, 41, 467–470.

Hornsby, J. (2000). Personal and sub-personal: A defence of Dennett's early distinction. *Philosophical Explorations*, 3, 6–24.

Hursh, S.R. (1980). Economic concepts for the analysis of behavior. *Journal of the Experimental Analysis of Behavior*, 34, 219–238.

Hursh, S.R. (1984). Behavioral economics. *Journal of the Experimental Analysis of Behavior*, 42, 435–452.

Hursh, S.R. and Roma, P.G. (in press). Behavioral economics and the analysis of consumption and choice. *Managerial and Decision Economics*.

Hursh, S.R. and Silberberg, A. (2008). Economic demand and essential value. *Psychological Review*, 115, 186–198.

Hursh, S.R., Madden, G.J., Spiga, R., DeLeon, I.G., and Francisco, M.T. (2012). The translational utility of behavioral economics: The experimental analysis of consumption and choice. In Madden, G.J., Dube, W.V., Hanley, G.P., and Lattal, K.A. (Eds) *APA Handbook of Behavior Analysis. Vol. 2. Translating Principles into Practice* (pp. 191–224). Washington, DC: American Psychological Association.

Hyman, S.E. and Malenka, R.C. (2001). Addiction and the brain: The neurobiology of compulsion and its persistence. *Nature Reviews Neuroscience*, 2, 695–703.

Jarmolowicz, D.P., Mueller, E.T., Koffarnus, M.N., Carter, A.E., Gatchalian, K.M., and Bickel, W.K. (2013). Executive dysfunction in addiction. In MacKillop, J. and de Wit, H. (Eds) *The Wiley-Blackwell Handbook of Addiction Pharmacology* (pp. 27–61). Chichester: Wiley.

Jentsch, J.D. and Taylor, J.R. (1999). Impulsivity resulting from frontostriatal dysfunction in drug abuse: Implications for the control of behavior by reward-related stimuli. *Psychopharmacology*, 146, 373–390.

Johnson, M.W., Bickel, W.K., and Baker, F. (2007). Moderate drug use and delay discounting: A comparison of heavy, light, and never smokers. *Experimental and Clinical Psychopharmacology*, 15, 187–194.

Joseph, J. (2003). *The Gene Illusion: Genetic Research in Psychiatry and Psychology Under theMicroscope.* Ross-on-Wye: PCCS Books.

Jurado, M.B. and Rosselli, M. (2007). The elusive nature of executive functions: A review of our current understanding. *Neuropsychology Reviews*, 17, 213–233.

Kable, J.W. and Glimcher, P.W. (2007). People the neural correlates of subjective value during intertemporal choice. *Nature Neuroscience*, 10, 1625–1632.

Kable, J.W. and Glimcher, P.W. (2010). An "as soon as poss" effect in human intertemporal decision making: Behavioral evidence and neural mechanism. *Journal of Neurophysiology*, 103, 2013–2023.

Kacelnik, A. (1997). Normative and descriptive models of decision making: Time discounting and risk sensitivity. In Bock, G.R. and Cardew, G. (Eds) *Characterizing Human Psychological Adaptations* (pp. 51–70). Chichester: John Wiley.

Kagel, J.H., Battalio, R.C., and Green, L. (1995). *Economic Choice Theory: An Experimental Analysis of Animal Behavior.* Cambridge: Cambridge University Press.

Kahneman, D. (2003). A perspective on judgment and choice: Mapping bounded rationality. *American Psychologist*, 58, 697–720.

Kahneman, D. (2011). *Thinking, Fast and Slow.* London: Allen Lane.

Kahneman, D. and Tversky, A. (1979). Prospect theory: An analysis of decision under risk. *Econometrica*, 47, 263–291.

Kaplan, H.S. and Gangestad, S.W. (2005). Life history theory and evolutionary psychology. In Buss, D.M. (Ed.) *The Handbook of Evolutionary Psychology* (pp. 68–95). Hoboken, NJ: Wiley.

Karlsen, F. (2013). *A World of Excesses: Online Games and Excessive Playing.* Farnham, Surrey, and Burlington, VT: Ashgate.

Kassinove, J.I. and Schare, M.L. (2001). Effects of the "near miss" and the "big win" on persistence at slot machine gambling. *Psychology of Addictive Behaviors*, 15, 155–158.

Kelley, J.F. and White, W.L. (Eds) (2011). *Addiction Recovery Management: Theory, Research and Practice.* New York: Humana Press.

Kendler, K.S., Karkowski, L.M., Neale, M.C., and Prescott, C.A. (2000). Illicit psychoactive substance use, heavy use, abuse, and dependence in a U.S. population-based sample of male twins. *Archives of General Psychiatry*, 57, 261–269.

Kendrick, D.T., Sadalla, E.K., and O'Keefe, R.C. (1998). Evolutionary cognitive psychology: The missing heart of modern cognitive science. In Crawford, C. and Krebs, D.L. (Eds) *Handbook of Evolutionary Psychology* (pp. 485–515). Mahawa, NJ: Erlbaum.

Kennerley, S.W. and Walton, M.E. (2011). Decision making and reward in frontal cortex: Complementary evidence from neurophysiological and neuropsychological studies. *Behavioral Neuroscience*, 125, 297–317.

Kennerley, S.W., Behrens, T.E.J., and Wallis, J. (2011). Double dissociation of value computations in orbitofrontal and anterior cingulated neurons. *Nature Neuroscience*, 14, 1581–1589.

Kennett, J. (2001). *Agency and Responsibility: A Common-sense Moral Psychology.* Oxford: Oxford University Press.

Kirby, K.N. and Petry, N.M. (2004). Heroin and cocaine abusers have higher discount rates for delayed rewards than alcoholics or non-drug using controls. *Addiction*, 99, 461–471.

Kirby, K.N., Petry, N.M., and Bickel, W.K. (1999). Heroin addicts have higher discounting rates for delayed rewards than non-drug using controls. *Journal of Experimental Psychology: General*, 128, 1167–1173.

Kirton, M.J. (2003). Adaption-Innovation: In the Context of Diversity and Change. London: Routledge.

Knutson, B., Wolkowitz, O., Cole, S.W., Chan, T., Moore, E., and Johnson, R. (1998). Selective alteration of personality and social behavior by serotonergic intervention. *American Journal of Psychiatry*, 155, 373–379.

Koob, G.F. (2013). Neuroscience of addiction. In McCrady, B.S. and Epstein, E.E. (Eds) *Addictions: A Comprehensive Guidebook*, 2nd edn (pp. 17–35). New York: Oxford University Press.

Koob, G.F. and Le Moal, M. (2001). Drug addiction, dysregulation of reward, and allostasis. *Neuropsychopharmacology*, 24, 97–129.

Koob, G.F. and Le Moal, M. (2006). *Neurobiology of Addiction*. London: Academic Press.

Koob, G.F., Arends, M.A., and Le Moal, M. (2014). *Drugs, Addiction, and the Brain*. Oxford: Academic Press.

Koole, S.L., van Dillen, L.F., and Sheppes, G. (2013). The self-regulation of emotion. In Vohs, K.D. and Baumeister, R.F. (Eds) *Handbook of Self-regulation: Research, Theory, and Applications*, 2nd edn (pp. 22–40). New York: Guilford Press.

Kringelbach, M.L. (2010). The hedonic brain: A functional neuroanatomy of human pleasure. In Kringelbach, M.L. and Berridge, K.C. (Eds) *Pleasures of the Brain* (pp. 202–221). Oxford: Oxford University Press.

Ladouceur, R. and Walker, M. (1996). A cognitive perspective gambling. In Salkovskis, P.M. (Ed.) *Trends in Cognitive and Behavioral Therapies* (pp. 89–120). Chichester: Wiley.

Ladouceur, R., Gaboury, A., Dumont, M., and Rochette, P. (1988). Gambling: Relationship between the frequency of wins and irrational thinking. *The Journal of Psychology*, 122, 409–414.

Langer, E.J. (1975). The illusion of control. *Journal of Personality and Social Psychology*, 32, 311–328.

Lawrence, A.D. and Calder, A.J. (2004). Homologizing human emotions. In Evans, D. and Cruse, P. (Eds) *Emotion, Evolution and Rationality* (pp. 15–47). Oxford: Oxford University Press.

Lea, S.E.G. (1984). *Instinct, Environment and Behaviour*. London: Methuen.

Ledgerwood, A. and Trope, Y. (2013). Local and global evaluations: Attitudes as self-regulatory guides for near and distant responding. In Vohs, K.D. and Baumeister, R.F. (Eds) *Handbook of Self-regulation: Research, Theory, and Applications*, 2nd edn (pp. 226–243). New York: Guilford Press.

LeDoux, J. (1998). *The Emotional Brain*. London: Weidenfeld & Nicolson.

Ledoux, S.F. (2015). *Origins and Components of Behaviorology*, 3rd edn. Ottawa, Ontario: BehaveTech Publishing.

Legrenzi, P. and Umità, C. (2011). *Neuromania: On the Limits of Brain Science*. Oxford: Oxford University Press.

Levesque, H.J. (1986). Making believers out of computers. *Artificial Intelligence*, 30, 81–108.

Levesque, H.J. (1989). Logic and the complexity of reasoning. In Thomason, R.H. (Ed.) *Philosophical Logic and Artificial Intelligence* (pp. 73–107). Amsterdam: Kluwer.

London, E.D., Ernst, M., Grant, S., Bonson, K., and Weinstein, A. (2000). Orbitofrontal cortex and human drug abuse: Functional imaging. *Cerebral Cortex*, 10, 334–342.

Luria, A.R. (1966). *Human Brain and Psychological Processes*. New York: Harper & Row.

Lyon, G.R. and Krasnegor, N.A. (Eds). (1996). *Attention, Memory, and Executive Function*. Baltimore, MD: Paul H. Brookes.

MacKay, T.-L. and Hodgins, T.C. (2012). Cognitive distortions as a problem gambling risk factor in Internet gambling. *International Gambling Studies*, 12(2), 163–175.

MacKillop, J. and de Wit, H. (Eds) (2012). *The Wiley-Blackwell Handbook of Addiction Pharmacology*. Chichester: John Wiley.

MacLin, O.H., Dixon, M.R., Daugherty, D., and Small, S.L. (2007). Using a computer simulation of three slot machines to investigate a gambler's preference among varying densities of near-miss alternatives. *Behavior Research Methods*, 39, 237–241.

Madden, G.J. and Bickel, W.K. (Eds) (2010). *Impulsivity: The Behavioral and Neurological Science of Discounting*. Washington, DC: American Psychological Association.

Madden, G.J., Petry, N.M., Badger, G., and Bickel, W.K. (1997). Impulsive and self-control choices in opioid-dependent subjects and non-drug using controls: Drug and monetary rewards. *Experimental and Clinical Psychopharmacology*, 5, 256–262.

Mazur, J. (1987). An adjusting procedure for studying delayed reinforcement. In Commons, M., Mazur, J., Nevin, J., and Rachlin, H. (Eds) *Quantitative Analysis of Behavior. Vol. 5: The Effect of Delay and of Intervening Events on Reinforcement Value* (pp. 55–73). Hillsdale, IL: Erlbaum.

McClure, S.M., Laibson, D.L., Loewenstein, G., and Cohen, J.D. (2004). Separate neural systems value immediate and delayed monetary rewards. *Science*, 306(5695), 503–507.

McCrady, B.S. and Epstein, E.E. (Eds) (2013). *Addictions: A Comprehensive Guidebook*, 2nd edn. New York: Oxford University Press.

McFarland, D. (1991). Defining motivation and cognition in animals and robots. *International Studies in the Philosophy of Science*, 5, 153–170.

McIlvane, W.J., Dube, W.V., and Serna, R.W. (1996). Analysis of behavioral selection by consequences and its potential contributions to understanding brain–behavior relations. In Pribram, K.H. and King, J.S. (Eds) *Learning as Self-organization*. Mahwah, NJ: Earlbaum.

McKim, W.A. and Hancock, S.D. (2013). *Drugs and Behavior: An Introduction to Behavioral Pharmacology*. Boston, MA: Pearson.

McNaughton, N. and Corr, P.J. (2004). A two-dimensional neuropsychology of defense: Fear/anxiety and defence distance. *Neuroscience and Biobehavioral Reviews*, 28, 285–305.

McRae, K., Ochsner, K.N., and Gross, J.J. (2013). The reason in passion: A social cognitive neuroscience approach to emotion regulation. In Vohs, K.D. and Baumeister, R.F. (Eds) *Handbook of Self-regulation: Research, Theory, and Applications*, 2nd edn (pp. 186–203). New York: Guilford Press.

Mehrabian A. (1980). *Basic Dimensions for a General Psychological Theory*. Cambridge, MA: Oelgeschlager, Gunn & Hain.

Mehrabian, A. and Russell, J.A. (1974). *An Approach to Environmental Psychology*. Cambridge, MA: MIT Press.

Meichenbaum, D. (1977). *Cognitive-behavior Modification: An Integrative Approach*. New York: Plenum.

Mellars, P.M. (1991). Cognitive changes and the emergence of modern humans in Europe. *Cambridge Archaeological Journal*, 1, 63–76.

Mellars, P.M., Boyle, K., Bar-Yosef, O., and Stringer, C. (Eds) (2007). *Rethinking the Human Revolution: New Behavioural and Biological Perspectives on the Origin and Dispersal of Modern Humans*. Cambridge: McDonald Institute for Archaeological Research.

Miller, E.K. and Wallis, J.D. (2009). Executive function and higher-order cognition: Definition and neural substrates. In Squire, L.R. (Ed.) *Encyclopedia of Neuroscience*, Vol. 4 (pp. 99–104). Oxford: Academic Press.

Miller, J.C., Dixon, M.R., Parker, A., Kulland, A.M., and Weatherly, J.N. (2010). Concurrent validity of the gambling function assessment (GFA): Correlations with the South Oaks Gambling Screen (SOGS) and indicators of diagnostic efficiency. *Analysis of Gambling Behavior*, 4, 61–75.

Mischel, W. and Ayduk, O. (2013). Willpower in a cognitive affective processing system: The dynamics of delay of gratification. In Vohs, K.D. and Baumeister, R.F. (Eds) *Handbook of Self-regulation: Research, Theory, and Applications*, 2nd edn (pp. 83–105). New York: Guilford Press.

Mitchell, J.M., Fields, H.L., D'Esposito, M., and Boettiger, C.A. (2005). Impulsive responding in alcoholics. *Alcoholism, Clinical and Experimental Research*, 29, 2158–2169.

Mitchell, S.H. (1999). Measures of impulsivity in cigarette smokers and non-smokers. *Psychopharmacology*, 146, 455–464.

Mithen, S. (1996). *The Prehistory of the Mind*. London: Thames and Hudson.

Mojzisch, A. and Schultz-Hardt, S. (2007). Being fed-up: A social cognitive neuroscience approach to mental satiation. *Annals of the New York Academy of Sciences*, 1118, 186–205.

Moll, J. and Grafman, J. (2011). Well, what do you want to do? A cognitive neuroscience view of plan decision making. In Vartanian, O. and Mandel, D.R. (Eds) *Neuroscience of Decision Making* (pp. 285–309). New York and Hove: Psychology Press.

Montague, P.R. and Berns, G.S. (2002). Neural economics and biological substrates of valuation. *Neuron*, 36, 265–284.

Monterosso, J.R., Ainslie, G., Xu, J., Cordova, X., Domier, C.P., and London, E.D. (2007). Frontoparietal cortical activity of methamphetamine-dependent and comparison subjects performing a delay discounting task. *Human Brain Mapping*, 28, 383–393.

Müller, A. and Mitchell, J.E. (Eds) (2011). *Compulsive Buying: Clinical Foundations and Treatment*. London and New York: Routledge.

Murphy, N. and Brown, W.S. (2007). *Did My Neurons Make Me Do It?* Oxford: Oxford University Press.

Naqvi, N.H. and Bechara, A. (2008). The hidden island of addiction: The insula. *Trends in Neurosciences*, 32, 56–67.

Naqvi, N.H., Shiv, B., and Bechara, A. (2006). The role of emotion in decision making. *Current Directions in Psychological Science*, 15, 260–264.

Nastally, B.L. (2010). *Functional Investigation of and Treatment Strategies for the Near Miss Effect in Gambling*. PhD dissertation, Southern Illinois University.

Nastally, B.L., Dixon, M.R., and Jackson, J.W. (2010). Manipulating slot machine preference in problem gambling through contextual control. *Journal of Applied Behavior Analysis*, 43, 125–129.

Nester, E.J. and Landsman, D. (2001). Learning about addiction from the genome. *Nature*, 409, 834–835.

Nichols, S. and Stitch, S.P. (2003). *Mindreading: An Integrated Account of Pretence, Self-awareness, and Understanding Other Minds*. Oxford: Oxford University Press.

Nichols, T.T. and Wilson, S.J. (2015). Working memory functioning and addictive behavior: Insights from cognitive neuroscience. In Wilson, S.J. (Ed.) *The Wiley Handbook on the Cognitive Neuroscience of Addiction* (pp. 55–77). Chichester: Wiley-Blackwell.

Odum, A.L., Madden, G.J., and Bickel, W.K. (2002). Discounting of delayed health gains and losses by current, never-, and ex-smokers of cigarettes. *Nicotine and Tobacco Research*, 4, 295–303.

Odum, A.L., Madden, G.J., Badger, G.J., and Bickel, W.K. (2000). Needle-sharing in opioid-dependent outpatients: Psychological processes underlying risk. *Drug and Alcohol Dependence*, 60, 259–266.

Ohmura, Y., Takahashi, T., and Kitamura, N. (2005). Discounting delayed and probabilistic monetary gains and losses by smokers of cigarettes, *Psychopharmacology (Berlin)*, 182, 508–515.

Oliveira-Castro, J.M. and Foxall, G.R. (2015). Dimensions of demand elasticity. In Foxall, G.R. (Ed.) *The Routledge Companion to Consumer Behavior Analysis* (pp. 121–137). London and New York: Routledge.

Oliveira-Castro, J.M., Foxall, G.R., and Schrezenmaier, T.C. (2005). Patterns of consumer response to retail price differentials. *Service Industries Journal*, 25, 309–327.

Oliveira-Castro, J.M., Foxall, G.R., and James, V.K. (2008). Individual differences in price responsiveness within and across food brands. *Service Industries Journal*, 28, 733–753.

Oliveira-Castro, J.M., Foxall, G.R., James V.K., Pohl, R.H.B., Dias, M.B., and Chang, S.W. (2008). Consumer-based brand equity and brand performance. *Service Industries Journal*, 28, 445–461.

Oliveira-Castro, J.M., Foxall, G.R., Yan, J., and Wells, V.K. (2011). A behavioural-economic analysis of the essential value of brands. *Behavioural Processes*, 87, 106–114.

Oliveira-Castro, J.M., Cavalcanti, P., and Foxall, G.R. (2015a). What consumers maximize: Brand choice as a function of utilitarian and informational reinforcement. *Managerial and Decision Economics* DOI: 10.1002/mde.2722 (published online May 2015).

Oliveira-Castro, J.M., Cavalcanti, P., and Foxall, G.R. (2015b). What do consumers maximize? The analysis of utility functions in light of the Behavioral Perspective Model. In Foxall, G.R. (Ed.) *The Routledge Companion to Consumer Behavior Analysis* (pp. 202–212). London and New York: Routledge.

O'Shea, M., Gottfredson, L., and Foster, J.K. (2014). *The Human Brain, Intelligence and Memory*. London: Reed Business Information.

Over, D.E. (2003). *Evolution and the Psychology of Thinking: The Debate*. Hove and New York: Psychology Press.

Panksepp, J. (1998). *Affective Neuroscience: The Foundations of Human and Animal Emotions*. New York: Oxford University Press.

Panksepp, J. (2007). The neuroevolutionary and neuroaffective psychobiology of the prosocial brain, in Dunbar, R.I.M. and Barrett, L. (Eds) *The Oxford Handbook of Evolutionary Psychology* (pp. 145–162.) Oxford: Oxford University Press.

Papaleontiou-Louca, E. (2008). *Metacognition and Theory of Mind*. Newcastle upon Tyne: Scholars Publishing.

Peters, J. and Buchel, C. (2011). The neural mechanisms of inter-temporal decision making: Understanding variability. *Trends in Cognitive Science*, 15, 227–239.

Peterson, R.L. (2007). *Inside the Investor's Brain: The Power of Mind over Money.* Hoboken, NJ: Wiley.

Petry, N.M. (2001a). Delay discounting of money and alcohol in actively using alcoholics, current abstinent alcoholics, and controls. *Psychopharmacology (Berlin)*, 154, 243–250.

Petry, N.M. (2001b). Pathological gamblers, with and without substance use diorders, discount rewards at high rates. *Journal of Abnormal Psychology*, 110, 482–487.

Petry, N.M. (2005). *Pathological Gambling: Etiology, Comorbidity, and Treatment.* Washington, DC: American Psychological Association.

Petry, N.M. and Casarella, T. (1999). Excessive discounting of delayed rewards in substance abusers with gambling problems. *Drug and Alcohol Dependence*, 56, 25–32.

Phelps, E.A. and Sokol-Hessner, P. (2012). Social and emotional factors in decision-making: Appraisal and value. In Dolan, R.J. and Sharot, T. (Eds) *Neuroscience of Preference and Choice: Cognitive and Neural Mechanisms* (pp. 207–223). Amsterdam: Academic Press.

Pickering, A.D. and Smillie, L.D. (2008). The behavioral activation system: Challenges and opportunities. In Corr, P.J. (Ed.) *The Reinforcement Sensitivity Theory of Personality* (pp. 120–154). Cambridge: Cambridge University Press.

Poland, J. and Graham, G. (Eds) (2011). *Addiction and Responsibility.* Cambridge, MA: MIT Press.

Politser, P. (2008). *Neuroeconomics: A Guide to the New Science of Making Choices.* New York: Oxford University Press.

Popper, K. (1959). *The Logic of Scientific Discovery.* London: Hutchinson.

Porcelli, A.J. and Delgado, M.R. (2009). Reward processing in the human brain: Insights from fMRI. In Dreher, J.-C. and Tremblay, L. (Eds) *Handbook of Reward and Decision Making* (pp. 165–184). Amsterdam: Academic Press.

Potenza, N.M. (2006). Should addictive disorders include non-substance-related conditions? *Addiction*, 101(Suppl. 1), 142–151.

Potenza, N.M. (2008). The neurobiology of pathological gambling and drug addiction: An overview and new findings. *Transactions of the Royal Philosophical Society B-Biological Sciences*, 363, 3181–3189.

Qi, S., Ding, C., Song, Y., and Yang. D. (2011). Neural correlates of near-misses effect in gambling. *Neuroscience Letters*, 493, 80–85.

Quine, W.O. (1960). *Word and Object.* Cambridge, MA: MIT Press.

Raab, G., Elger, C.E., Neuner, M., and Weber, B. (2011). The neural basis of compulsive buying. In Müller, A. and Mitchell, J.E. (Eds) *Compulsive Buying: Clinical Foundations and Treatment* (pp. 63–86). London and New York: Routledge.

Rachlin, H. (1989). *Judgment, Decision, and Choice: A Cognitive/Behavioral Synthesis.* New York: Freeman.

Rachlin, H. (1994). *Behavior and Mind: The Roots of Modern Psychology.* Oxford: Oxford University Press.

Rachlin, H. (2000a). *The Science of Self Control.* Cambridge, MA: Harvard University Press.

Rachlin, H. (2000b). The lonely addict. In Bickel, W.K. and Vuchinich, R.E. (Eds) *Reframing Health Behavior Change with Behavioral Economics.* Mahwah, NJ: Erlbaum.

Radoilska, L. (2013). *Addiction and Weakness of Will.* Oxford: Oxford University Press.

Read, D. (2003). Subadditive intertemporal choice. In Loewenstein, G., Read, D., and Baumesiter, R.F. (Eds) *Time and Decision: Economic and Psychological Perspectives on Intertemporal Choice* (pp. 301–322). New York: Russell Sage Foundation.

Reader, S.M. and Laland, K.N. (Eds) (2003). *Animal Innovation*. Oxford: Oxford University Press.

Redish, A.D. and Kurth-Nelson, Z. (2010). Neural models of delay discounting. In Madden, G.J. and Bickel, W.K. (Eds) *Impulsivity: The Behavioral and Neurological Science of Discounting* (pp. 123–158). Washington, DC: American Psychological Association.

Reid, R.L. (1986). The psychology of the near-miss. *Journal of Gambling Behavior*, 2, 32–39.

Renfrew, C. (1994). Towards a cognitive archaeology. In Renfrew, C. and Zubrow, E.B.W. (Eds) *The Ancient Mind: Elements of Cognitive Archaeology* (pp. 3–12). Cambridge: Cambridge University Press.

Renfrew, C. (2007). *Prehistory: The Making of the Human Mind*. London: Weidenfeld & Nicolson.

Renfrew, C. and Zubrow, E.B.W. (Eds) (1994). *The Ancient Mind: Elements of Cognitive Archaeology*. Cambridge: Cambridge University Press.

Reynolds, B., Richards, J.B., Horn, K., and Karraker, K. (2004). Delay and probability discounting in a model of impulsive behavior: Effect of alcohol. *Journal of the Experimental Analysis of Behavior*, 71, 121–143.

Rick, S. and Loewenstein, G. (2008). The role of emotion in economic behavior. In Lewis, M., Haviland-Jones, J.M., and Barrett, L.F. (Eds) *Handbook of Emotions*, 3rd edn (pp. 138–156). New York: Guilford Press.

Ridgway, N., Kukar-Kinney, M., and Monroe, K.B. (2008). An expanded conceptualization and a new measure of compulsive buying. *Journal of Consumer Research*, 35, 622–639.

Robbins, L. (1935). *An Essay on the Nature and Significance of Economic Science*, 2nd edn. London: Macmillan.

Robbins, T.W. and Everitt, B.J. (1999). Drug addiction: Bad habits add up. *Nature*, 398, 567–570.

Robbins, T.W. and Everitt, B.J. (2002). Dopamine – Its role in behavior and cognition in experimental animals and humans. In Di Chiara, G. (Ed.) *Dopamine in the CNS II* (pp. 173–211). Berlin: Springer.

Robbins, T.W., Cardinal, R., DiCiano, P., Halligan, P., Hellemans, J.L., and Everitt, B. (2007). Neuroscience of drugs and addiction. In Nutt, D., Robbins, T.W., Stimson, G.V., Ince, M., and Jackson, A. (Eds) *Drugs and the Future: Brain Science, Addiction and Society* (pp. 11–87). Oxford: Elsevier.

Robins, L.N., Helzer, J.E., and Davis, D.H. (1975). Narcotic use in Southeast Asia and afterward. *Archives of General Psychiatry*, 32, 955–961.

Rogers, A.R. (1994). Evolution of time preference by natural selection. *American Economic Review*, 84, 460–481.

Rogers, A., Morgan, P., and Foxall, G.R. (2015). Triple jeopardy in behavioral perspective. In Foxall, G.R. (Ed.) *The Routledge Companion to Consumer Behavior Analysis* (pp. 150–174). London and New York: Routledge.

Rolls, E.T. (1999). *Emotion and the Brain*. Oxford: Oxford University Press.

Rolls, E.T. (2005). *Emotion Explained*. Oxford: Oxford University Press.

Rolls, E.T. (2008). *Memory, Attention, and Decision-making*. Oxford: Oxford University Press.

Rolls, E.T. (2009). From reward value to decision-making: Neuronal and computational principles. In Dreher, J.-C. and Tremblay, L. (Eds) *Handbook of Reward and Decision Making* (pp. 97–133). Amsterdam: Academic Press.

Rolls, E.T. (2012). *Neuroculture: On the Implications of Brain Science.* Oxford: Oxford University Press.

Rolls, E.T. (2014*). Emotion and Decision-making Explained.* Oxford: Oxford University Press.

Romero, S., Foxall, G.R., Schrezenmaier, T.C., Oliveira-Castro, J., and James, V.K. (2006). Deviations from matching in consumer choice. *European Journal of Behavior Analysis*, 7, 15–40.

Rosenberg, A. (1988). *Philosophy of Social Science.* Oxford: Oxford University Press.

Rosenberg, A. (1992). *Economics – Mathematical Politics or Science of Diminishing Returns?* Chicago, IL: Chicago University Press.

Ross, D. (2000a). Introduction: The Dennettian Stance. In Ross, D., Brook, A., and Thompson, D. (Eds) *Dennett's Philosophy: A Comprehensive Assessment* (pp. 1–40). Cambridge, MA: MIT Press.

Ross, D. (2000b). Rainforest realism: A Dennettian theory of existence. In Ross, D., Brook, A., and Thompson, D. (Eds) *Dennett's Philosophy: A Comprehensive Assessment* (pp. 147–168). Cambridge, MA: MIT Press.

Ross, D. (2002). Dennettian behavioral explanations and the roles of the social sciences. In Brook, A. and Ross, D. (Eds) *Daniel Dennett* (pp. 140–183). Cambridge: Cambridge University Press.

Ross, D. (2005). *Economic Theory and Cognitive Science: Microexplanation.* Cambridge, MA: MIT Press.

Ross, D. (2008). Two styles of neuroeconomics. *Economics and Philosophy*, 24, 473–483.

Ross, D. (2009). Economic models of procrastination. In Andreou, C. and White, M. (Eds) *The Thief of Time* (pp. 28–50). Oxford: Oxford University Press.

Ross, D. (2012). The economic agent: Not human, but important. In Mäki, U. (Ed.) *Philosophy of Economics* (pp. 691–736). Amsterdam: Elsevier.

Ross, D., Brook, A., and Thompson, D. (Eds) (2000). *Dennett's Philosophy: A Comprehensive Assessment.* Cambridge, MA: MIT Press.

Ross, D., Sharp, C., Vuchinich, R.E., and Spurrett, D. (2008). *Midbrain Mutiny. The Picoeconomics and Neuroeconomics of Disordered Gambling.* Cambridge, MA: MIT Press.

Ross, D., Kincaid, H., Spurrett, D., and Collins, P. (Eds) (2010). *What is Addiction?* Cambridge, MA: MIT Press.

Rothbart, M.K., Ellis, L.K., and Posner, M.I. (2013). Temperament and self-regulation. In Vohs, K.D. and Baumeister, R.F. (Eds) *Handbook of Self-regulation: Research, Theory, and Applications*, 2nd edn (pp. 441–460). New York: Guilford Press.

Roy, A., Adinoff, B., Roerich, L., Custer, R., Lorenz, V., Barbaccia, M., Guidotti, A., Costa, E., and Linnoila, M. (1988). Pathological gambling: A psychobiological study. *Archives of General Psychiatry*, 45, 369–373.

Rueda, W.R., Posner, M.I., and Rothbart, M.K. (2013). Attentional control and self-regulation. In Vohs, K.D. and Baumeister, R.F. (Eds) *Handbook of Self-regulation: Research, Theory, and Applications*, 2nd edn (pp. 284–299). New York: Guilford Press.

Runyan, J.D. (2014). *Human Agency and Neural Causes: Philosophy of Action and the Neuroscience of Voluntary Agency.* New York: Palgrave Macmillan.

Sadler-Smith, E. (2009). A duplex model of cognitive style. In Zhang, L. and Sternberg, R.J. (Eds) *Perspectives on the Nature of Intellectual Styles* (pp. 3–28). New York: Springer.

Samuelson, P. (1937). A note on measurement of utility. *Review of Economic Stuides*, 4, 155–161.

Sayette, M.A. and Griffin, K.M. (2013). Self-regulatory failure and addiction. In Vohs, K.D. and Baumeister, R.F. (Eds) *Handbook of Self-regulation: Research, Theory, and Applications*, 2nd edn (pp. 505–521). New York: Guilford Press.

Schoenbaum, G., Setlow, B., Saddoris, M.P., and Gallagher, M. (2003). Encoding predicted outcome and acquired value in orbitofrontal cortex during cue sampling depends upon input from basolateral amygdala. *Neuron*, 39, 855–867.

Schott, B.H., Minuzzi, L., Krebs, R.M., Elmenhurst, D., Lang, M., Winz, O.H., Seidenbecher, C., Hoenen, H.H., Heinze, H.J., Ziles, K., Durzel, E., and Bauer, A. (2008). Mesolimbic functional magnetic resonance image activations during reward-related ventral striatal dopamine release. *Journal of Neuroscience*, 28, 14311–14319.

Schüll, N.D. (2012). *Addiction by Design: Machine Gambling in Las Vegas*. Princeton, NJ, and Oxford: Princeton University Press.

Schultz, W. (1992). Activity of dopamine neurons in the behaving primate. *Seminars in Neuroscience*, 4, 129–138.

Schultz, W. (2000). Multiple reward signals in the brain. *Nature Reviews/Neuroscience*, 1, 199–207.

Schultz, W. (2002). Getting formal with dopamine and reward. *Neuron*, 36, 241–263.

Schultz, W. (2006). Behavioral theories and the neurophysiology of reward. *Annual Review of Psychology*, 57, 87–115.

Schultz, W. (2010). Dopamine signals for reward value and risk: basic and recent data. *Behavioral and Brain Functions*, 6, 24.

Schultz, W. and Dickinson, A. (2000). Neuronal coding of prediction errors. *Annual Review of Neuroscience*, 23, 473–500.

Schultz, W., Dayan, P. and Montague, P.R. (1997). A neural substrate of prediction and reward. *Science*, 275, 1593–1599.

Schultz, W., Preuschoff, K., Camerer, C., Hsu, M., Fiorillo, C.D., Tobler, P.N., and Bossaerts, P. (2008). Explicit neural signals reflecting reward uncertainty. *Philosophical Transactions of the Royal Society B*, 363, 3801–3811.

Searle, J. (2001). *Rationality in Action*. Cambridge, MA: MIT Press.

Shaffer, H.J. (Ed.) (2012). *APA Addiction Syndrome Handbook*. Washington, DC: American Psychological Association.

Shallice, T. and Cooper, R.P. (2011). *The Organisation of Mind*. Oxford; Oxford University Press.

Shea, N., Boldt, A., Bang, D., Yeung, N., Heyes, C., and Frith, C.D. (2014). Suprapersonal cognitive control and metacognition. *Trends in Cognitive Sciences*, 18, 186–193.

Shettleworth, S.J. (2000). Modularity and the evolution of cognition. In Heyes, C. and Huber, L. (Eds) *The Evolution of Cognition* (pp. 43–60). Cambridge, MA: MIT Press.

Shettleworth, S.J. (2010). *Cognition, Evolution, and Behavior*. Oxford: Oxford University Press.

Sidman, M. (1994). *Equivalence Relations and Behavior: A Research Story*. Boston, MA: Authors Cooperative.

Sigurdsson, V. and Foxall, G.R. (2015). Experimental analyses of choice and matching: From the animal laboratory to the marketplace. In Foxall, G.R. (Ed.) *The Routledge Companion to Consumer Behavior Analysis* (pp. 78–95). London and New York: Routledge.

Sigurdsson, V., Larsen, N.M., and Gunnarsson, D. (2011). An in-store experimental analysis of consumers' selection of fruits and vegetables. *Service Industries Journal*, 31, 2587–2602.

Sigurdsson, V., Kahamseh, S., Gunnarsson, D., Larsen, N.M., and Foxall, G.R. (2013a). An econometric examination of the Behavioral Perspective Model in the context of Norwegian retailing. *The Psychological Record*, 62, 277–294.

Sigurdsson, V., Menon, R.G.V., Sigurdarson, J.P., Kristjansson, J.K., and Foxall, G.R. (2013b). A test of the Behavioral Perspective Model in the context of an e-mail marketing experiment. *The Psychological Record*, 62, 295–307.

Sigurdsson, V., Larsen, N.M., and Fagerstrom, A. (2015). Behavior analysis of in-store consumer behavior. In Foxall, G.R. (Ed.) *The Routledge Companion to Consumer Behavior Analysis* (pp. 40–50). London and New York: Routledge.

Simon, H.A. (1977). *The New Science of Management Decision*, revised edn. Upper Saddle River, NJ: Prentice-Hall.

Simon, H.A. (1987). Rational decision making in business organizations. In Green, L. and Kagel, J.H. (Eds) *Advances in Behavioral Economics*, Vol. 1 (pp. 18–47). New York: Academic Press.

Skinner, B.F. (1931). The concept of the reflex in the description of behavior. *Journal of General Psychology*, 5, 427–458.

Skinner, B.F. (1935a). The generic nature of the concepts of stimulus and response. *Journal of General Psychology*, 12, 40–65.

Skinner, B.F. (1935b). Two types of conditioned reflex and a pseudo-type. *Journal of General Psychology*, 12, 66–77.

Skinner, B.F. (1937). Two types of conditioned reflex: A reply to Konorski and Miller. *Journal of General Psychology*, 16, 272–279.

Skinner, B.F. (1938). *The Behavior of Organisms*. New York: Appleton-Century-Crofts.

Skinner, B.F. (1945). The operational analysis of psychological terms. *Psychological Review*, 52, 270–277.

Skinner, B.F. (1950). Are theories of learning necessary? *Psychological Review*, 57, 193–216.

Skinner, B.F. (1953). *Science and Human Behavior*. New York: Macmillan.

Skinner, B.F. (1957). *Verbal Behavior*. New York: Century.

Skinner, B.F. (1963). Behaviorism at fifty. *Science*, 140, 951–958.

Skinner, B.F. (1969). *Contingencies of Reinforcement: A Theoretical Analysis*. Englewood Cliffs, NJ: Prentice-Hall.

Skinner, B.F. (1971). *Beyond Freedom and Dignity*. New York: Knopf.

Skinner, B.F. (1974). *About Behaviorism*. New York: Knopf.

Skinner, B.F. (1977). Why I am not a cognitive psychologist. *Behaviorism*, 5, 1–10.

Skinner, B.F. (1981). Selection by consequences. *Science*, 213, 501–504.

Skinner, B.F. (1983). Can the experimental analysis of behavior rescue psychology? *The Behavior Analyst*, 6, 9–17.

Skinner, N. and Fox-Francoeur, C. (2013). Personality implications of adaption-innovation: VI. Adaption-innovation as a predictor of disease proneness. *Social Behavior and Personality: An International Journal*, 41, 223–227.

Smillie, L.D. (2008). What is reinforcement sensitivity? Neuroscience paradigms for approach–avoidance process theories of personality. *European Journal of Personality*, 22, 359–384.

Staddon, J.E.R. (1980). *Limits to Action: The Allocation of Individual Behavior*. New York: Academic Press.

Stanovich, K.E. (2004). *The Robot's Rebellion*. Chicago, IL: Chicago University Press.

Stanovich, K.E. (2009a). Distinguishing the reflective, algorithmic, and autonomous minds: Is it time for a tri-process theory? In Evans, J.St.B.T. and Frankish, K. (Eds) *In Two Minds: Dual Processes and Beyond* (pp. 55–88). Oxford: Oxford University Press.

Stanovich, K.E. (2009b). *What Intelligence Tests Miss: The Psychology of Rational Thought*. New Haven, CT, and London: Yale University Press.

Stanovich, K.E. (2011). *Rationality and the Reflective Mind*. Oxford: Oxford University Press.

Stanovich, K.E. and West, R.F. (2000). Individual differences in reasoning: Implications for the rationality debate? *Brain and Behavioral Sciences*, 23, 645–726.

Stanovich, K.E. and West, R.F. (2003). Evolutionary versus instrumental goals: How evolutionary psychology misconceives human rationality. In Over, D.E. (Ed.) *Evolution and the Psychology of Thinking: The Debate*. Hove and New York: Psychology Press.

Stanovich, K.E., West, R.F., and Toplak, M.E. (2012). Intelligence and rationality. In Sternberg, R. and Kaufman, S.B. (Eds) *Cambridge Handbook of Intelligence* (pp. 784–826). Cambridge: Cambridge University Press.

Stein, J.S. and Madden, G.J. (2013). Delay discounting and drug abuse: Empirical, conceptual, and methodological considerations. In MacKillop, J. and de Wit, H. (Eds) *The Wiley-Blackwell Handbook of Addiction Psychopharmacology* (pp. 165–208). Chichester: Wiley.

Sternberg, S. (2011). Modular processes in brain and mind. *Cognitive Neuropsychology*, 28, 156–208.

Story, G.W., Vlaev, I., Seymour, B., Darzi, A., and Dolan, R.J. (2014). Does temporal discounting explain unhealthy behavior? A systematic review and reinforcement learning perspective. *Frontiers in Behavioral Neuroscience*, Vol. 8, Article 76.

Strickland, L.H. and Grote, F.W. (1967). Temporal presentation of winning symbols and slot-machine playing. *Journal of Experimental Psychology*, 74, 10–13.

Subramaniyan, M. and Dani, J.A. (2015). Dopaminergic and cholinergic learning mechanisms in nicotine addiction. *Annals of the New York Academy of Sciences*, 1349, 46–63.

Sundali, J.A., Safford, A.H., and Croson, R. (2012). The impact of near-miss events on betting behavior: An examination of casino rapid roulette play *Judgment and Decision Making*, 7, 768–778.

Symmonds, M. and Dolan, R.J. (2012). The neurobiology of preferences. In Dolan, R.J. and Sharot, T. (Eds) *Neuroscience of Preference and Choice: Cognitive and Neural Mechanisms* (pp. 3–31). Amsterdam: Academic Press.

Taylor, S.E., Klein, L.C., Lewis, B.P., Gruenewald, T.L., Gurung, R.A.R., and Updegraff, J.A. (2000). Biobehavioral responses to stress in females: Tend-and-befriend, not fight-or-flight. *Psychological Review*, 107, 411–429.

Terrace., H.S. (1984). Animal cognition. In Roitblatt, H.L., Bever, TG., and Terrace, H.S. (Eds) *Animal Cognition* (pp. 7–28). Hillsdale, NJ: Erlbaum.

Tiffany, S.T. (1999). Cognitive concepts of craving. *Alcohol Research and Health*, 23, 215–224.

Toates, F. (2011). *Biological Psychology*, 3rd edn. Harlow, Essex: Pearson.

Toates, F. and Dommett, E. (2011). *Addictions*. Milton Keynes: The Open University.

Tobler, P.N. and Kobayashi, S. (2009). Electrophysiological correlates of reward processing in dopamine neurons. In Dreher, J.-C. and Tremblay, L. (Eds) *Handbook of Reward and Decision Making* (pp. 29–50). Amsterdam: Academic Press

Tomasello, M. (2014). *A Natural History of Human Thinking*. Cambridge, MA: Harvard University Press.

Tooby, J. and Cosmides, L. (1992). The psychological foundations of culture. In Barkow, J.H., Cosmides, L., and Tooby, J. (Eds) *The Adapted Mind* (pp. 19–136). Oxford: Oxford University Press.

Toronchuk, J.A. and Ellis, G.F.R. (2013). Affective neuronal selection: The nature of the primordial emotion systems. *Frontiers in Psychology*, Vol. 3, Article 589.

Tsuang, M.T., Bar, J.L., Harley, R.M., and Lyons, M.J. (2001). The Harvard Twin Study of substance abuse: What we have learned. *Harvard Review of Psychiatry*, 9, 267–279.

Tsuang, M.T., Lyons, M.J., Meyer, J.M., Doyle, T., Eisen, S.A., Goldberg, J., True, W., Lin, N., Toomey, R., and Eaves, L. (1998). Co-occurrence of abuse of different drugs in men: The role of drug-specific and shared vulnerabilities. *Archives of General Psychiatry*, 55, 967–972.

Tucker, B. (2006). A future discounting explanation for the persistence of a mixed foraging-horticulture strategy among the Mikea of Madagascar. In Kennett, J. and Winterhalter, B. (Eds) *Behavioral Ecology and the Transition to Agriculture* (pp. 22–40). Berkeley, CA: University of California Press.

Van der Molen, P.P. (1994). Adaption-innovation and changes in social structure: On the anatomy of catastrophe. In Kirton, M.J. (Ed.) *Adaptors and Innovators: Styles of Creativity and Problem Solving* (pp. 137–172). London: Routledge.

Van der Wal, A.J., Schade, H.M., Krabbendam, L., and van Vugt, M. (2015). Do natural landscapes reduce future discounting in humans? *Proceedings of the Royal Society B*, 280, 2013–2295.

Vaughan, W., Jr. and Herrnstein, R.J. (1997). Stability, melioration, and natural selection. In Rachlin, H. and Laibson, D.I. (Eds) *The Matching Law: Papers in Psychology and Economics* (pp. 194–225). New York: Russel Sage Foundation.

Vella, K.J. (2015). From consumer response to corporate response. In Foxall, G.R. (Ed.) *The Routledge Companion to Consumer Behavior Analysis* (pp. 272–295). London and New York: Routledge.

Vella, K.J. and Foxall, G.R. (2011). *The Marketing Firm: Economic Psychology of Corporate Behaviour*. Cheltenham, Glos, and Northampton, MA: Edward Elgar.

Verdejo-García, A. and Bechara, A. (2009). A somatic-marker theory of addiction. *Neuropharmacology*, 56(Suppl. 1), 48–62.

Vohs, K.D. and Baumeister, R.F. (Eds) (2011). *Handbook of Self-regulation: Research, Theory, and Applications*, 2nd edn. New York: Guilford Press.

Volkov, N.D., Fowlder, J.S., Wang, G.J., Swanson, J.M., and Telang, F. (2007). Dopamine in drug abuse and addiction: Results of imaging studies and treatment implications. *Archives of Neurology*, 64, 1575–1579.

Voorneveld, M. (2008). From preferences to Cobb–Douglas utility. *SSE/EFI Working Paper Series in Economics and Finance*, 701, 1–6.

Vuchinich, R.E. and Heather, N. (Eds) (2003). *Choice, Behavioral Economics and Addiction*. Amsterdam: Pergamon.

Vuchinich, R.E. and Simpson, C.A. (1998). Hyperbolic temporal discounting in social drinkers and problem drinkers. *Experimental and Clinical Psychopharmacology*, 6, 292–305.

Wagenaar, W. (1988). *Paradoxes of Gambling Behaviour*. London: Erlbaum.

Wagner, D.D. and Heatherton, T.F. (2013). Giving in to temptation: The emerging cognitive neuroscience of self-regulatory failure. In Vohs, K.D. and Baumeister, R.F. (Eds) *Handbook of Self-regulation: Research, Theory, and Applications*, 2nd edn (pp. 41–63). New York: Guilford Press.

Walker, M. (1992). Irrational thinking among slot machine players. *Journal of Gambling Studies*, 8, 245–262.

Walton, M.E., Rudeback, P.H., Behrens, E.J., and Rushworth, M.F.A. (2011). Cingulate and orbitofrontal contributions to valuing knowns and unknowns in a changeable world. In Delgado, M.R., Phelps, E.A., and Robbins, T.W. (Eds) *Decision Making, Affect and Learning: Attention and Performance XXIII* (pp. 235–261). Oxford: Oxford University Press.

Wargo, D.T., Baglini, N.A., and Nelson, K.A. (2010a). The new millennium's first global financial crisis: The neuroeconomics of greed, self-interest, deception, false trust, overconfidence and risk perception. In Stanton, A.A., Day, M., and Welpe, I.M. (Eds) *Neuroeconomics and the Firm* (pp. 78–98). Cheltenham, Glos: Edward Elgar.

Wargo, D.T., Baglini, N.A., and Nelson, K.A. (2010b). Dopamine, expected utility and decision-making in the firm. In Stanton, A.A., Day, M., and Welpe, I.M. (Eds) *Neuroeconomics and the Firm* (pp. 151–170). Cheltenham, Glos: Edward Elgar.

Watanabe, H., Henriksson, R., Ohnishi, Y.N., Ohnishi, Y.H, Harper, C., Sheedy, D., Garrick, T., Nyberg, F., Nestler, E.J., Bakalkin, G., and Yakovleva, T. (2009). FOSB proteins in the orbitofrontal and dorsolateral prefrontal cortices of human alcoholic. *Addiction Biology*, 14, 294–297.

Watson, K. and Platt, M. (2008). Neuroethology of reward and decision-making. *Philosophical Transactions of the Royal Society B*, 363, 3825–3835.

Weatherly, J.N. and Flannery-Woehl, K.A. (2009). Do cognitive fallacies predict behavior when non-pathological gamblers play slot machines and video poker? *Analysis of Gambling Behavior*, 3, 7–14.

Weatherly, J.N., Thompson, B.J., Hodny, M., and Meier, E. (2009). Choice behavior of nonpathological women playing concurrently available slot machines: Effect of changes in payback percentages. *Journal of Applied Behavior Analysis*, 42, 895–900.

Weatherly, J.N., Montes, K.S., and Christopher, D.M. (2010). Investigating the relationship between escape and gambling behavior. *Analysis of Gambling Behavior*, 4, 79–87.

Wells, V.K. and Foxall, G.R. (Eds). (2012). *Handbook of Developments in Consumer Behaviour*. Cheltenham, Glos, and Northampton, MA: Edward Elgar.

Wells, V.K. and Foxall, G.R. (2013). Matching, demand, maximization, and consumer choice. *The Psychological Record*, 62, 239–257.

West, R. and Brown, J. (2013). *Theory of Addiction*, 2nd edn. Chichester: Wiley-Blackwell.

Williams, D.R. and Williams, H. (1969). Auto-maintenance in the pigeon: Sustained pecking despite contingent non-reinforcement. *Journal of the Experimental Analysis of Behavior*, 12, 511–520.

Wills, T.A., Vaccaro, D., and McNamara, G. (1994). Novelty seeking, risk taking, and related constructs as predictors of adolescent substance use: An application of Cloninger's theory. *Journal of Substance Abuse*, 6, 1–20.

Winstanley, C.A. (2010). The neural and neurochemical basis of delay discounting. In Madden, G.J. and Bickel, W.K. (Eds) *Impulsivity: The Behavioral and Neurological Science of Discounting* (pp. 95–122). Washington, DC: American Psychological Association.

Winstanley, C.A., Eagle, D.M., and Robbins, T.W. (2006). Behavioral models of impulsivity in relation to ADHD: Translation between clinical and preclinical studies. *Clinical Psychology Reviews*, 26, 379–395.

Winstanley, C.A., Cocker, P.J., and Rogers, R.D. (2011). Dopamine modulates reward expectancy during performance of a slot machine task in rats: Evidence for a "near-miss" effect. *Neuropsychopharmacology*, 36, 913–925.

Winterhalter, B. (2007). Risk and decision-making. In Dunbar, R.I.M. and Barrett, L. (Eds) *The Oxford Handbook of Evolutionary Psychology* (pp. 433–445). Oxford: Oxford University Press.

Wise, R.A. (1980) The dopamine synapse and the notion of "pleasure centers" in the brain. *Trends in Neuroscience*, 3, 91–95.

Wohl, M.J.A. and Enzle, M.E. (2003). The effects of near wins and near losses on self-perceived personal luck and subsequent gambling behavior. *Journal of Experimental Social Psychology*, 39, 184–191.

Wood, W.S. and Clapham, M.M. (2006). Rules gamblers play by – and shouldn't. In Ghezzi, P.M., Lyons, C.A., Dixon, M.R., and Wilson, G.R. (Eds) *Gambling: Behavior Theory, Research and Application* (pp. 191–205). Reno, NV: Context Press.

Wynn, T. and Coolidge, F.L. (2004). The expert Neanderthal mind. *Journal of Human Evolution*, 46, 467–487.

Yan, J. and Foxall, G.R. (2015). The BPM and essential value. In Foxall, G.R. (Ed.) *The Routledge Companion to Consumer Behavior Analysis* (pp. 138–149). London and New York: Routledge.

Yan, J., Foxall, G.R., and Doyle, J.R. (2012a). Patterns of reinforcement and the essential value of brands: I. Incorporation of utilitarian and informational reinforcement into the estimation of demand. *The Psychological Record*, 62, 361–376.

Yan, J., Foxall, G.R., and Doyle, J.R. (2012b). Patterns of reinforcement and the essential value of brands: II. Evaluation of a model of consumer choice. *The Psychological Record*, 62, 377–394.

Yani-de-Soriano, M., Foxall, G.R., and Newman, A. (2013). The impact of the interaction of utilitarian and informational reinforcement and behaviour setting scope on consumer response. *Psychology and Marketing*, 30, 148–159.

Yi, R., Mitchell, S.H., and Bickel, W.K. (2010). Delay discounting and substance abuse-dependence. In Madden, G.J. and Bickel, W.K. (Eds) *Impulsivity: The Behavioral and Neurological Science of Discounting* (pp. 191–211). Washington, DC: American Psychological Association.

Zak, P.J. (2004). Neuroeconomics. In Zeki, S. and Goodenough, O. (Eds) *Law and the Brain* (pp. 133–153). Oxford: Oxford University Press.

Zak, P.J. (2007). The neuroeconomics of trust. In Franz, R. (Ed.) *Renaissance in Behavioral Economics: Essays in Honor of Harvey Leibenstein* (pp. 17–33). London and New York: Routledge.

Zak, P.J. and Nadler, A. (2010). Using brains to create trust: A manager's toolbox. In Stanton, A.A., Day, M., and Welpe, I.M. (Eds) *Neuroeconomics and the Firm* (pp. 69–77). Cheltenham, Glos: Edward Elgar.

Zeeb, F.D., Robbins, T.W., and Winstanley, C.A. (2009). Serotonergic and dopaminergic modulation of gambling behaviour as assessed using a novel rat gambling task. *Neuropsychopharmacology*, 34, 2329–2343.

Zettle, R.D. and Hayes, S.C. (1982). Rule-governed behavior: A potential framework for cognitive-behavioral therapy. In Kendall, P.C. (Ed.) *Advances in Cognitive-behavioral Research and Therapy* (pp. 73–117). New York: Academic Press.

Zlomke, K.R. and Dixon, M.R. (2006). Modification of slot-machine preferences through use of a conditioned discrimination paradigm. *Journal of Applied Behavior Analysis*, 39, 351–361.

Zuckerman, M. (1979). *Sensation Seeking: Beyond the Optimum Level of Arousal*. Hillsdale, IL: Erlbaum.

Zuckerman, M. (1994). *Behavioral Expressions and Biosocial Bases of Sensation Seeking*. Cambridge: Cambridge University Press.

Index

Page numbers in *italics* denote tables, those in **bold** denote figures.